THIS GREAT ARGUMENT: THE RIGHTS OF WOMEN

Edited by
HAMIDA BOSMAJIAN / Seattle University
HAIG BOSMAJIAN / University of Washington

▲ **Addison-Wesley Publishing Company**

Reading, Massachusetts

Menlo Park, California / London / Don Mills, Ontario

This book is in the
ADDISON-WESLEY SERIES IN SPEECH

Consulting Editor
FREDERICK W. HABERMAN

Contents

Introduction

Introduction

This great argument on the rights of women has persisted, as the selections in this book indicate, through the centuries. The argument, however, has brought small improvement to the status of women and no great liberation. To the large masses of people, female and male, the argument has remained unpersuasive, never powerful enough to break out into a revolution. While other groups which have experienced injustice, persecution, and suppression have through peaceful and violent revolution achieved liberation, there has never been a revolution for the liberation of women. We have had religious revolutions, workers' revolutions, slave revolutions, but we never have had a sexual revolution. Although some contemporary women's liberation writers and speakers refer to the evolution of some women's rights over the past century and a half as a "sexual revolution," it is difficult to view the slow evolutionary process as a "revolution." Over a century ago, feminist and abolitionist Lucy Stone, speaking at a women's rights convention in October 1855, delivered a speech which expressed the injustices against women and their grievances, injustices and grievances sounding very similar to those expressed by contemporary women's liberation spokeswomen. Over one hundred years ago, Lucy Stone told her audience:

> The last speaker alluded to this movement as being that of a few disappointed women. From the first years to which my memory stretches, I have been a disappointed woman. When, with my brothers, I reached forth after the sources of knowledge, I was reproved with "It isn't fit for you; it doesn't belong to women." Then there was but one college in the world where women were admitted, and that was in Brazil. I would have found my way there, but by the time I was prepared to go, one was opened in the young state of Ohio—the first in the United States where women and Negroes could

3

enjoy opportunities with white men. I was disappointed when I came to seek a profession worthy an immortal being—every employment was closed to me, except those of the teacher, the seamstress, and the housekeeper. In education, in marriage, in religion, in everything, disappointment is the lot of woman. It shall be the business of my life to deepen this disappointment in every woman's heart until she bows down to it no longer. I wish that women, instead of being walking show-cases, instead of begging of their fathers and brothers the latest and gayest new bonnet, would ask of them their rights. . . . We want rights. The flour-merchant, the house-builder, and the postman charge us no less on account of our sex; but when we endeavor to earn money to pay all these, then, indeed, we find the difference. . . . Women working in tailor-shops are paid one-third as much as men. . . . The present condition of woman causes a horrible perversion of the marriage relation. It is asked of a lady, "Has she married well?" "Oh, yes, her husband is rich." Woman must marry for a home, and you men are the sufferers by this; for a woman who loathes you may marry you because you have the means to get money which she can not have. But when woman can enter the lists with you and make money for herself, she will marry you only for deep and earnest affection.[1]

Consider the many specific grievances that Lucy Stone expressed: (1) the charge that women who take part in the women's liberation movement are disappointed and frustrated women; (2) unequal educational opportunities; (3) unequal professional opportunities; (4) women as objects of display for the benefit of men; (5) women receiving lower pay for the same job performed by men; (6) the economic dependence of women on men— all of these issues and problems mentioned by Lucy Stone in 1855 are an integral part of the women's liberation movement in the second half of the twentieth century. Decade after decade, century after century, women have expressed these grievances and have proposed remedies for doing away with the inequalities and injustices. The 1966 Statement of Purpose of the National Organization for Women (NOW), for example, is concerned with almost all of the items discussed by Lucy Stone. There has been no sexual revolution, statements by contemporary feminists to the contrary. The great argument on the rights of women persists.

The selections in this book present the various and diverse aspects of this great argument, its strengths and weaknesses and some of the attacks upon it. As in the "liberation" of other groups, the arguments for the rights of women are at times strident, militant, and emotional; at other times, they are calm, detached, and reasoned. The same observation can be applied to the antifeminist argument, although there is a greater element of fear in the voice of the critics of women's liberation, whether those voices are from several centuries past or from the present. The frantic, *ad hominem* voice of the New York *Herald*, reporting on a women's rights convention in September 1852, is the voice of some antifeminists today; said the *Herald*:

> Who are these women? What do they want? What are the motives that impel them to this course of action?... Some of them are old maids, whose personal charms were never very attractive, and who have been slighted by the masculine gender in general; some of them women who have been badly mated, whose own temper, or their husbands', has made life anything but agreeable to them, and they are therefore down upon the whole of the opposite sex; some, having so much of the virago in their disposition, that nature appears to have made a mistake in their gender—mannish women, like hens that crow; some of boundless vanity and egotism, who believe that they are superior in intellectual ability to "all the world and the rest of mankind," and delight to see their speeches and addresses in print; and man shall be consigned to his proper sphere—nursing the babies, washing the dishes, mending stockings, and sweeping the house. This is "the good time coming."

> What do the leaders of the Woman's Rights Convention want? They want to vote, and to hustle with the rowdies at the polls. They want to be members of Congress, and in the heat of debate to subject themselves to coarse jests and indecent language. . . . They want to fill all other posts which men are ambitious to occupy—to be lawyers, doctors, captains of vessels, and generals in the field. How funny it would sound in the newspapers, that Lucy Stone, pleading a cause, took suddenly ill in the pains of parturition, and perhaps gave birth to a fine bouncing boy in court![2]

The *Herald's* editorial continued in the same vein, jesting about leading feminists doing "men's jobs." Much of this derision and *ad hominem* attack is still part of the anti-feminist argument in the second half of the twentieth century.

The "humor" of women's demands for equal job opportunities, equal pay, and equal treatment before the law was not lost in the halls of Congress on February 8, 1964. Laughter resounded in the House of Representatives when on that day Congressman Howard W. Smith, eighty-one-year-old representative from Virginia, proposed to amend the Civil Rights Bill by adding the word "sex" to Title VII of that bill, which prohibited discrimination on the basis of race, color, or national origin. Smith and other Southerners were fighting a losing battle to defeat the Civil Rights Bill, and Smith's amendment was more a parliamentary tactic to hamper passage of the bill than a sincere desire by Smith to see equal opportunities in employment extended to women. His sincerity can be judged from the following passage from his speech introducing the amendment; with a straight face he said:

> Mr. Chairman, this amendment is offered to the fair employment practices title of this bill to include within our desire to prevent discrimination against another minority group, the women, but a very essential minority group, in the absence of which the majority group would not be here today.
>
> Now, I am very serious about this amendment. . . . I do not think it can do any harm to this legislation; maybe it can do some good. I think it will do some good for the minority sex.
>
> . . . to show you how some of the ladies feel about discrimination against them, I want to read you an extract from a letter that I received the other day. This lady has a real grievance on behalf of the minority sex. She said that she had seen that I was going to present an amendment to protect the most important sex, and she says: "I suggest that you might also favor an amendment or a bill to correct the present 'imbalance' which exists between males and females in the United States."
>
> Then she goes on to say—and she has her statistics, which is the reason why I am reading it to you, because this is serious—"The census of 1960 shows that we had 88,331,000 males living in this country, and 90,992,000 females, which leaves the country with an 'imbalance' of 2,661,000 females." Now another paragraph: "Just why the Creator would set up such an imbalance of spinsters, shutting off the 'right' of every female to have a husband of her own, is, of course, known only to nature. But I am sure you will agree that this is a grave injustice. . . ."
>
> And I do agree, and I am reading you the letter because I want all of the rest of you to agree, you of the majority—"But I am sure you will agree this is a grave injustice to womankind and something the Congress and President Johnson should take immediate steps to correct . . ." And you interrupted me just now before I could finish reading the sentence, which continues on: ". . . immediate steps to correct, especially in this election year."
>
> Now, I just want to remind you here that in this election year it is pretty nearly half of the voters in this country that are affected, so you had better sit up and take notice.
>
> She also says this, and this is a very cogent argument, too: "Up until now, instead of assisting these poor unfortunate females in obtaining their 'right' to happiness, the Government has on several occasions engaged in wars which killed off a large number of eligible males, creating an 'imbalance' in our male and female population that was even worse than before. Would you have any suggestions as to what course our Government might pursue to protect our spinster friends in their 'right' to a nice husband and family?"

I read that letter just to illustrate that women have some real grievances and some real rights to be protected. I am serious about this thing. . . . [3]

Humorous and sarcastic as he may have been in introducing the amendment, Congressman Smith's colleagues saw some merit in it and the 1964 Civil Rights Act emerged with Smith's amendment intact.

With the *ad hominem* and humorous "arguments" used to deprecate the grievances and demands of women, there have persisted through the centuries several arguments ritualistically uttered from time to time to convince men and women that females cannot be allowed complete freedom of choice, that the status of women carries with it prohibitions not applied to men. Like old wives' tales these arguments persist in spite of all evidence to the contrary.

One of the old arguments is that there are jobs and tasks which are for men to do, not for women; it is argued that women cannot handle certain jobs as well as the men who have traditionally done them. This argument has been used through the centuries until it has almost become a commonplace. The refutations of the argument have also spanned the centuries. An often quoted passage in contemporary women's liberation publications comes from an 1851 speech delivered by Sojourner Truth, who stated simply and forcefully the idea that women have done "men's work." In May 1851, a women's convention was held in Akron, Ohio, and some of what transpired there and parts of Sojourner Truth's speech were recorded by Frances D. Gage, chairwoman of the convention:

> The second day the work waxed warm. Methodist, Baptist, Episcopal, Presbyterian, and Universalist ministers came in to hear and discuss the resolutions presented. One claimed superior rights and privileges for man, on the ground of "superior intellect"; another, because of the "manhood of Christ; if God had desired the equality of woman, He would have given some token of His will through the birth, life, and death of the Saviour." Another gave us a theological view of the "sin of our first mother."
>
> --
>
> I rose and announced "Sojourner Truth," and begged the audience to keep silence for a few moments.
>
> "Wall, chilern, whar dar is so much racket dar must be somethin' out o' kilter. I tink dat 'twixt de niggers of de Souf and de womin at de Norf, all talkin' 'bout rights, de white men will be in a fix pretty soon. But what's all dis here talkin' 'bout?
>
> "Dar man ober dar say dat womin needs to be helped into carriages, and lifted ober ditches, and to hab de best place everywhar. Nobody eber helps me

into carriages, or ober mud-puddles, or gibs me any best place!" And raising herself to her full height, and her voice to a pitch like rolling thunder, she asked, "And a'n't I a woman? Look at me! Look at my arm! (and she bared her right arm to the shoulder, showing her tremendous muscular power.) I have ploughed, and planted, and gathered into barns, and no man could head me! And a'n't I a woman? I could work as much and eat as much as a man——when I could get it——and bear de lash as well! And a'n't I a woman? I have borne thirteen chilern, and seen 'em mos' all sold off to slavery, and when I cried out with my mother's grief, none but Jesus heard me! And a'n't I a woman?

"Den dat little man in black dar, he say women can't have as much rights as men, 'cause Christ wan't a woman! Whar did your Christ come from?" Rolling thunder couldn't have stilled that crowd, as did those deep, wonderful tones, as she stood there with outstretched arms and eyes of fire. Raising her voice still louder, she repeated, "Whar did your Christ come from? From God and a woman! Man had nothin' to do wid Him."[4]

During World War II, with a manpower shortage, we found that women could indeed work well and efficiently at jobs traditionally limited to men; the shipyards and airplane factories hired women to do "men's work." Even the Nazis, who attempted to relegate women to küche, kinde, and kirche, increased the use of women at men's jobs as the war progressed and the shortage of manpower increased. In the Soviet Union, a nation which had higher casualties in World War II than any other country, women became an integral part of the job force during the postwar period, working as doctors, bricklayers, dentists, and in many professions commonly thought of as limited to men. What is obvious is that in times of crisis, the taboos against women working at "male jobs" are temporarily lifted; as soon as the crisis is past, society evidently goes back to believing that there are jobs which women cannot do, jobs which they handled quite well during the emergency.

In reviewing the arguments used in the middle of the twentieth century for and against the Equal Rights Amendment, attorney Elizabeth C. Crable has written: "The arguments for and against the Equal Rights Amendment sound very much like the ones that were made for and against the Suffrage Amendment." At the time (summer 1949) that she wrote her article on the pros and cons of the Equal Rights Amendment (which had been introduced in every Congress since 1923), some of the arguments against the amendment were as follows:

1. The Amendment would violate states' rights; each state should be left to correct its own abuses.

2. The Amendment would cause confusion and clutter up the courts with litigation.
3. The Amendment might deprive states of the power to legislate for the protection of the health, safety, morals, and welfare of the community.
4. The Amendment might affect a wife's right to support and alimony.
5. The Amendment would change the age of majority and the age of consent to marriage.
6. The Amendment might affect maternity legislation.
7. The Amendment might do away with so-called "protective" labor laws for women.[5]

Several of these 1949 objections, used decades earlier against the Suffragettes, are still to be heard in the 1970s, especially argument number seven. Labor leaders and congressmen opposing passage of the 1970 Equal Rights Amendment have relied heavily in committee hearings and congressional speeches on the argument that such equality amendments would threaten protective laws which have been instituted to assure that women would not be overworked, mistreated, or allowed to engage in "men's work." (See the selections by Mortimer Furay and Emanuel Celler.)

The male's power of defining women's place and women's work, the power of defining what is respected, what is superior, and what is desirable is a power which women will have to minimize before they will be liberated. This power to define has been used for centuries to subjugate peoples. Those who have allowed themselves to be defined by the law, education, religion, parents, politicians, racists, et cetera, have found themselves dominated by those who held the power to define. The Nazis defined the Jews as "disease," "bacilli," "the plague," as subhumans; the success of the redefinition led to the suppression and execution of the Jewish population. As the blacks in the United States have recognized, one way in which whites have suppressed them for so long has been by defining who and what a "Negro" was. The whites characterized him as lazy, slow, dumb, happy, et cetera. As long as the blacks did not take away from the whites this power to define, they were trapped in their suppression.

The same appears to be the case with women. The male-dominated culture has defined what a woman is and who and what she should be. If being male is by definition to be superior, being female is by the same definition, to be inferior. When the male has lost all other arguments, he can always resort to the argument of his "manliness." The extent and force of this "argument" is discussed by Kate Millett in her *Sexual Politics*:

It is in the area of class that the castelike status of the female within patriarchy is most liable to confusion, for sexual status often operates in a superficially confusing way within the variable of class. In a society where status is dependent upon the economic, social, and educational circumstances of class, it is possible for certain females to appear to stand higher than some males. Yet not when one looks more closely at the subject. This is perhaps easier to see by means of an analogy: a black doctor or lawyer has higher social status than a poor white sharecropper. But race, itself a caste system which subsumes class, persuades the latter citizen that he belongs to a higher order of life, just as it oppresses the black professional in spirit, whatever his material success may be. In much the same manner, a truck driver or butcher has always his "manhood" to fall back upon. Should this final vanity be offended, he may contemplate more violent methods.[6]

The resort to arguments based on "manliness," or ridicule loaded with sarcasm, innuendo, and assertions of penis envy (and usually hardly worthy of attention) can place a woman on the defensive. Such arguments revolve around motive and not the specific grievances and problems which legitimately should be the subject under discussion and debate. Whether a woman warrants equal pay or equal job opportunities or economic freedom cannot be determined if the woman discusses the inequalities which exist and the man insists on discussing penis envy as the motivating force behind the woman's demands. Using the penis envy argument as an answer to women's demands for equality in jobs and education makes about as much sense as whites using the "You want to marry my daughter" argument as a reason for refusing blacks equal pay, equal jobs, equal educational opportunities, and equality under the law. The whites' fears of liberated blacks have led to various types of irrational red herrings conjured up to keep the race subjugated. Similarly, the males' fears of liberated women have driven them to use arguments hardly relevant to the immediate issues and grievances being presented by women.

The clichés and axioms used over the centuries to answer women's demands are dogma of the most dangerous kind. Often encompassing Nature, God, and Sex, they become "irrefutable" dogma. No matter how many times they are demonstrated to be false by the behavior and actions of women, they persist as arguments. The extent to which men are committed to them reflects the depth of their fears and their uncompromising position.

One of the conclusions which stands out after one has read the selections in this book is that in our society, as in preceding ones, there exists an institutionalized sexism. For years, the blacks have distinguished between institutionalized racism and individual racism—racism which is practiced through our institutions (government, church, business, education, courts) and racism which is practiced by individuals in the society. The distinction is a valuable one and we find that much of the discrimination against women is institutionalized in religion, government, the schools, labor, and the courts. All have built within them a structured sexism, one of the effects of which is a kind of vicious circle. What attorney Diane B. Schulder says about the legal discriminations against women, discriminations institutionalized by the law, applies equally to other institutions in our society:

> . . . prejudice (the mythology of class oppression) is enshrined in laws. Laws lead to enforcement or practices. Practices reinforce and lead to prejudice. The cycle continues. . . . Women who feel oppressed, women involved in the fight for women's liberation, are not paranoid. Their feelings of oppression are not imaginary. Indeed their oppression, in more areas than generally realized, is built into the law.[7]

"The cycle continues." Question-begging, circular arguments are difficult to attack, and they are vicious because when one attempts to break out of the circle, one is forced back into it. As Professor Knudsen states: "Women, ambivalent about careers and convinced that they will face discrimination, make lesser efforts than men, permitting employers to justify discrimination by appealing to evidence of lower achievement and commitment to employment. The effect is the perpetuation of a belief that sexual equality exists and that only effort is lacking. . . . "[8] The vicious circle is recognized by Professor Karen Sacks when she writes: "The family ideal is fine for the owners. Men and women are pitted against each other in competition for wages. Women are made to feel out of place in a work situation, treated less seriously, and given less pay for equal work. This is justified by the 'well-known fact' that women do not stay on the job for long. So despite the work or career plans of any individual women, certain types of work are reserved for us as a group: the most underpaid in any given category of work. Women do not put up with this kind of situation any longer than they absolutely must. But in quitting, we only reinforce the woman-home ideology, and help perpetuate the System."[9]

Just as there is the "well-known fact" that women do not stay on the job for long, there are numerous other "well-known facts," commonplace "truths" about women which have led to arguments in which the premise is assumed and never examined. These "obvious truths" are employed to keep women "in their place"; that the women have "their place" is itself one of the "truths" which "everyone knows." "Woman's place is in the home" has not really been a point at issue; it has been accepted as a truth, not as a premise yet to be established. Nevertheless, it has long been used to justify discrimination against women.

These unexamined arguments about the rights of women have their roots deep in the past, as the selections in this book indicate. The "second sex" forever becomes the "second sex" simply because, as the first selection tells us, ". . . the rib, which the Lord God had taken from man, made he a woman, and brought her unto the man. And Adam said, "This is now bone of my bones, and flesh of my flesh: she shall be called Woman, because she was taken out of Man." Not only is she second in time, but she is second simply because she "was taken out of Man." Not only is she ordained to be the "second sex," she is destined to be the more evil of the two sexes since it is she who tempted Adam to evil; and because of her sinfulness the Lord said to her: ". . . I will greatly multiply thy sorrow and thy conception; in sorrow thou shalt bring forth children; and thy desire shall be to thy husband, and he shall rule over thee." From the Beginning, she was the sinful second sex destined to be ruled over by man. The injustices, discriminations, and oppression which the women's liberation movements of the twentieth century are attempting to eradicate have a lineage which goes back to the beliefs and attitudes expressed as part of the mythic statement in Genesis, the mythic statement with which we begin our survey of This Great Argument: The Rights of Women.

Notes

1. Quoted in *History of Woman Suffrage*, eds. Elizabeth Cady Stanton, Susan B. Anthony, and Matilda Joslyn Gage (Rochester, New York, 1889), I, 165—166.

2. *Ibid.*, pp. 853—854.

3. 110 *Congressional Record* 2577 (1964).

4. *History of Woman Suffrage*, p. 116.

5. Elizabeth C. Crable, "Pros and Cons of the Equal Rights Amendment," *Women Lawyers Journal*, XXXV (Summer 1949), p. 9.

6. Kate Millett, *Sexual Politics* (Doubleday: New York, 1970), p. 36.

7. Diane B. Schulder, "Does the Law Oppress Women?" in Robin Morgan, ed., *Sisterhood Is Powerful* (Vintage Books: New York, 1970), pp. 156—157.

8. Hacker, "Women as a Minority Group," pp. 127—145 in this book.

9. Karen Sacks, "Social Bases for Sexual Equality: A Comparative View," in Robin Morgan, ed., *Sisterhood Is Powerful* (Vintage Books: New York, 1970), p. 463.

The Tradition of the Argument

Part Two of the Agent

The Mythic Statement

Myth is not written in a book; in its true form it is a vital force that forms the behavior and actions of living men and women in a community. Since it springs from the very primal drives and fears of mankind, it is associated with dangers and must be controlled with taboos and, in civilized societies, with laws. This is the reason why the mythic statement is so often a mystery or a riddle, for by the time the scribe of Genesis or the Greek farmer-poet Hesiod recorded their versions of the creation of men and women and the origin of evil, the primal drives and acts had already been heavily censored by the various civilizing powers in tribal communities. We can, therefore, only speculate what the original *mythos* (action) was. Theodor Reik, for example, offers in his *The Creation of Woman* the theory that the genesis of Eve is but the censored version of a primitive initiation rite in which young men are re-born, thus proving to the elders of the tribe "that men, too, can bear children," even female children, as in the case of Eve. In his *Myth and Guilt*, Reik interprets the story of the fall as a displacement of a primal act of guilt in which sons devoured their father-god in a cannibalistic ritual. Eve does not take part in that act. If Reik's theory should be true, then the story of woman as the cause of man's woes is one of the biggest hoaxes ever perpetrated on mankind. On the other hand, to absolve half of mankind from the capacity for evil would make woman less than human.

Theologians, psychologists, anthropologists, and poets have used these basic stories for inspiration and speculation. The problem is that one analogy is used to explain another, and one enigmatic metaphor is used to elucidate another. It cannot be denied, however, that the simple lines in Genesis had a profound impact on the development of western civilization. In Genesis the subjection of women received divine sanction, and thereafter, no matter how non-Christian or anti-Christian a man of imagination or science might be, he would write about women as the second sex. The inferiority of women is still a vital myth in the community of men.

"But I suffer not woman to teach, nor to usurp authority over man, but to be in silence," exhorts the Apostle Paul (Timothy 2:12). Over a thousand years later, St. Thomas Aquinas, accepting the story of Genesis literally, says about women: "As regards the individual nature, woman is defective and misbegotten, for the active force in the male tends to the production of a perfect likeness in the masculine sex; while the production of woman comes from a defect in the active force, or some material indisposition, or even from some external influence; such as that of the south wind, which is moist, as the Philosopher [Aristotle, *Generation of Animals*, IV, 2] says." Woman has a place in the general plan of God, but not as an individual. Strange as it may seem, Aquinas and Freud are not really so far apart. Freud's theory of penis envy in women is in line with the idea of woman as an imperfection and defect, and though he is less direct than the theologians, he too subscribes to the view that women are "naturally" submissive: "It may be that the part played by women in the sexual function leads them to incline towards passive behavior and passive aims." The difference in attitude lies primarily in the shift that has taken place from the divine order to the natural order of things. Whatever the primal cause of the story in Genesis, the impact of the literal meaning of the words on the page cannot be denied.

The accounts in Genesis, which were part of the oral tradition well before 1000 B.C., and in Hesiod's *Works and Days* and *Theogeny* (written in the eighth century B.C.) share certain similarities. Both include conflicting statements as to the origin of a female figure. Pandora is created differently in each version, and in Genesis God creates first male and female together and later forms Eve from the already created Adam. Both the Greek and the Judaic tradition have as the ruler of the universe a patriarchal figure who is easily offended when his taboos are violated. Totemic and magical objects and rituals provoke in each case the opposition of a male force, Prometheus and the serpent, who promises mankind benefits that the tyrannical father-god is keeping from them. Prometheus brings mankind fire hidden in a hollow reed, and the serpent promises Eve the knowledge of good and evil. A transgression is committed, with the result that woman becomes associated with the loss of innocence, with guilt and punishment. A difference is that Pandora represents a luxurious and superfluous creature who releases ills upon mankind while subjecting men to her beauty, whereas Eve is condemned to subordination for her one act of rebellion. History as we know it begins with both women, and perhaps as long as it will last, Pandora and her box and Eve and her apple will remain among man's most powerful symbols, projecting what each age wants to see in them and shrouding forever the primal energies that lie hidden in an unknowable and forgotten past.

Genesis

And God said, Let us make man in our image, after our likeness: and let them have dominion over the fish of the sea, and over the fowl of the air, and over the cattle, and over all the earth, and over every creeping thing that creepeth upon the earth.

So God created man in his own image, in the image of God created he him; male and female created he them.

Genesis 1: 26—27

And the Lord God said, It is not good that man should be alone; I will make him an help meet for him.

And out of the ground the Lord God formed every beast of the field, and every fowl of the air; and brought them unto Adam to see what he would call them: and whatsoever Adam called every living creature, that was the name thereof.

And Adam gave names to all cattle, and to the fowl of the air, and to every beast of the field; but for Adam there was not found an help meet for him.

And the Lord God caused a deep sleep to fall upon Adam, and he slept: and he took one of his ribs, and closed up the flesh thereof;

And the rib, which the Lord God had taken from man, made he a woman, and brought her unto the man.

And Adam said, This is now bone of my bones, and flesh of my flesh: she shall be called Woman, because she was taken out of Man.

Genesis 2:18—23

And the Lord God called unto Adam, and said unto him, Where art thou?

And he said, I heard thy voice in the garden, and I was afraid, because I was naked; and I hid myself.

And he said, Who told thee that thou wast naked? hast thou eaten of the tree, whereof I commanded thee that thou shouldst not eat?

And the man said, The woman whom thou gavest to be with me, she gave me of the tree, and I did eat.

And the Lord God said unto the woman, What is this that thou hast done? And the woman said, The serpent beguiled me, and I did eat.

And the Lord God said unto the serpent, Because thou hast done this, thou art cursed above all cattle, and above every beast of the field; upon thy belly shalt thou go, and dust shalt thou eat all the days of thy life:

And I will put enmity between thee and the woman, and between thy seed and her seed; it shall bruise thy head, and thou shalt bruise his heel.

Unto the woman he said, I will greatly multiply thy sorrow and thy conception; in sorrow thou shalt bring forth children; and thy desire shall be to thy husband, and he shall rule over thee.

And unto Adam he said, Because thou hast harkened unto the voice of thy wife, and hast eaten of the tree, of which I commanded thee, saying, Thou shalt not eat of it: cursed is the ground for thy sake; in sorrow shalt thou eat of it all the days of thy life;

Thorns also and thistles shall it bring forth to thee; and thou shalt eat the herb of the field;

In the sweat of thy face shalt thou eat bread, till thou return unto the ground; for out of it wast thou taken: for dust thou art, and unto dust shalt thou return.

And Adam called his wife's name Eve; because she was the mother of all living.

Genesis 3:9–20.

Hesiod/Prometheus and Pandora

Now Iapetus took to wife the neat-ankled maid Clymene, daughter of Ocean, and went up with her into one bed. And she bare him a stout-hearted son, Atlas: also she bare very glorious Menoetius and clever Prometheus, full of various wiles, and scatter-brained Epimetheus who from the first was a mischief to men who eat bread; for it was he who first took of Zeus the woman, the maiden whom he had formed. But Menoetius was outrageous, and far-seeing Zeus struck him with a lurid thunderbolt and sent him down to Erebus because of his mad presumption and exceed-

From Hesiod's *Theogeny*. Reprinted by permission of the publishers and The Loeb Classical Library from Hugh G. Evelyn White, tr., Hesiod, *The Homeric Hymns and Homerica* (Harvard University Press: Cambridge, Mass.).

ing pride. And Atlas through hard constraint upholds the wide heaven with unwearying head and arms, standing at the borders of the earth before the clear-voiced Hesperides; for this lot wise Zeus assigned to him. And ready-witted Prometheus he bound with inextricable bonds, cruel chains, and drove a shaft through his middle, and set on him a long-winged eagle, which used to eat his immortal liver; but by night the liver grew as much again everyway as the long-winged bird devoured in the whole day. That bird Heracles, the valiant son of shapely-ankled Alcmene, slew; and delivered the son of Iapetus from the cruel plague, and released him from affliction—not without the will of Olympian Zeus who reigns on high, that the glory of Heracles the Theban-born might be yet greater than it was before over the plenteous earth. This, then, he regarded, and honoured his famous son; though he was angry, he ceased from the wrath which he had before because Prometheus matched himself in wit with the almighty son of Cronos. For when the gods and mortal men were divided at Mecone, even then Prometheus was forward to cut up a great ox and set portions before them, trying to befool the mind of Zeus. Before the rest he set flesh and inner parts thick with fat upon the hide, covering them with an ox paunch; but for Zeus he put the white bones dressed up with cunning art and covered with shining fat. Then the father of men and of gods said to him:

"Son of Iapetus, most glorious of all lords, good sir, how unfairly you have divided the portions!"

So said Zeus whose wisdom is everlasting, rebuking him. But wily Prometheus answered him, smiling softly and not forgetting his cunning trick:

"Zeus, most glorious and greatest of the eternal gods, take which ever of these portions your heart within you bids." So he said, thinking trickery. But Zeus, whose wisdom is everlasting, saw and failed not to perceive the trick, and in his heart he thought mischief against mortal men which also was to be fulfilled. With both hands he took up the white fat and was angry at heart, and wrath came to his spirit when he saw the white ox-bones craftily tricked out: and because of this the tribes of men upon earth burn white bones to the deathless gods upon fragrant altars. But Zeus who drives the clouds was greatly vexed and said to him:

"Son of Iapetus, clever above all. So, sir, you have not yet forgotten your cunning arts!"

So spake Zeus in anger, whose wisdom is everlasting; and from that time he was always mindful of the trick, and would not give the power of unwearying fire to the Melian race of mortal men who live on the earth. But the noble son of Iapetus outwitted him and stole the farseen gleam of unwearying fire in a hollow fennel stalk. And Zeus who thunders on high was stung in spirit, and his dear heart was angered when he saw amongst men the far-seen ray of fire. Forthwith he made an evil thing for men as the price of fire; for the very famous Limping God formed of earth the likeness of a shy maiden as the son of Cronos willed. And the goddess bright-eyed Athene girded and clothed her with silvery raiment, and down from her head she spread with her hands a broidered veil, a wonder to see; and she, Pallas Athene, put about her head lovely garlands, flowers of new-grown herbs. Also she put upon her head a crown of gold which the very famous Limping God made himself and worked with his own hands as a favour to Zeus his father. On it was much curious work, wonderful to see; for of the many creatures which the land and sea rear up, he put most upon it, wonderful things, like living beings with voices: and great beauty shone out from it.

But when he had made the beautiful evil to be the price for the blessing, he brought her out, delighting in the finery which the bright-eyed daughter of a mighty father had given her, to the place where the other gods and men were. And wonder took hold of the deathless gods and mortal men when they saw that which was sheer guile, not to be withstood by men.

For from her is the race of women and female kind: of her is the deadly race and tribe of women who live amongst mortal men to their great trouble, no helpmeets in hateful poverty, but only in wealth. And as in thatched hives bees feed the drones whose nature is to do mischief—by day and throughout the day until the sun goes down the bees are busy and lay the white combs, while the drones stay at home in the covered skeps and reap the toil of others into their own bellies—even so Zeus who thunders on high made women to be an evil to mortal men, with a nature to do evil. And he gave them a second evil to be the price for the good they had: whoever avoids marriage and the sorrows that women cause, and will not wed, reaches deadly old age without anyone to tend his years, and though he at least has no lack of livelihood while he lives, yet, when he is dead, his kinsfolk divide his possessions amongst them. And as for the man who chooses the lot of marriage and takes a good wife suited to his mind, evil continually contends with good; for whoever happens to have mischievous children, lives always with unceasing grief in his spirit and heart within him; and this evil cannot be healed.

So it is not possible to deceive or go beyond the will of Zeus; for not even the son of Iapetus, kindly Prometheus, escaped his heavy anger, but of necessity strong bands confined him, although he knew many a wile.

Zeus in the wrath of his heart hath hidden the means of subsistence—
Wrathful because he once was deceived by the wily Prometheus.
Therefore it was he devised most grievous troubles for mortals.
Fire he hid: yet that, for men, did the gallant Prometheus
Steal in a hollow reed, from the dwelling of Zeus the Adviser,
Nor was he seen by the ruler of gods, who delights in the thunder.
Then, in his rage at the deed, cloud-gathering Zeus did address him:
Iapetionides, in cunning greater than any,
"Thou in the theft of fire and deceit of me art exulting,
Source of regret for thyself and for men who shall be hereafter.
I, in the place of fire, will give them a bane, so that all men
May in spirit exult and find in their misery comfort!"
Speaking thus, loud laughed he, the father of gods and of mortals.
Then he commanded Hephaistos, the cunning artificer, straightway
Mixing water and earth, with speech and force to endow it,
Making it like in face to the gods whose life is eternal.
Virginal, winning and fair was the shape: and he ordered Athene
Skilful devices to teach her, the beautiful works of the weaver.
Then did he bid Aphrodite the golden endow her with beauty,
Eager desire and passion that wasteth the bodies of mortals.
Hermes, guider of men, the destroyer of Argus, he ordered,
Lastly, a shameless mind to bestow and a treacherous nature.
So did he speak. They obeyed Lord Zeus, who is offspring of Kronos.
Straightway, out of the earth, the renowned artificer fashioned
One like a shame-faced maid, at the will of the ruler of Heaven.
Girdle and ornaments added the bright-eyed goddess Athene.
Over her body the Graces divine and noble Persuasion
Hung their golden chains; and the Hours with beautiful tresses
Wove her garlands of flowers that bloom in the season of Springtime.
All her adornments Pallas Athene fitted upon her.
Into her bosom, Hermes the guide, the destroyer of Argus,
Falsehood, treacherous thoughts and a thievish nature imparted:
Such was the bidding of Zeus who heavily thunders; and lastly,

Hermes, herald of gods, endowed her with speech, and the woman
Named Pandora, because all the gods who dwell in Olympos
Gave her presents, to make her a fatal bane unto mortals.
When now Zeus had finished this snare so deadly and certain,
Famous Argus slayer, the herald of gods, he commanded,
Leading her thence, as a gift to bestow her upon Epimetheus.
He, then, failed to remember Prometheus had bidden him never
Gifts to accept from Olympian Zeus, but still to return them
Straightway, lest some evil befall thereby unto mortals.
So he received her—and then, when the evil befell, he remembered.
Till that time, upon earth were dwelling the races of mortals,
Free and secure from trouble and free from wearisome labour;
Safe from painful diseases that bring mankind to destruction
Since full swiftly in misery age unto mortals approacheth.
Now with her hands, Pandora the great lid raised from the vessel,
Letting them loose: and grievous the evil for men she provided.
Hope yet lingered, alone, in the dwelling securely imprisoned,
Since she under the edge of the lid had tarried and flew not
Forth: too soon Pandora had fastened the lid of the vessel.
Such was the will of Zeus, cloud-gatherer, lord of the aegis.
Numberless evils beside to the haunts of men had departed,
Full is the earth of ills, and full no less are the waters.
Freely diseases among mankind, by day and in darkness
Hither and thither may pass and bring much woe upon mortals:
Voiceless, since of speech high-counselling Zeus has bereft them.

Plato / On Matrimony and Philosophy

As we have seen, the mythic view of women in the Graeco-Judaic-Christian
tradition often perpetuated the false concepts of the dangerousness and
inferiority of the second sex and advocated its subjugation to divine or human
male authority. Yet the concept of the equality of women, as well as their
self-sufficiency, was not foreign to the ancient Greeks. There were self-
sufficient females like the legendary warlike Amazons and the historical

---

From *The Republic*, Book V.

though mysterious poet Sappho of Lesbos. In Aristophanes' comedy *Lysistrata* (412 B.C.) we have one of the first examples of sexual politics, for the women of Athens and Sparta refused to have sexual relations with their men unless the latter ended the futile war between the two states. Although Aristophanes had great fun with this battle of the sexes, he had his characters occasionally utter lines that express sympathy for woman's plight. Lysistrata's "I am only a woman I know; but I have a mind, and I can distinguish between sense and nonsense" establishes the traditional complaint of the oppressed: I am human; recognize my humanity.

Such a feeling of humanity is often lacking in Plato's *Republic*, where individuation is subordinated to the good of the state. It is interesting that Plato (ca. 427–348 B.C.) turns to Athens' rival, Sparta, when he discusses the need for equal education of men and women. It was a logical choice, for Athenian women had no rights, and Plato considered democracy, which was at his time in serious trouble, just one degree above anarchy. He envisions a socialistic state governed by a benign patriarchy of philosopher kings. Simone de Beauvoir has pointed out in her book *The Second Sex* that "all forms of socialism, wresting woman away from the family, favor her liberation: Plato envisioned a communal regime and promised women an autonomy in it such as they enjoyed in Sparta." In his utopia is the starting point for the concept of equality that we will find in the ideas of Fourier, Marx, Engels, and Lenin.

We must keep in mind, though, that Plato considered women inferior in degree. A female guardian was somewhat inferior to her male counterpart, but she was superior to an artisan. In order to liberate women for her public duties, they had to be freed from childcare. Parents did not know their children, who were to be raised in "pens" supervised by special personnel. In the following excerpts, the reader is likely to notice a certain dehumanizing element, to which Plato's repeated use of animal imagery contributes not a little.

. . . For men born and educated like our citizens, the only way, in my opinion, of arriving at a right conclusion about the possession and use of women and children is to follow the path on which we originally started, when we said that the men were to be the guardians and watch-dogs of the herd.

True.

Let us further suppose the birth and education of our women to be subject to similar or nearly similar regulations; then we shall see whether the result accords with our design.

What do you mean?

What I mean may be put into the form of a question, I said: Are dogs divided into he's and she's, or do they both share equally in hunting and in keeping watch and in the other duties of dogs? or do we intrust to the males the entire and exclusive care of the flocks, while we leave the females at home, under the idea that the bearing and the suckling of their puppies are labor enough for them?

No, he said, they share alike; the only difference between them is that the males are stronger and the females weaker.

But can you use different animals for the same purpose, unless they are bred and fed in the same way?

You cannot.

Then, if women are to have the same duties as men, they must have the same nurture and education?

Yes.

The education which was assigned to the men was music and gymnastics.

Yes.

Then women must be taught music and gymnastics and also the art of war, which they must practise like the men?

That is the inference, I suppose.

I should rather expect, I said, that several of our proposals, if they are carried out, being unusual, may appear ridiculous.

No doubt of it.

Yes, and the most ridiculous thing of all will be the sight of women naked in the palæstra, exercising with the men, especially when they are no longer young; they certainly will not be a vision of beauty, any more than the enthusiastic old men who, in spite of wrinkles and ugliness, continue to frequent the gymnasia.

Yes, indeed, he said: according to present notions the proposal would be thought ridiculous.

First, then, whether the question is to be put in jest or in earnest, let us come to an understanding about the nature of woman: Is she capable of sharing either wholly or partially in the actions of men, or not at all? And is the art of war one of those arts in which she can or cannot share? That will be the best way of commencing the inquiry, and will probably lead to the fairest conclusion.

That will be much the best way...

...And if, I said, the male and female sex appear to differ in their fitness for any art or pursuit, we should say that such pursuit or art ought to be assigned to one or the other of them; but if the difference consists only in women bearing and men begetting children, this does not amount to a proof that a woman differs from a man in respect of the sort of education she should receive; and we shall therefore continue to maintain that our guardians and their wives ought to have the same pursuits.

Very true, he said.

Next, we shall ask our opponent how, in reference to any of the pursuits or arts of civic life, the nature of a woman differs from that of a man?

That will be quite fair.

And perhaps he, like yourself, will reply that to give a sufficient answer on the instant is not easy; but after a little reflection there is no difficulty.

Yes, perhaps.

Suppose then that we invite him to accompany us in the argument, and then we may hope to show him that there is nothing peculiar in the constitution of women which would affect them in the administration of the State.

By all means.

Let us say to him: Come now, and we will ask you a question: When you spoke of a nature gifted or not gifted in any respect, did you mean to say that one man will acquire a thing easily, another with difficulty; a little learning will lead the one to discover a great deal, whereas the other, after much study and application, no sooner learns than he forgets; or again, did you mean, that the one has a body which is a good servant to his mind, while the body of the other is a hinderance to him?—would not these be the sort of differences which distinguish the man gifted by nature from the one who is ungifted?

No one will deny that.

And can you mention any pursuit of mankind in which the male sex has not all these gifts and qualities in a higher degree than the female? Need I waste time in speaking of the art of weaving, and the management of pancakes and preserves, in which womankind does really appear to be great, and in which for her to be beaten by a man is of all things the most absurd?

You are quite right, he replied, in maintaining the general inferiority

of the female sex: although many women are in many things superior to
many men, yet on the whole what you say is true.

And if so, my friend, I said, there is no special faculty of adminstration
in a State which a woman has because she is a woman, or which a man
has by virtue of his sex, but the gifts of nature are alike diffused in both; all
the pursuits of men are the pursuits of women also, but in all of them a
woman is inferior to a man.

Very true.

Then are we to impose all our enactments on men and none of them
on women?

That will never do.

One woman has a gift of healing, another not; one is a musician, and
another has no music in her nature?

Very true.

And one woman has a turn for gymnastic and military exercises, and
another is unwarlike and hates gymnastics?

Certainly.

And one woman is a philosopher, and another is an enemy of
philosophy; one has spirit, and another is without spirit?

That is also true.

Then one woman will have the temper of a guardian, and another not.
Was the selection of the male guardians determined by differences of this
sort?

Yes.

Men and women alike possess the qualities which make a guardian;
they differ only in their comparative strength or weakness.

Obviously.

And those women who have such qualities are to be selected as the
companions and colleagues of men who have similar qualities and whom
they resemble in capacity and in character?

Very true.

And ought not the same natures to have the same pursuits?

They ought.

Then, as we were saying before, there is nothing unnatural in as-
signing music and gymnastics to the wives of the guardians—to that point
we come round again.

Certainly not.

The law which we then enacted was agreeable to nature, and therefore not an impossibility or mere aspiration; and the contrary practice, which prevails at present, is in reality a violation of nature.

That appears to be true.

We had to consider, first, whether our proposals were possible, and secondly whether they were the most beneficial?

Yes.

And the possibility has been acknowledged?

Yes.

The very great benefit has next to be established?

Quite so.

You will admit that the same education which makes a man a good guardian will make a woman a good guardian; for their original nature is the same?

Yes.

I should like to ask you a question.

What is it?

Would you say that all men are equal in excellence, or is one man better than another?

The latter.

And in the commonwealth which we were founding do you conceive the guardians who have been brought up on our model system to be more perfect men, or the cobblers whose education has been cobbling?

What a ridiculous question!

You have answered me, I replied: Well, and may we not further say that our guardians are the best of our citizens?

By far the best.

And will not their wives be the best women?

Yes, by far the best.

And can there be anything better for the interests of the State than that the men and women of a State should be as good as possible?

There can be nothing better.

And this is what the arts of music and gymnastics, when present in such a manner as we have described, will accomplish?

Certainly.

Then we have made an enactment not only possible but in the highest degree beneficial to the State?

True.

Then let the wives of our guardians strip, for their virtue will be their robe, and let them share in the toils of war and the defence of their country; only in the distribution of labors the lighter are to be assigned to the women, who are the weaker natures, but in other respects their duties are to be the same. And as for the man who laughs at naked women exercising their bodies from the best of motives, in his laughter he is plucking

"A fruit of unripe wisdom,"

and he himself is ignorant of what he is laughing at, or what he is about; for that is, and ever will be, the best of sayings, "that the useful is the noble, and the hurtful is the base." . . .

Very true.

[After a brief digression, Socrates proceeds to discuss selective mating.] . . . Well, I said, I submit to my fate. Yet grant me a little favor: let me feast my mind with the dream as day-dreamers are in the habit of feasting themselves when they are walking alone; for before they have discovered any means of effecting their wishes—that is a matter which never troubles them—they would rather not tire themselves by thinking about possibilities; but assuming that what they desire is already granted to them, they proceed with their plan, and delight in detailing what they mean to do when their wish has come true—that is a way which they have of not doing much good to a capacity which was never good for much. Now I myself am beginning to lose heart, and I should like, with your permission, to pass over the question of possibility at present. Assuming therefore the possibility of the proposal, I shall now proceed to inquire how the rulers will carry out these arrangements, and I shall demonstrate that our plan, if executed, will be of the greatest benefit to the State and to the guardians. First of all, then, if you have no objection, I will endeavor with your help to consider the advantages of the measure; and hereafter the question of possibility.

I have no objection; proceed.

First, I think that if our rulers and their auxiliaries are to be worthy of the name which they bear, there must be willingness to obey in the one and the power of command in the other; the guardians themselves must obey the laws, and they must also imitate the spirit of them in any details which are intrusted to their care.

That is right, he said.

You, I said, who are their legislator, having selected the men, will now select the women and give them to them; they must be as far as possible of like natures with them; and they must live in common houses and meet at common meals. None of them will have anything specially his or her own; they will be together, and will be brought up together, and will associate at gymnastic exercises. And so they will be drawn by a necessity of their natures to have intercourse with each other—necessity is not too strong a word, I think?

Yes, he said; necessity, not geometrical, but another sort of necessity which lovers know, and which is far more convincing and constraining to the mass of mankind.

True, I said; and this, Glaucon, like all the rest, must proceed after an orderly fashion; in a city of the blessed, licentiousness is an unholy thing which the rulers will forbid.

Yes, he said, and it ought not to be permitted.

Then clearly the next thing will be to make matrimony sacred in the highest degree, and what is most beneficial will be deemed sacred?

Exactly.

And how can marriages be made most beneficial? that is a question which I put to you, because I see in your house dogs for hunting, and of the nobler sort of birds not a few. Now, I beseech you, do tell me, have you ever attended to their pairing and breeding?

In what particulars?

Why, in the first place, although they are all of a good sort, are not some better than others?

True.

And do you breed from them all indifferently; or do you take care to breed from the best only?

From the best.

And do you take the oldest or the youngest, or only those of ripe age?

I choose only those of ripe age.

And if care was not taken in the breeding, your dogs and birds would greatly deteriorate?

Certainly.

And the same of horses and of animals in general?

Undoubtedly.

Good heavens! my dear friend, I said, what consummate skill will our rulers need if the same principle holds of the human species!

Certainly, the same principle holds; but why does this involve any particular skill?

Because, I said our rulers will often have to practise upon the body corporate with medicines. Now you know that when patients do not require medicines, but have only to be put under a regimen, the inferior sort of practitioner is deemed to be good enough; but when medicine has to be given, then the doctor should be more of a man.

That is quite true, he said; but to what are you alluding?

I mean, I replied, that our rulers will find a considerable dose of falsehood and deceit necessary for the good of their subjects: we were saying that the use of all these things regarded as medicines might be of advantage.

And we were very right.

And this lawful use of them seems likely to be often needed in the regulations of marriages and births.

How so?

Why, I said, the principle has been already laid down that the best of either sex should be united with the best as often, and the inferior with the inferior as seldom, as possible; and that they should rear the offspring of the one sort of union, but not of the other, if the flock is to be maintained in first-rate condition. Now these goings on must be a secret which the rulers only know, or there will be a further danger of our herd, as the guardians may be termed, breaking out into rebellion.

Very true.

Had we better not appoint certain festivals at which we will bring together the brides and bridegrooms, and sacrifices will be offered and suitable hymeneal songs composed by our poets: the number of weddings is a matter which must be left to the discretion of the rulers, whose aim will be to preserve the average of population? There are many other things which they will have to consider, such as the effects of wars and diseases and any similar agencies, in order as far as this is possible to prevent the State from becoming either too large or too small.

Certainly, he replied.

We shall have to invent some ingenious kind of lots which the less worthy may draw on each occasion of our bringing them together, and then they will accuse their own ill-luck and not the rulers.

To be sure, he said.

And to think that our braver and better youth, besides their other honors and rewards, might have greater facilities of intercourse with women given them; their bravery will be a reason, and such fathers ought to have as many sons as possible.

True.

And the proper officers, whether male or female or both, for offices are to be held by women as well as by men———.

Yes———.

The proper officers will take the offspring of the good parents to the pen or fold, and there they will deposit them with certain nurses who dwell in a separate quarter; but the offspring of the inferior, or of the better when they chance to be deformed, will be put away in some mysterious, unknown place, as they should be.

Yes, he said, that must be done if the breed of the guardians is to be kept pure.

They will provide for their nurture, and will bring the mothers to the fold when they are full of milk, taking the greatest possible care that no mother recognizes her own child; and other wet-nurses may be engaged if more are required. Care will also be taken that the process of suckling shall not be protracted too long; and the mothers will have no getting up at night or other trouble, but will hand over all this sort of thing to the nurses and attendants.

You suppose the wives of our guardians to have a fine easy time of it when they are having children.

Why, said I, and so they ought. Let us, however, proceed with our scheme. We were saying that the parents should be in the prime of life?

Very true.

And what is the prime of life? May it not be defined as a period of about twenty years in a woman's life, and thirty years in a man's?

Which years do you mean to include?

A woman, I said, at twenty years of age may begin to bear children to the State, and continue to bear them until forty; a man may begin at five-and-twenty, when he has passed the point at which the pulse of life beats quickest, and continue to beget children until he be fifty-five.

Certainly, he said, both in men and women those years are the prime of physical as well as of intellectual vigor.

Anyone above or below the prescribed ages who takes part in the public hymeneals shall be said to have done an unholy and unrighteous thing; the child of which he is the father, if it steals into life, will have been conceived under auspices very unlike the sacrifices and prayers, which at each hymeneal priestesses and priests and the whole city will offer, that the new generation may be better and more useful than their good and useful parents, whereas his child will be the offspring of darkness and strange lust.

Very true, he replied.

And the same law will apply to any one of those within the prescribed age who forms a connection with any woman in the prime of life without the sanction of the rulers; for we shall say that he is raising up a bastard to the State, uncertified and unconsecrated.

Very true, he replied.

This applies, however, only to those who are within the specified age: after that we will allow them to range at will, except that a man may not marry his daughter or his daughter's daughter, or his mother or his mother's mother; and women, on the other hand, are prohibited from marrying their sons or fathers, or son's son or father's father, and so on in either direction. And we grant all this, accompanying the permission with strict orders to prevent any embryo which may come into being from seeing the light; and if any force a way to the birth, the parents must understand that the offspring of such a union cannot be maintained, and arrange accordingly.

That also, he said, is a reasonable proposition. But how will they know who are fathers and daughters, and so on?

They will never know. The way will be this: dating from the day of the hymeneal, the bridegroom who was then married will call all the male children who are born in the seventh and the tenth month afterward his sons, and the female children his daughters, and they will call him father, and he will call their children his grandchildren, and they will call the elder generation grandfathers and grandmothers. All who were begotten at the time when their fathers and mothers came together will be called their brothers and sisters, and these, as I was saying, will be forbidden to intermarry. This, however, is not to be understood as an absolute prohibition of marriage of brothers and sisters; if the lot favors them, and they receive the sanction of the Pythian oracle, the law will allow them.

Quite right, he replied.

Such is the scheme, Glaucon, according to which the guardians of our State are to have their wives and families in common.

The Poetic Statement

The following poems are an infinitesimal part of the thousands of poems written about women, not to speak of the important role of women in plays and novels. The sonnets are basically an idealization of the position of women in the world. However, the poem by Anne Finch, Countess of Winchilsea, is an outcry against the real situation of women, and Swift's poem "The Lady's Dressing Room" is a satire on men who have idealized women into goddesses.

Women, relegated to cupbearers and childbearers in heroic Anglo-Saxon literature, played an important role in medieval romances and in the love lyrics that influenced so much of the poetry in the Renaissance. The pinnacle of womanhood in the romance and courtly love tradition is probably Beatrice, in Dante's *Divine Comedy*, a virginal woman who leads the poet ever upward and on to a vision of eternity and everlasting life. In the more secular love lyrics, too, the traditional roles of men and women are reversed. The man becomes the woman's vassal and even her slave as he cringes for her favor. She is the general in the army of Cupid and the master of her admirer's life, and she holds his salvation or damnation in her little hand. The real situation of women was, of course, not at all like this. Women had no rights, marriages were often arranged between infants, wives were regularly beaten. Love between husband and wife was rare, but love between a married woman and a secret as well as an often younger admirer remained an interesting possibility. In his fantasies, the young man would endow the usually inferior sex with powers that bordered on the supernatural. She was a taboo, and infinitely attractive.

A genuine union between two people who accepted each other as human beings remained, however, an impossibility. Instead, there evolved an intricate sexual and political relationship. For a further exploration of this fascinating subject the reader is referred to Cappelanus' *The Art of Courtly Love*, to Castiglione's *The Courtier*, and to two modern works: Denis de Rougemont's *Love in the Western World* and C. S. Lewis's *The Allegory of Courtly Love*. The sonnet by Petrarch (1304—1374) and the sonnet "Like some weak lords" by Sidney (1554—1586) well illustrate the sexual-political relationships in the warfare of love. Here the woman is given power and glory, and she subdues and even enslaves the man, but by doing so she also becomes guilty. The reader cannot help but wonder if the entire sequence is not a subconscious expression of guilt by the male sex for having subjugated women. By taking upon themselves momentarily the woman's role, they experience her suffering, alleviate some of their guilt, and find justification for hidden or open hostility against the second sex.

This hostility is very pronounced in Shakespeare's sonnet "Two loves I have of comfort and despair." Here the woman is associated with the forces of hell, and the young man, whom Shakespeare woos, is the bright angel. To him the sonnet cycle is dedicated, and it is in that cycle that we find some of the finest love lyrics in the English language. The depth and range of Shakespeare's sonnets can be largely attributed to his sexually ambiguous attitude. In his waiting and yearning he knows how a woman feels, even though he is hostile to women.

An attitude of spiritual homosexuality is taken by Donne in "Batter my heart, three person'd God," where sexual, political, and religious images are combined. The lover general is the patriarch of the universe, who has to conquer the human heart. Donne expresses that conquest through the image of a besieged town for which the forces of good and evil are battling. The town is traditionally a feminine symbol: for example, the whore of Babylon, and the New Jerusalem as the bride of Christ. In Donne's poem the human soul is waiting to be overpowered, to be raped by a superior force, and only through this rape will the soul be fulfilled and become a greater self. The reader is advised to read more of Donne's poems, which give a varied portrayal of the manifold possibilities in love relationships between men and women, between the human and the divine.

Petrarch / Sonnet*

A thousand times, O my sweet warrior,
Burning to purchase peace of those proud eyes,
Have I held forth the heart your heart denies,
Which your nobility will not bend for.
And if some other lady love it more,
Vain is her hope and false: what you despise
I must disdain, since what you do not prize
I spurn, and what you hate cannot adore.
Exiled by me, what then if it shall find
With you no word of mercy now or later.
And so, when others call it stay behind,
Afraid to go, afraid of its dear hater?
Though guilt to both of us must be assigned,
It loves you more, and thus your guilt is greater.

Sir Philip Sidney / Sonnet 29†

Like some weak Lords, neighboured by mighty kings,
    To keep themselves and their chief cities free,
    Do easily yield, that all their coasts may be
Ready to store their camps of needful things:
So *Stella's* heart, finding what power *Love* brings,
    To keep itself in life and liberty,
    Doth willing grant, that in the frontiers he
Use all to help his other conquerings:
And thus her heart escapes, but thus her eyes
    Serve him with shot, her lips his heralds are:
    Her breasts his tents, her legs his triumphal car:
Her flesh his food, her skin his armour brave,
And I, but for because my prospect lies
Upon that coast, am given up for a slave.

---

*   Translated by Joseph Auslander, *The Sonnets of Petrarch* (London: Longman, Green and Co., 1931).

†   From *Astrophel and Stella*.

Sir Philip Sidney / Sonnet 76

She comes, and straight therewith her shining twins do move
    Their rays to me, who in her tedious absence lay
    Benighted in cold woe, but now appears my day,
The only light of joy, the only warmth of Love.
She comes with light and warmth, which like Aurora prove
    Of gentle force, so that mine eyes dare gladly play
    With such a rosy morn, whose beams most freshly gay
Scorch not, but only do dark chilling sprites remove.
    But lo, while I do speak, it groweth noon with me,
Her flamy glist'ring lights increase with time and place;
My heart cries, "Ah, it burns!" Mine eyes now dazzled be:
No wind, no shade can cool. What help then in my case,
    But with short breath, long looks, staid feet, and walking head,
    Pray that my sun go down with meeker beams to bed.

William Shakespeare / Sonnet CXLIV

Two loves I have of comfort and despair,
Which like two spirits do suggest me still:
The better angel is a man right fair,
The worser spirit a woman colour'd ill.
To win me soon to hell, my female evil
Tempteth my better angel from my side,
And would corrupt my saint to be a devil,
Wooing his purity with her foul pride.
And whether that my angel be turn'd fiend
Suspect I may, yet not directly tell;
But being both from me, both to each friend,
I guess one angel in another's hell:
    Yet this shall I ne'er know, but live in doubt,
    Till my bad angel fire my good one out.

John Donne/Holy Sonnet XIV

Batter my heart, three person'd God; for, you
As yet but knocke, breathe, shine, and seeke to mend;
That I may rise, and stand, o'erthrow mee, and bend
Your force, to breake, blowe, burn and make me new.
I, like an usurpt towne, to'another due,
Labour to'admit you, but Oh, to no end,
Reason your viceroy in mee should defend,
But is captiv'd, and proves weak or untrue.
Yet dearly I love you, and would be loved faine,
But am betroth'd unto your enemie:
Divorce mee, untie, or break that knot againe,
Take me to you, imprison me, for I
Except you enthrall mee, never shall be free,
Nor ever chast, except you ravish mee.

Anne Finch, Countess of Winchilsea/The Introduction

Very little is known about the Countess of Winchilsea (1661–1720). She
came from an aristocratic family and married an aristocrat. Her education
"trained" her for little else other than marriage. That is probably the reason
that she speaks out repeatedly against the lack of education for women. Her
marriage, though childless, was very happy and she did not hesitate to write
poetry to her husband, who encouraged her in her endeavors. Anne was very
much aware that poetry was written almost exclusively by men and very
seldom by a woman. She brings this to light in a mocking manner in a poem
written for her husband during his absence. Here the muses are aghast at
her presumption

> "A husband!" echoed all around;
> And to Parnassus sure that sound
>   Had never yet been sent;
> Amazement in each face was read.
> In haste the affrighted sisters fled,
>   And to a council went.

Anne was not a great poet, but that she even dared to express herself
in that medium was an accomplishment. Moreover, as the poem "The Intro-
duction" reveals, she was very much aware that the injustices committed

against women had their origin not in nature but in education. The wits of the age—Swift, Pope, Gay—did not exactly admire her, though Pope did not hesitate to "borrow" occasionally a line from her verse. She wrote not always well, but she wrote.

In order to understand what that implies, we must remind ourselves that illiteracy was very common among women and that the skill of writing was considered dangerous to the "female sex." When more women did learn to write, their prose left much to be desired, as the many satires by men about female writings reveal. Anne, then, wrote surprisingly well considering all the handicaps, prejudices, and conditionings that forged her character. Her poetry is a private statement; she did not make money with it as did her contemporary, Aphra Behn, who supported herself partially by her writings. A fictional example of the power of the written word for women is Samuel Richardson's prodigious and interminable scribbler, Pamela.

Did I my lines intend for public view,
How many censures would their faults pursue!
Some would, because such words they do affect,
Cry they're insipid, empty, incorrect.
And many have attained, dull and untaught,
The name of wit, only by finding fault.
True judges might condemn their want of wit;
And all might say, they're by a woman writ.
Alas! a woman that attempts the pen,
Such an intruder on the rights of men,
Such a presumptuous creature is esteemed,
The fault can by no virtue be redeemed.
They tell us we mistake our sex and way;
Good breeding, fashion, dancing, dressing, play,
Are the accomplishments we should desire;
To write, or read, or think, or to enquire,
Would cloud our beauty, and exhaust our time,
And interrupt the conquests of our prime;
Whilst the dull manage of a servile house
Is held by some our utmost art and use.
   Sure, 'twas not ever thus, nor are we told
Fables, of women that excelled of old;
To whom, by the diffusive hand of heaven,
Some share of wit and poetry was given.

On that glad day, on which the Ark returned,
The holy pledge, for which the land had mourned,
The joyful tribes attend it on the way,
The Levites do the sacred charge convey,
Whilst various instruments before it play;
Here, holy virgins in the concert join,
The louder notes to soften and refine,
And with alternate verse complete the hymn divine.
   Lo! the young poet, after God's own heart,
By Him inspired and taught the Muses' art,
Returned from conquest a bright chorus meets,
That sing his slain ten thousand in the streets.
In such loud numbers they his acts declare,
Proclaim the wonders of his early war,
That Saul upon the vast applause does frown,
And feels its mighty thunder shake the crown.
What can the threatened judgment now prolong?
Half of the kingdom is already gone:
The fairest half, whose judgment guides the rest,
Have David's empire o'er their hearts confessed.
   A woman here leads fainting Israel on,
She fights, she wins, she triumphs with a song,
Devout, majestic, for the subject fit,
And far above her arms, exalts her wit,
Then to the peaceful, shady palm withdraws,
And rules the rescued nation with her laws.
   How are we fallen! fallen by mistaken rules,
And Education's, more than Nature's fools;
Debarred from all improvements of the mind,
And to be dull, expected and designed;
And if some one would soar above the rest,
With warmer fancy, and ambition pressed,
So strong the opposing faction still appears,
The hopes to thrive can ne'er outweigh the fears.
Be cautioned, then, my Muse, and still retired;
Nor be despised, aiming to be admired;
Conscious of wants, still with contracted wing,
To some few friends, and to thy sorrows sing.
For groves of laurel thou wert never meant:
Be dark enough thy shades, and be thou there content.

Jonathan Swift / The Lady's Dressing Room

Swift's poem about a lover who explores his lady's dressing room provides
a stark contrast to the poems written in the courtly love tradition. Swift
(1667–1745) has many times been accused of being a misogynist, but
though his satire against Celia is in very strong terms, his anger is even more
directed at the foolish male who made a mortal woman into a goddess. The
poem is mainly about an idealist whose illusions have been crushed and who,
to use Blake's words, lays himself down among the swine as a result.
Because of idealizing courtly or pastoral romanticism, a healthy relationship
between men and women is impossible. Neither Celia, nor Strephon, nor
the speaker of the poem express Swift's view: men and women should base
their relationship on reason, common sense, and affection. Swift thought
that the ability to converse intelligently with each other is a sounder basis
for marriage than infatuation with a pretty or handsome face.

Five Hours, (and who can do it less in?)
By haughty *Celia* spent in Dressing;
The Goddess from her Chamber issues,
Array'd in Lace, Brocades and Tissues.

Strephon, who found the Room was void,
And *Betty* otherwise employ'd;
Stole in, and took a strict Survey,
Of all the Litter as it lay;
Whereof, to make the Matter clear,
An Inventory follows here.

And first a dirty Smock appear'd,
Beneath the Arm-pits well besmear'd.
Strephon, the Rogue, display'd it wide,
And turn'd it round on every Side.
On such a Point few Words are best,
And *Strephon* bids us guess the rest;
But swears how damnably the Men lie,
In calling *Celia* sweet and cleanly.
Now listen while he next produces,
The various Combs for various Uses,

Fill'd up with Dirt so closely fixt,
No Brush could force a way betwixt.
A Paste of Composition rare,
Sweat, Dandriff, Powder, Lead and Hair;
A Forehead Cloth with Oyl upon't
To smooth the Wrinkles on her Front;
Here Allum Flower to stop the Steams,
Exhal'd from sour unsavoury Streams,
There Night-gloves made of *Tripsy's* Hide,
Bequeath'd by *Tripsy* when she dy'd,
With Puppy Water, Beauty's Help
Distill'd from *Tripsy's* darling Whelp;
Here Gallypots and Vials plac'd,
Some fill'd with Washes, some with Paste,
Some with Pomatum, Paints and Slops,
And Ointments good for scabby Chops.
Hard by a filthy Bason stands,
Fowl'd with the Scouring of her Hands;
The Bason takes whatever comes
The Scrapings of her Teeth and Gums,
A nasty Compound of all Hues,
For here she spits, and here she spues.
But oh! it turn'd poor *Strephon's* Bowels,
When he beheld and smelt the Towels,
Begumm'd, bematter'd, and beslim'd
With Dirt, and Sweat, and Ear-Wax grim'd.
No Object *Strephon's* Eye escapes,
Here Pettycoats in frowzy Heaps;
Nor be the Handkerchiefs forgot
All varnish'd o'er with Snuff and Snot.
The Stockings, why shou'd I expose,
Stain'd with the Marks of stinking Toes;
Or greasy Coifs and Pinners reeking,
Which *Celia* slept at least a Week in?
A Pair of Tweezers next he found
To pluck her Brows in Arches round,
Or Hairs that sink the Forehead low,
Or on her Chin like Bristles grow.

The Virtues we must not let pass,
Of *Celia's* magnifying Glass.
When frighted *Strephon* cast his Eye on't
It shew'd the Visage of a Gyant.
A Glass that can to Sight disclose,
The smallest Worm in *Celia's* Nose,
And faithfully direct her Nail
To squeeze it out from Head to Tail;
For catch it nicely by the Head,
It must come out alive or dead.

Why *Strephon* will you tell the rest?
And must you needs describe the Chest?
That careless Wench! no Creature warn her
To move it out from yonder Corner;
But leave it standing full in Sight
For you to exercise your Spight.
In vain, the Workmen shew'd his Wit
With Rings and Hinges counterfeit
To make it seem in this Disguise,
A Cabinet to vulgar Eyes;
For *Strephon* ventur'd to look in,
Resolv'd to go thro' thick and thin;
He lifts the Lid, there needs no more,
He smelt it all the Time before.
As from within *Pandora's* Box,
When *Epimetheus* op'd the Locks,
A sudden universal Crew
Of humane Evils upwards flew;
He still was comforted to find
That *Hope* at last remain'd behind;
So *Strephon* lifting up the Lid,
To view what in the Chest was hid.
The Vapours flew from out the Vent,
But *Strephon* cautious never meant
The Bottom of the Pan to grope,
And fowl his Hands in Search of *Hope*.
O never may such vile Machine
Be once in *Celia's* Chamber seen!

O may she better learn to keep
"Those Secrets of the hoary deep!"

As Mutton Cutlets, Prime of Meat,
Which tho' with Art you salt and beat,
As Laws of Cookery require,
And toast them at the clearest Fire;
If from adown the hopeful Chops
The Fat upon a Cinder drops,
To stinking Smoak it turns the Flame
Pois'ning the Flesh from whence it came;
And up exhales a greasy Stench,
For which you curse the careless Wench;
So Things, which must not be exprest,
When plumpt into the reeking Chest;
Send up an excremental Smell
To taint the Parts from whence they fell.
The Pettycoats and Gown perfume,
Which waft a Stink round every Room.

Thus finishing his grand Survey,
Disgusted *Strephon* stole away
Repeating in his amorous Fits,
Oh! *Celia, Celia, Celia* shits!

But Vengeance, Goddess never sleeping
Soon punish'd *Strephon* for his Peeping;
His foul Imagination links
Each Dame he sees with all her Stinks:
And, if unsav'ry Odours fly,
Conceives a Lady standing by:
All Women his Description fits,
And both Idea's jump like Wits:
By vicious Fancy coupled fast,
And still appearing in Contrast.
I pity wretched *Strephon* blind
To all the Charms of Female Kind;
Should I the Queen of Love refuse,
Because she rose from stinking Ooze?
To him that looks behind the Scene,

> *Satira*'s but some pocky Quean.
> When *Celia* in her Glory shows,
> If *Strephon* would but stop his Nose;
> (Who now so impiously blasphemes
> Her Ointments, Daubs, and Paints and Creams,
> Her Washes, Slops, and every Clout,
> With which he makes so foul a Rout;)
> He soon would learn to think like me,
> And bless his ravisht Sight to see
> Such Order from Confusion sprung,
> Such gaudy Tulips rais'd from Dung.

John Milton / from *Paradise Lost*

When Milton (1608–1674) published the complete version of *Paradise Lost* in 1674, he was a disappointed revolutionary who had been afflicted with blindness for over twenty-two years, who had been married three times, and who had published in 1643 a pamphlet called *The Doctrine and Discipline of Divorce*, wherein he argued for divorce on grounds of incompatibility. His *Paradise Lost* is a final grand encyclopaedic Christian apology about the cause and reason for man's condition in the world. His Universe, though cracked by sinful rebellion, is still ordered and governed by a divine patriarchal potentate whose image, Adam, rules over the creatures of the earth and over Eve. His portrait of Eve is generally considered in terms of the antifeminist tradition, for Eve is not only the one who first brings into the world "all our woe," but she is also intellectually and morally inferior to Adam. It is through Satan's eyes that we first see the human pair in their unfallen state:

> . . . though both
> Not equal, as thir sex not equal seem'd;
> For contemplation he and valor form'd,
> For softness she and sweet attractive Grace,
> He for God only, she for God in him:
> His fair large Front and Eye sublime declar'd
> Absolute rule . . .

During a visit by the Archangel Raphael, Adam tells how he had asked the creator to give him a companion, since the animals over which he rules are so far beneath him. It is interesting to note that Adam pleads for a truly equal partner:

> Let not my words offend thee, Heavenly Power,
> My Maker, be propitious while I speak.
> Hast thou not made me here thy substitute,
> And these inferior far beneath me set?
> Among unequals what society
> Can sort, what harmony or true delight?
> Which must be mutual, in proportion due
> Giv'n and receiv'd; but in disparity
> The one intense, the other still remiss
> Cannot well suit with either, but soon prove
> Tedious alike: Of fellowship I speak
> Such as I seek, fit to participate
> All rational delight, wherein the brute
> Cannot be human consort . . .

> VIII, 379—392

After God has fashioned Eve from Adam's rib, He leads her to him not only as flesh of his flesh, but also as a gift. Enchanted with Eve, Adam will eventually fall because of his love for her, because of his uxoriousness and sexual submissiveness, against which the archangel warns him:

> But if the sense of touch whereby mankind
> Is propagated seem such dear delight
> Beyond all other, think the same voutsaf't
> To Cattle and each Beast; which would not be
> To them made common and divulg'd, if aught
> Therein enjoy'd were worthy to subdue
> The Soul of Man, or passion in him move.
> What higher in her society thou find'st
> Attractive, human, rational, love still;
> In loving thou dost well, in passion not,
> Wherein true Love consists not; Love refines
> The thoughts, and heart enlarges, hath his seat
> In Reason, and is judicious, is the scale
> By which to heavenly Love thou may'st ascend,
> Not sunk in carnal pleasure . . .

> VIII, 579—593

The creator did not make for Adam an equal mate. Eve is inferior to Adam in degree, and as a result she is less capable of reason and moral choice, but she is also less responsible for her crime of disobedience than Adam. After Eve received being, she is at first not in love with Adam but with herself, and displays in this way from the beginning a tendency to rebel. As she tells Adam about her first moments of consciousness, Milton casts her lines in terms of the temptation of Narcissus:

> ... and laid me down
> On the green bank, to look into the clear
> Smooth Lake, that to me seem'd another Sky.
> As I bent down to look, just opposite,
> A Shape within the wat'ry gleam appeared
> Bending to look on me, I started back,
> It started back, but pleas'd I soon return'd,
> Pleas'd it return'd as soon with answering looks
> Of sympathy and love; there I had fixt
> Mine eyes till now, and pin'd with vain desire,
> Had not a voice thus warn'd me, What thou seest,
> What there thou seest fair Creature is thyself,
> With thee it came and goes: but follow me,
> And I will bring thee where no shadow stays
> Thy coming, and thy soft embraces, he
> Whose image thou art, him thou shalt enjoy
> Inseparably thine, to him shalt bear
> Multitudes like thyself, and thence be call'd
> Mother of human Race: what could I do,
> But follow straight, invisibly thus led?
> Till I espi'd thee, fair indeed and tall,
> Under a Plantan, yet methought less fair,
> Less winning soft, less amiably mild,
> Than that smooth wat'ry image; back I turn'd,
> Thou following cri'd'st aloud, Return fair *Eve*,
> Whom fli'st thou? whom thou fli'st, of him thou art,
> His flesh, his bone; to give thee being I lent
> Out of my side to thee, nearest my heart
> Substantial Life, to have thee by my side
> Henceforth an individual solace dear;
> Part of my Soul I seek thee, and thee claim

My other half: with that thy gentle hand
Seiz'd mine, I yielded, and from that time see
How beauty is excell'd by manly grace
And wisdom, which alone is truly fair.

IV, 457—491

In spite of her willing submission to Adam, Eve seems to be moved by a vague but deep-seated sense of inferiority. It is to this feeling that the serpent directs his outrageous flatteries to Eve as "Empress of this fair World," "Sovran Mistress," and "Goddess humane," endowing her with political and sexual powers she does not have. After the fall, Eve reflects precisely on these newly gained powers as she decides if Adam should have a share in her new-found glory:

> But to *Adam* in what sort
> Shall I appear? shall I to him make known
> As yet my change, and give him to partake
> Full happiness with me, or rather not,
> But keep the odds of Knowledge in my power
> Without Copartner? so to add what wants
> In Female Sex, the more to draw his Love,
> And render me more equal, and perhaps,
> A thing not undesirable, sometime
> Superior: for inferior who is free?
> This may be well: but what if God has seen,
> And Death ensue? then I shall be no more,
> And *Adam* wedded to another *Eve*,
> Shall live with her enjoying, I extinct;
> A death to think. Confirm'd then I resolve,
> *Adam* shall share with me in bliss or woe:
> So dear I love him, that with him all deaths
> I could endure, without him live no life.

IX, 816—833

As a fallen creature, she plays a game of power politics and Adam "scrupl'd not to eat/ Against his better knowledge, not deceiv'd,/ But fondly overcome with Female charm." When divine punishment is dealt to man, Eve is given the punishment of biological and sexual submission:

> Thy sorrow I will greatly multiply
> By thy Conception; Children thou shalt bring

> In sorrow forth, and to thy Husband's will
> Thine shall submit, he over thee shall rule.
>
> X, 193—197

Milton sees then the tyranny of the sexes over each other as a direct result of the fall. Yet the last lines of the poem leave the reader with an image of man and woman equally united as they seek a place in a fallen world ruled by the all-powerful patriarchy of the universe:

> The World was all before them, where to choose
> Thir place of rest, and Providence thir guide:
> They hand in hand with wand'ring steps and slow,
> Through *Eden* took thir solitary way.

Jean Jacques Rousseau / Sophy, or Woman

Those who consider Rousseau, (1712—1778) too radical have blamed him for the French revolution, and those who are for women's rights consider him a conservative, a secular Thomas Aquinas at best. His views on the nature, education, and duties of women are most clearly stated in the last book of *Emile* (1757—1760), a novel of education. The woman destined for Emile is Sophy, who grows up in what Rousseau considered the ideal environment. She lives, with her highly respectable but poor parents, a simple country life strictly in accordance with the laws of nature. Since Emile's education is in terms of these same laws, both will eventually be united as the perfect couple and live in harmony with nature and justice. Rousseau envisioned such a unit in his *Julie, ou la Nouvelle Héloïse* and applied it to political life in *Le Contrat Social*. Both works are controlled by the thesis that man is basically good if he lives in accord with nature and that he becomes evil only through the corruption of social institutions. *Emile*, then, reveals the development and education of Rousseau's ideal man. The book was a bestseller at the time, but it also caused such a scandal that Rousseau had to flee Paris. He went first to Geneva and then to England, where he stayed until 1767.

From the book *Emile: or, Education*, by Jean Jacques Rousseau. Translated by Barbara Foxley. Everyman's Library Edition. Published by E. P. Dutton & Co., and reprinted with their permission.

Mary Wollstonecraft, a most ardent advocate for the rights of women, was the first to take issue with Rousseau's concept of women. She claims in her *Vindication of the Rights of Women* that if Rousseau's argument that man's moral sense is formed by his development of reason is correct, then women, whom he sees as dependent on and subservient to men, can have no moral sense because their reason has not been allowed to develop. In reply to Rousseau's theory on the education of women, she exclaims: "What nonsense! when will a great man arise with sufficient strength of mind to puff away the fumes which pride and sensuality have thus spread over the subject! If women are by nature inferior to men, their virtues must be the same in quality, if not in degree, or virtue is a relative idea; consequently, their conduct should be founded on the same principles, and have the same aim." Her wish for a great champion of women's rights came true in the person of John Stuart Mill.

The reader will note in the selections from *Emile* that opposition to Rousseau's notions about the education of women depends on the question: What is and what is not in accordance with nature? He views the education of women so much in terms of the social institution of marriage that he perpetrates the very evils he sought to avoid, for if the institution should in any way be corrupt, then the partners will be corrupt too. Thus, in spite of his revolutionary ideas in other areas, his views on women are in accord with the tradition of antifeminism. Since she brought about the fall of man, her individualism must be curbed. As Rousseau says: "The life of a good woman is a perpetual struggle against self; it is only fair that woman should bear her share of the ills she has brought upon man."

... Sophy should be as truly a woman as Emile is a man, i.e., she must possess all those characters of her sex which are required to enable her to play her part in the physical and moral order. Let us inquire to begin with in what respects her sex differs from our own.

But for her sex, a woman is a man; she has the same organs, the same needs, the same faculties. The machine is the same in its construction; its parts, its working, and its appearance are similar. Regard it as you will the difference is only in degree.

Yet where sex is concerned man and woman are unlike; each is the complement of the other; the difficulty in comparing them lies in our inability to decide, in either case, what is a matter of sex, and what is not. General differences present themselves to the comparative anatomist and even to the superficial observer; they seem not to be a matter of sex; yet they are really sex differences, though the connection eludes our observation. How far such differences may extend we cannot tell; all we know for certain is that where man and woman are alike we have to do with the characteristics of the species; where they are unlike, we have to do with the characteristics of sex. Considered from these two stand-points, we find so many instances of likeness and unlikeness that it is perhaps one of the greatest of marvels how nature has contrived to make two beings so like and yet so different.

These resemblances and differences must have an influence on the moral nature; this inference is obvious, and it is confirmed by experience; it shows the vanity of the disputes as to the superiority or the equality of the sexes; as if each sex, pursuing the path marked out for it by nature, were not more perfect in that very divergence than if it more closely resembled the other. A perfect man and a perfect woman should no more be alike in mind than in face, and perfection admits of neither less nor more.

In the union of the sexes each alike contributes to the common end, but in different ways. From this diversity springs the first difference which may be observed between man and woman in their moral relations. The man should be strong and active; the woman should be weak and passive; the one must have both the power and the will; it is enough that the other should offer little resistance. . . .

. . . The mutual duties of the two sexes are not, and cannot be, equally binding on both. Women do wrong to complain of the inequality of man-made laws; this inequality is not of man's making, or at any rate it is not the result of mere prejudice, but of reason. She to whom nature has entrusted the care of the children must hold herself responsible for them to their father. No doubt every breach of faith is wrong, and every faithless husband, who robs his wife of the sole reward of the stern duties of her sex, is cruel and unjust; but the faithless wife is worse; she destroys the family and breaks the bonds of nature; when she gives her husband children who are not his own, she is false both to him and them, her crime is not infidelity but treason. To my mind, it is the source of dissension and of crime of every kind. Can any position be more wretched than that of the unhappy father who, when he clasps his child to his breast, is haunted by the suspicion that this is the child of another, the badge of his own dishonour, a thief who is robbing his own children of their inheritance. Under such circumstances the family is little more than a group of secret enemies, armed against each other by a guilty woman, who compels them to pretend to love one another.

Thus it is not enough that a wife should be faithful; her husband, along with his friends and neighbours, must believe in her fidelity; she must be modest, devoted, retiring; she should have the witness not only of a good conscience, but of a good reputation. In a word, if a father must love his children, he must be able to respect their mother. For these reasons it is not enough that the woman should be chaste, she must preserve her reputation and her good name. From these principles there arises not only a moral difference between the sexes, but also a fresh motive for duty and propriety, which prescribes to women in particular the most scrupulous attention to their conduct, their manners, their behaviour. Vague assertions as to the equality of the sexes and the similarity of their duties are only empty words; they are no answer to my argument.

. . . The children's health depends in the first place on the mother's, and the early education of man is also in a woman's hands; his morals, his passions, his tastes, his pleasures, his happiness itself, depend on her. A woman's education must therefore be planned in relation to man. To be pleasing in his sight, to win his respect and love, to train him in childhood, to tend him in manhood, to counsel and console, to make his life pleasant and happy, these are the duties of woman for all time, and this is what she should be taught while she is young. The further we depart from this principle, the further we shall be from our goal, and all our precepts will fail to secure her happiness or our own. . . .

. . . The woman who loves true manhood and seeks to find favour in its sight will adopt means adapted to her ends. Woman is a coquette by profession, but her coquetry varies with her aims; let these aims be in accordance with those of nature, and a woman will receive a fitting education.

Even the tiniest little girls love finery; they are not content to be pretty, they must be admired; their little airs and graces show that their heads are full of this idea, and as soon as they can understand they are controlled by "What will people think of you?" If you are foolish enough to try this way with little boys, it will not have the same effect; give them their freedom and their sports, and they care very little what people think; it is a work of time to bring them under the control of this law. . . .

. . . Show the sense of the tasks you set your little girls, but keep them busy. Idleness and insubordination are two very dangerous faults, and very hard to cure when once established. Girls should be attentive and industrious, but this is not enough by itself; they should early be accustomed to restraint. This misfortune, if such it be, is inherent in their sex, and they will never escape from it, unless to endure more cruel sufferings. All their life long, they will have to submit to the strictest and most enduring restraints, those of propriety. They must be trained to bear the yoke from the first, so that they may not feel it, to master their own caprices and to submit themselves to the will of others. If they were always eager to be at work, they should sometimes be compelled to do nothing. Their childish faults, unchecked and unheeded, may easily lead to dissipation, frivolity, and inconstancy. To guard against this, teach them above all things self-control. Under our senseless conditions, the life of a good woman is a perpetual struggle against self; it is only fair that woman should bear her share of the ills she has brought upon man. . . .

. . . Just because they have, or ought to have, little freedom, they are apt to indulge themselves too fully with regard to such freedom as they have; they carry everything to extremes, and they devote themselves to their games with an enthusiasm even greater than that of boys. This is the second difficulty to which I referred. This enthusiasm must be kept in check, for it is the source of several vices commonly found among women, caprice and that extravagant admiration which leads a woman to regard a thing with rapture to-day and to be quite indifferent to it to-morrow. This fickleness of taste is as dangerous as exaggeration; and both spring from the same cause. Do not deprive them of mirth, laughter, noise, and romping games, but do not let them tire of one game and go off to another; do not leave them for a moment without restraint. Train them to break off their games and return to their other occupations without a murmur. Habit is all that is needed, as you have nature on your side.

This habitual restraint produces a docility which woman requires all her life long, for she will always be in subjection to a man, or to man's judgment, and she will never be free to set her own opinion above his. What is most wanted in a woman is gentleness; formed to obey a creature so imperfect as man, a creature often vicious and always faulty, she should early learn to submit to injustice and to suffer the wrongs inflicted on her by her husband without complaint; she must be gentle for her own sake, not his. Bitterness and obstinacy only multiply the sufferings of the wife and the misdeeds of the husband; the man feels that these are not the weapons to be used against him. Heaven did not make women attractive and persuasive that they might degenerate into bitterness, or meek that they should desire the mastery; their soft voice was not meant for hard words, nor their delicate features for the frowns of anger. When they lose their temper they forget themselves; often enough they have just cause of complaint; but when they scold they always put themselves in the wrong. We should each adopt the tone which befits our sex; a soft-hearted husband may make an overbearing wife, but a man, unless he is a perfect monster, will sooner or later yield to his wife's gentleness, and the victory will be hers.

Daughters must always be obedient, but mothers need not always be harsh. To make a girl docile you need not make her miserable; to make her modest you need not terrify her; on the contrary, I should not be sorry to see her allowed occasionally to exercise a little ingenuity, not to escape punishment for her disobedience, but to evade the necessity for obedience. Her dependence need not be made unpleasant, it is enough that she should realise that she is dependent. Cunning is a natural gift of woman, and so convinced am I that all our natural inclinations are right, that I would cultivate this among others, only guarding against its abuse. . . .

. . . it is not fitting that a man of education should choose a wife who has none, or take her from a class where she cannot be expected to have any education. But I would a thousand times rather have a homely girl, simply brought up, than a learned lady and a wit who would make a literary circle of my house and install herself as its president. A female wit is a scourge to her husband, her children, her friends, her servants, to everbody. From the lofty height of her genius she scorns every womanly duty, and she is always trying to make a man of herself after the fashion of Mlle. de L'Enclos. Outside her home she always makes herself ridiculous and she is very rightly a butt for criticism, as we always are when we try to escape from our own position into one for which we are unfitted. These highly talented women only get a hold over fools. We can always tell what artist or friend holds the pen or pencil when they are at work; we know what discreet man of letters dictates their oracles in private. This trickery is unworthy of a decent woman. If she really had talents, her pretentiousness would degrade them. Her honour is to be unknown; her glory is the respect of her husband; her joys the happiness of her family. I appeal to my readers to give me an honest answer; when you enter a woman's room what makes you think more highly of her, what makes you address her with more respect—to see her busy with feminine occupations, with her household duties, with her children's clothes about her, or to find her writing verses at her toilet table surrounded with pamphlets of every kind and with notes on tinted paper?

Mary Wollstonecraft / A Vindication of the Rights of Women

Mary Wollstonecraft (1759—1797), daughter of a tyrannical father and a meek mother, was born into a time of revolution. At the age of twenty-eight she decided to make her way as a writer and joined the society around Joseph Johnson, her publisher, where she met revolutionary thinkers like Blake, Paine, and Godwin. Five weeks after Edmund Burke came out with his conservative *Reflections on the Revolution in France*, she published *A Vindication of the Rights of Men* (1790), which was to be followed in 1792 by *A Vindication of the Rights of Women*, the first revolutionary book on women's rights. She is against all the inequalities that result from social structures based on the pattern of commander and subordinates, and she attacks that very pattern as the cause of evil, for "every profession, in which great subordination of rank constitutes its power, is highly injurious to morality."

In the first of the following two selections, we find her argument against the prevailing view that women should render themselves pleasing through ornament and dress. The second selection is the peroration of her book, her final plea for the freedom and equality of women. The entire book is not only a reply to male commentators about women, but is addressed to a male audience as well: "Be just then, O ye men of understanding."

After several stormy love affairs, Mary Wollstonecraft quietly married William Godwin when she discovered that she was pregnant. Their daughter was born on August 30, 1797. Mary died on the tenth of September due to complications resulting from childbirth. Her daughter was to be Mary Wollstonecraft Shelley, a poet's wife and author of the famous Gothic novel *Frankenstein*.

Why Women Are Fond of Dress and Ornament

Ignorance and the mistaken cunning that nature sharpens in weak heads as a principle of self-preservation, render women very fond of dress, and produce all the vanity which such a fondness may naturally be expected to generate, to the exclusion of emulation and magnanimity.

I agree with Rousseau that the physical part of the art of pleasing consists in ornaments, and for that very reason I should guard girls against the contagious fondness for dress so common to weak women, that they may not rest in the physical part. Yet, weak are the women who imagine that they can long please without the aid of the mind, or, in other words, without the moral art of pleasing. But the moral art, if it be not a profanation to use the word art, when alluding to the grace which is an effect of virtue, and not the motive of action, is never to be found with ignorance; the sportiveness of innocence, so pleasing to refined libertines of both sexes, is widely different in its essence from this superior gracefulness.

A strong inclination for external ornaments ever appears in barbarous states, only the men not the women adorn themselves; for where women are allowed to be so far on a level with men, society has advanced, at least, one step in civilization.

The attention to dress, therefore, which has been thought a sexual propensity, I think natural to mankind. But I ought to express myself with more precision. When the mind is not sufficiently opened to take pleasure in reflection, the body will be adorned with sedulous care; and ambition will appear in tattooing or painting it.

So far is this first inclination carried, that even the hellish yoke of slavery cannot stifle the savage desire of admiration which the black heroes inherit from both their parents, for all the hardly earned savings of a slave are commonly expended in a little tawdry finery. And I have seldom known a good male or female servant that was not particularly fond of dress. Their cloths were their riches; and, I argue from analogy, that the fondness for dress so extravagant in females, arises from the same cause—want of cultivation of mind. When men meet they converse about business, politics, or literature; but, says Swift, "how naturally do women apply their hands to each other's lappets and ruffles." And very natural is it—for they have not any business to interest them, have not a taste for literature, and they find politics dry, because they have not acquired a love for mankind by turning their thoughts to the grand pursuits that exalt the human race, and promote general happiness.

Besides, various are the paths to power and fame which by accident or choice men pursue, and though they jostle against each other—for men of the same profession are seldom friends—yet there is a much greater number of their fellow-creatures with whom they never clash. But women are very differently situated with respect to each other—for they are all rivals.

Before marriage it is their business to please men; and after, with a few exceptions, they follow the same scent with all the persevering pertinacity of instinct. Even virtuous women never forget their sex in company, for they are for ever trying to make themselves *agreeable*. A female beauty, and a male wit, appear to be equally anxious to draw the attention of the company to themselves; and the animosity of contemporary wits is proverbial.

Is it then surprising that when the sole ambition of woman centres in beauty, and interest gives vanity additional force, perpetual rivalships should ensue? They are all running the same race, and would rise above the virtue of mortals if they did not view each other with a suspicious and even envious eye.

An immoderate fondness for dress, for pleasure, and for sway, are the passions of savages; the passions that occupy those uncivilized beings who have not yet extended the dominion of the mind, or even learned to think with the energy necessary to concatenate that abstract train of thought which produces principles. And that women from their education and the present state of civilized life are in the same condition, cannot, I think, be controverted. To laugh at them then, or satirize the follies of a being who is never to be allowed to act freely from the light of her own reason, is as absurd as cruel; for, that they who are taught blindly to obey authority will endeavour cunningly to elude it, is most natural and certain.

Yet let it be proved that they ought to obey man implicitly, and I shall immediately agree that it is woman's duty to cultivate a fondness for dress, in order to please, and a propensity to cunning for her own preservation.

The virtues, however, which are supported by ignorance must ever be wavering—the house built on sand could not endure a storm. It is almost unnecessary to draw the inference. If women are to be made virtuous by authority, which is a contradiction in terms, let them be immured in seraglios and watched with a jealous eye. Fear not that the iron will enter into their souls—for the souls that can bear such treatment are made of yielding materials, just animated enough to give life to the body.

> "Matter too soft a lasting mark to bear,
> And best distinguish'd by black, brown, or fair."

The most cruel wounds will of course soon heal, and they may still people the world, and dress to please man—all the purposes which certain celebrated writers have allowed that they were created to fulfil.

Men of Sense, Be Just

It is not necessary to inform the sagacious reader, now I enter on my concluding reflections, that the discussion of this subject merely consists in opening a few simple principles and clearing away the rubbish which obscured them. But as all readers are not sagacious, I must be allowed to add some explanatory remarks to bring the subject home to reason—to that sluggish reason which supinely takes opinions on trust, and obstinately supports them to spare itself the labour of thinking.

Moralists have unanimously agreed, that unless virtue be nursed by liberty, it will never attain due strength—and what they say of man I extend to mankind, insisting that in all cases morals must be fixed on immutable principles; and that the being cannot be termed rational or virtuous who obeys any authority but that of reason.

To render women truly useful members of society, I argue that they should be led, by having their understandings cultivated on a large scale, to acquire a rational affection for their country, founded on knowledge, because it is obvious that we are little interested about what we do not understand. And to render this general knowledge of due importance, I have endeavoured to show that private duties are never properly fulfilled unless the understanding enlarges the heart; and that public virtue is only an aggregate of private. But the distinctions established in society undermine both, by beating out the solid gold of virtue, till it becomes only the tinsel-covering of vice; for whilst wealth renders a man more respectable than virtue, wealth will be sought before virtue; and whilst women's persons are caressed when a childish simper shows an absence of mind—the mind will lie fallow. Yet, true voluptuousness must proceed from the mind—for what can equal the sensations produced by mutual affection supported by mutual respect? What are the cold or feverish caresses of appetite, but sin embracing death, compared with the modest overflowings of a pure heart and exalted imagination? Yes, let me tell the libertine of fancy when he despises understanding in woman—that the mind, which he disregards, gives life to the enthusiastic affection from which rapture, shortlived as it is, alone can flow! And that without virtue a sexual attachment must expire, like a tallow candle in the socket, creating intolerable disgust. To prove this, I need only observe that men who have wasted great part of their lives with women, and with whom they have sought for pleasure with eager thirst, entertain the meanest opinion of the sex. —Virtue, true refiner of joy!—if foolish men were to fright thee from earth in order to give loose to all their appetites without a check—some sensual wight of taste would scale the heavens to invite thee back, to give a zest to pleasure!

That women at present are by ignorance rendered foolish or vicious, is, I think, not to be disputed; and that the most salutary effects tending to improve mankind might be expected from a revolution in female manners, appears, at least with a face of probability, to rise out of the observation. For as marriage has been termed the parent of those endearing charities which draw man from the brutal herd, the corrupting intercourse that wealth, idleness, and folly produce between the sexes, is more universally injurious to morality than all the other vices of mankind collectively considered. To adulterous lust the most sacred duties are sacrificed, because before marriage, men, by a promiscuous intimacy with women, learned to consider love as a selfish gratification—learned to separate it not only from esteem, but from the affection merely built on habit, which mixes a little humanity with it. Justice and friendship are also set at defiance, and that purity of taste is vitiated which would naturally lead a man to relish an artless display of affection rather than affected airs. But that noble simplicity of affection which dares to appear unadorned, has few attractions for the libertine, though it be the charm which, by cementing the matrimonial tie, secures to the pledges of a warmer passion the necessary parental attention; for children will never be properly educated till friendship subsists between parents. Virtue flies from a house divided against itself—and a whole legion of devils take up their residence there.

The affection of husbands and wives cannot be pure when they have so few sentiments in common, and when so little confidence is established at home, as must be the case when their pursuits are so different. That intimacy from which tenderness should flow, will not, cannot subsist between the vicious.

Contending, therefore, that the sexual distinction which men have so warmly insisted upon is arbitrary, I have dwelt on an observation that several sensible men, with whom I have conversed on the subject, allowed to be well founded; and it is simply this, that the little chastity to be found amongst men, and consequent disregard of modesty, tend to degrade both sexes; and further, that the modesty of women, characterized as such, will often be only the artful veil of wantonness instead of being the natural reflection of purity, till modesty be universally respected.

From the tyranny of man, I firmly believe, the greater number of female follies proceed; and the cunning, which I allow makes at present a part of their character, I likewise have repeatedly endeavoured to prove, is produced by oppression.

Were not dissenters, for instance, a class of people with strict truth characterized as cunning? And may I not lay some stress on this fact to prove, that when any power but reason curbs the free spirit of man, dissimulation is practised, and the various shifts of art are naturally called forth? Great attention to decorum which was carried to a degree of scrupulosity, and all that puerile bustle about trifles and consequential solemnity which Butler's caricature of a dissenter brings before the imagination, shaped their persons as well as their minds in the mould of prim littleness. I speak collectively, for I know how many ornaments to human nature have been enrolled amongst sectaries; yet, I assert that the same narrow prejudice for their sect which women have for their families, prevailed in the dissenting part of the community, however worthy in other respects; and also that the same timid prudence, or headstrong efforts, often disgraced the exertions of both. Oppression thus formed many of the features of their character perfectly to coincide with that of the oppressed half of mankind; for is it not notorious that dissenters were, like women, fond of deliberating together, and asking advice of each other, till by a complication of little contrivances some little end was brought about? A similar attention to preserve their reputation was conspicuous in the dissenting and female world, and was produced by a similar cause.

Asserting the rights which women in common with men ought to contend for, I have not attempted to extenuate their faults; but to prove them to be the natural consequence of their education and station in society. If so, it is reasonable to suppose that they will change their character, and correct their vices and follies, when they are allowed to be free in a physical, moral, and civil sense.*

Let women share the rights and she will emulate the virtues of man; for she must grow more perfect when emancipated, or justify the authority that chains such a weak being to her duty.—If the latter, it will be expedient to open a fresh trade with Russia for whips: a present which a father should always make to his son-in-law on his wedding day, that a husband may keep his whole family in order by the same means; and without any violation of justice reign, wielding this sceptre, sole master of his house, because he is the only being in it who has reason:—the divine, indefeasible earthly sovereignty breathed into man by the Master of the universe. Allowing this position, women have not any inherent rights to claim; and by the same rule their duties vanish, for rights and duties are inseparable.

Be just then, O ye men of understanding! and mark not more severely what women do amiss, than the vicious tricks of the horse or the ass for whom ye provide provender—and allow her the privileges of ignorance, to whom ye deny the rights of reason, or ye will be worse than Egyptian task-masters, expecting virtue where nature has not given understanding!

John Stuart Mill / The Subjection of Women

James Mill not only educated his son John Stuart Mill (1806—1873) to be a scholar and utilitarian, but he also taught him not to accept opinions on authority and to think always for himself. The value of this independence of thought is most evident in Mill's famous essay *On Liberty*, but he also displayed a more public independence when he supported women's suffrage after he became a member of Parliament in 1865. By this time he had

---

*   I had further enlarged on the advantages which might reasonably be expected to result from an improvement in female manners, towards the general reformation of society; but it appeared to me that such reflections would more properly close the last volume.

written, with the cooperation of his stepdaughter Helen Taylor and the inspiration of his wife Harriet Taylor, his *The Subjection of Women* (1861).

His essay is divided into four chapters. He begins by stating how difficult it is to apply rational arguments to attitudes that have been deeply rooted in human beings, especially when those attitudes are supported by a reliance on God and nature. He also does not think it likely that women will rebel, for they have been conditioned to their state since their earliest years. As Mill says: "The subjection of women to men being a universal custom, any departure from it appears unnatural."

In his second chapter Mill discusses the legal status of women and their need for equality and dignity. The foundation for woman's dignity is financial independence: "The power of earning is essential to the dignity of a woman if she has no independent property." Mill's belief is echoed in works such as Charlotte Brontë's *Villette* and Virginia Woolf's essay "A Room of One's Own." The classic symbolic gesture in line with Mill's belief was, of course, Nora's slamming of the door in Ibsen's *Doll's House*. In his third chapter Mill raises and attempts to answer such standard questions as: To what positions are women entitled? What are their capacities? Why aren't there any women composers? Why are women inferior in the arts?

Sections from his fourth chapter are printed below. Here Mill appeals directly to the "what's in it for me" motive in men by demonstrating that it would be to man's advantage if women were granted equal rights. Throughout his essay Mill's style is, as usual, clear and reasonable, and only occasionally, as in the discussion of marital harmony as opposed to incompatibility, does the reader detect an emotional undertone. His essay is directed to a male audience, but women could not wish for a more earnest and fervent advocate for their neglected rights and their humanity.

The Advantages of Women's Liberation in Public and Private Life

There remains a question, not of less importance than those already discussed, and which will be asked the most importunately by those opponents whose conviction is somewhat shaken on the main point. What good are we to expect from the changes proposed in our customs and institutions? Would mankind be at all better off if women were free? If not, why disturb their minds, and attempt to make a social revolution in the name of an abstract right?

It is hardly to be expected that this question will be asked in respect to the change proposed in the condition of women in marriage. The sufferings, immoralities, evils of all sorts, produced in innumerable cases by the subjection of individual women to individual men, are far too terrible to be overlooked. Unthinking or uncandid persons, counting those cases alone which are extreme, or which attain publicity, may say that the evils are exceptional; but no one can be blind to their existence, nor, in many cases, to their intensity. And it is perfectly obvious that the abuse of the power cannot be very much checked while the power remains. It is a power given, or offered, not to good men, or to decently respectable men, but to all men; the most brutal, and the most criminal. There is no check but that of opinion, and such men are in general within the reach of no opinion but that of men like themselves. If such men did not brutally tyrannise over the one human being whom the law compels to bear everything from them, society must already have reached a paradisiacal state. There could be no need any longer of laws to curb men's vicious propensities. Astræa must not only have returned to earth, but the heart of the worst man must have become her temple. The law of servitude in marriage is a monstrous contradiction to all the principles of the modern world, and to all the experience through which those principles have been slowly and painfully worked out. It is the sole case, now that negro slavery has been abolished, in which a human being in the plenitude of every faculty is delivered up to the tender mercies of another human being, in the hope forsooth that this other will use the power solely for the good of the person subjected to it. Marriage is the only actual bondage known to our law. There remain no legal slaves, except the mistress of every house.

It is not, therefore, on this part of the subject, that the question is likely to be asked, *Cui bono?* We may be told that the evil would outweigh the good, but the reality of the good admits of no dispute. In regard, however, to the larger question, the removal of women's disabilities—their recognition as the equals of men in all that belongs to citizenship—the opening to them of all honourable employments, and of the training and education which qualifies for those employments—there are many persons for whom it is not enough that the inequality has no just or legitimate defence; they require to be told what express advantage would be obtained by abolishing it.

To which let me first answer, the advantage of having the most universal and pervading of all human relations regulated by justice instead of injustice. The vast amount of this gain to human nature, it is hardly

possible, by any explanation or illustration, to place in a stronger light than
it is placed by the bare statement, to anyone who attaches a moral meaning to words. All the selfish propensities, the self-worship, the unjust
self-preference, which exist among mankind, have their source and
root in, and derive their principal nourishment from, the present constitution of the relation between men and women. Think what it is to a
boy, to grow up to manhood in the belief that without any merit or any
exertion of his own, though he may be the most frivolous and empty or
the most ignorant and stolid of mankind, by the mere fact of being born a
male he is by right the superior of all and every one of an entire half of
the human race: including probably some whose real superiority to himself he has daily or hourly occasion to feel; but even if in his whole conduct
he habitually follows a woman's guidance, still, if he is a fool, she thinks
that of course she is not, and cannot be, equal in ability and judgment to
himself; and if he is not a fool, he does worse—he sees that she is superior
to him, and believes that, notwithstanding her superiority, he is entitled
to command and she is bound to obey. What must be the effect on his
character, of this lesson? And men of the cultivated classes are often not
aware how deeply it sinks into the immense majority of male minds.
For, among right-feeling and well-bred people, the inequality is kept as
much as possible out of sight; above all, out of sight of the children. As
much obedience is required from boys to their mother as to their father:
they are not permitted to domineer over their sisters, nor are they accustomed to see these postponed to them, but the contrary; the compensa-
tions of the chivalrous feeling being made prominent, while the servitude
which requires them is kept in the background. Well brought-up youths
in the higher classes thus often escape the bad influences of the situation in
their early years, and only experience them when, arrived at manhood,
they fall under the dominion of facts as they really exist. Such people
are little aware, when a boy is differently brought up, how early the
notion of his inherent superiority to a girl arises in his mind; how it grows
with his growth and strengthens with his strength; how it is inoculated by
one schoolboy upon another; how early the youth thinks himself superior
to his mother, owing her perhaps forbearance, but no real respect; and
how sublime and sultan-like a sense of superiority he feels, above all,
over the woman whom he honors by admitting her to a partnership of his
life. Is it imagined that all this does not pervert the whole manner of
existence of the man, both as an individual and as a social being? It is
an exact parallel to the feeling of a hereditary king that he is excellent

above others by being born a king, or a noble by being born a noble. The relation between husband and wife is very like that between lord and vassal, except that the wife is held to more unlimited obedience than the vassal was. However the vassal's character may have been affected, for better and for worse, by his subordination, who can help seeing that the lord's was affected greatly for the worse? whether he was led to believe that his vassals were really superior to himself, or to feel that he was placed in command over people as good as himself, for no merits or labours of his own, but merely for having, as Figaro says, taken the trouble to be born. The self-worship of the monarch, or of the feudal superior, is matched by the self-worship of the male. Human beings do not grow up from childhood in the possession of unearned distinctions, without pluming themselves upon them. Those whom privileges not acquired by their merit, and which they feel to be disproportioned to it, inspire with additional humility, are always the few, and the best few. The rest are only inspired with pride, and the worst sort of pride, that which values itself upon accidental advantages, not of its own achieving. Above all, when the feeling of being raised above the whole of the other sex is combined with personal authority over one individual among them; the situation, if a school of conscientious and affectionate forbearance to those whose strongest points of character are conscience and affection, is to men of another quality a regularly constituted academy or gymnasium for training them in arrogance and and overbearingness; which vices, if curbed by the certainty of resistance in their intercourse with other men, their equals, break out towards all who are in a position to be obliged to tolerate them, and often revenge themselves upon the unfortunate wife for the involuntary restraint which they are obliged to submit to elsewhere.

The example afforded, and the education given to the sentiments, by laying the foundation of domestic existence upon a relation contradictory to the first principles of social justice, must, from the very nature of man, have a perverting influence of such magnitude, that it is hardly possible with our present experience to raise our imaginations to the conception of so great a change for the better as would be made by its removal. . . .

The second benefit to be expected from giving to women the free use of their faculties, by leaving them the free choice of their employments, and opening to them the same field of occupation and the same prizes and encouragements as to other human beings, would be that of doubling the mass of mental faculties available for the higher service of humanity. . . .

This great accession to the intellectual power of the species, and to the amount of intellect available for the good management of its affairs, would be obtained, partly, through the better and more complete intellectual education of women, which would then improve *pari passu* with that of men. Women in general would be brought up equally capable of understanding business, public affairs, and the higher matters of speculation, with men in the same class of society; and the select few of the one as well as of the other sex, who were qualified not only to comprehend what is done or thought by others, but to think or do something considerable themselves, would meet with the same facilities for improving and training their capacities in the one sex as in the other. In this way, the widening of the sphere of action for women would operate for good, by raising their education to the level of that of men, and making the one participate in all improvements made in the other. But independently of this, the mere breaking down of the barrier would of itself have an educational virtue of the highest worth. The mere getting rid of the idea that all the wider subjects of thought and action, all the things which are of general and not solely of private interest, are men's business, from which women are to be warned off—positively interdicted from most of it, coldly tolerated in the little which is allowed them—the mere consciousness a woman would then have of being a human being like any other, entitled to choose her pursuits, urged or invited by the same inducements as anyone else to interest herself in whatever is interesting to human beings, entitled to exert the share of influence on all human concerns which belongs to an individual opinion, whether she attempted actual participation in them or not—this alone would effect an immense expansion of the faculties of women, as well as enlargement of the range of their moral sentiments.

Besides the addition to the amount of individual talent available for the conduct of human affairs, which certainly are not at present so abundantly provided in that respect that they can afford to dispense with one-half of what nature proffers; the opinion of women would then possess a more beneficial, rather than a greater, influence upon the general mass of human belief and sentiment. I say a more beneficial, rather than a greater influence; for the influence of women over the general tone of opinion has always, or at least from the earliest known period, been very considerable. The influence of mothers on the early character of their sons, and the desire of young men to recommend themselves to young women, have in all recorded times been important agencies in the formation of character, and have determined some of the chief steps in the progress of civilisation.

[Mill discusses next the moral influence of women in classical and medieval times.]

At present the moral influence of women is no less real, but it is no longer of so marked and definite a character: it has more nearly merged in the general influence of public opinion. Both through the contagion of sympathy, and through the desire of men to shine in the eyes of women, their feelings have great effect in keeping alive what remains of the chivalrous ideal—in fostering the sentiments and continuing the traditions of spirit and generosity. In these points of character, their standard is higher than that of men; in the quality of justice, somewhat lower. As regards the relations of private life it may be said generally, that their influence is, on the whole, encouraging to the softer virtues, discouraging to the sterner: though the statement must be taken with all the modifications dependent on individual character. . . .

Women have, however, some share of influence in giving the tone to public moralities since their sphere of action has been a little widened, and since a considerable number of them have occupied themselves practically in the promotion of objects reaching beyond their own family and household. The influence of women counts for a great deal in two of the most marked features of modern European life—its aversion to war, and its addiction to philanthropy. Excellent characteristics both; but unhappily, if the influence of women is valuable in the encouragement it gives to these feelings in general, in the particular applications the direction it gives to them is at least as often mischievous as useful. In the philanthropic department more particularly, the two provinces chiefly cultivated by women are religious proselytism and charity. Religious proselytism at home, is but another word for embittering of religious animosities: abroad, it is usually a blind running at an object, without either knowing or heeding the fatal mischiefs—fatal to the religious object itself as well as to all other desirable objects—which may be produced by the means employed. As for charity, it is a matter in which the immediate effect on the persons directly concerned, and the ultimate consequence to the general good, are apt to be at complete war with one another: while the education given to women—an education of the sentiments rather than of the understanding—and the habit inculcated by their whole life, of looking to immediate effects on persons, and not to remote effects on classes of persons—make them both unable to see, and unwilling to admit, the ultimate evil tendency of any form of charity or philanthropy which commends itself to their sympathetic feelings.

These considerations show how usefully the part which women take in the formation of general opinion, would be modified for the better by that more enlarged instruction, and practical conversancy with the things which their opinions influence, that would necessarily arise from their social and political emancipation. But the improvement it would work through the influence they exercise, each in her own family, would be still more remarkable.

[Mill discusses next the negative results of a marriage between unequal partners. These results are aggravated if the female partner is inferior.]

Mere unlikeness, when it only means difference of good qualities, may be more a benefit in the way of mutual improvement, than a drawback from comfort. When each emulates, and desires and endeavours to acquire, the other's peculiar qualities the difference does not produce diversity of interest, but increased identity of it, and makes each still more valuable to the other. But when one is much the inferior of the two in mental ability and cultivation, and is not actively attempting by the other's aid to rise to the other's level, the whole influence of the connexion upon the development of the superior of the two is deteriorating: and still more so in a tolerably happy marriage than in an unhappy one. It is not with impunity that the superior in intellect shuts himself up with an inferior, and elects that inferior for his chosen, and sole completely intimate, associate. Any society which is not improving, is deteriorating: and the more so, the closer and more familiar it is. Even a really superior man almost always begins to deteriorate when he is habitually (as the phrase is) king of his company: and in his most habitual company the husband who has a wife inferior to him is always so. While his self-satisfaction is incessantly ministered to on the one hand, on the other he insensibly imbibes the modes of feeling, and of looking at things, which belong to a more vulgar or a more limited mind than his own. This evil differs from many of those which have hitherto been dwelt on, by being an increasing one. The association of men with women in daily life is much closer and more complete than it ever was before. Men's life is more domestic. Formerly, their pleasures and chosen occupations were among men, and in men's company: their wives had but a fragment of their lives. At the present time, the progress of civilisation, and the turn of opinion against the rough amusements and convivial excesses which formerly occupied most men in their hours of relaxation—together with (it must be said) the improved tone of modern feeling as to the reciprocity of duty which binds the husband towards the wife—have thrown the man very much more upon home and its inmates, for his personal and social pleasures: while the kind and degree of improvement which has been made in women's education, has made them in some degree capable of being his companions in ideas and mental taste, while leaving them, in most cases, still hopelessly inferior to him. His desire of mental communion is thus in general satisfied by a communion from which he learns nothing. An unimproving and unstimulating companionship is substituted for (what he might otherwise have been obliged to seek) the society of his equals in powers and his fellows in the higher pursuits. We see, accordingly, that young men of the greatest promise generally cease to improve as soon as they marry, and, not improving, inevitably degenerate. If the wife does not push the husband forward, she always holds him back. He ceases to care for what she does not care for; he no longer desires, and ends by disliking and shunning, society congenial to his former aspirations, and which would now shame his falling-off from them; his higher faculties both of mind and heart cease to be called into activity. And this change coinciding with the new and selfish interests which are created by the family, after a few years he differs in no material respect from those who have never had wishes for anything but the common vanities and the common pecuniary objects.

What marriage may be in the case of two persons of cultivated faculties, identical in opinions and purposes, between whom there exists that best kind of equality, similarity of powers and capacities with reciprocal superiority in them—so that each can enjoy the luxury of looking up to the other, and can have alternately the pleasure of leading and of being led in the path of development—I will not attempt to describe. To those who can conceive it, there is no need; to those who cannot, it would appear the dream of an enthusiast. But I maintain, with the profoundest conviction, that this, and this only, is the ideal of marriage; and that all opinions, customs, and institutions which favour any other notion of it, or turn the conceptions and aspirations connected with it into any other direction, by whatever pretences they may be coloured, are relics of primitive barbarism. The moral regeneration of mankind will only really commence, when the most fundamental of the social relations is placed under the rule of equal justice, and when human beings learn to cultivate their strongest sympathy with an equal in rights and in cultivation.

Thus far, the benefits which it has appeared that the world would gain by ceasing to make sex a disqualification for privileges and a badge of subjection, are social rather than individual; consisting in an increase of the general fund of thinking and acting power, and an improvement in the general conditions of the association of men with women. But it would be a grievous understatement of the case to omit the most direct benefit of all, the unspeakable gain in private happiness to the liberated half of the species; the difference to them between a life of subjection to the will of others, and a life of rational freedom. After the primary necessities of food and raiment, freedom is the first and strongest want of human nature. While mankind are lawless, their desire is for lawless freedom. When they have learnt to understand the meaning of duty and the value of reason, they incline more and more to be guided and restrained by these in the exercise of their freedom; but they do not therefore desire freedom less; they do not become disposed to accept the will of other people as the representative and interpreter of those guiding principles. On the contrary, the communities in which the reason has been most cultivated, and in which the idea of social duty has been most powerful, are those which have most strongly asserted the freedom of action of the individual—the liberty of each to govern his conduct by his own feelings of duty, and by such laws and social restraints as his own conscience can subscribe to.

He who would rightly appreciate the worth of personal independence as an element of happiness, should consider the value he himself puts upon it as an ingredient of his own. There is no subject on which there is a greater habitual difference of judgment between a man judging for himself, and the same man judging for other people. When he hears others complaining that they are not allowed freedom of action—that their own will has not sufficient influence in the regulation of their affairs—his inclination is, to ask, what are their grievances? what positive damage they sustain? and in what respect they consider their affairs to be mismanaged? and if they fail to make out, in answer to these questions, what appears to him a sufficient case, he turns a deaf ear, and regards their complaint as the fanciful querulousness of people whom nothing reasonable will satisfy. But he has a quite different standard of judgment when he is deciding for himself. Then, the most unexceptionable administration of his interests by a tutor set over him, does not satisfy his feelings: his personal exclusion from the deciding authority appears itself the greatest grievance of all, rendering it superfluous even to enter into the question of mismanagement. It is the same with nations. What citizen of a free country would listen to any offers of good and skilful administration, in return for the abdication of freedom? Even if he could believe that good and skilful administration can exist among a people ruled by a will not their own, would not the consciousness of working out their own destiny under their own moral responsibility be a compensation to his feelings for great rudeness and imperfection in the details of public affairs? Let him rest assured that whatever he feels on this point, women feel in a fully equal degree.

An active and energetic mind, if denied liberty will seek for power: refused the command of itself, it will assert its personality by attempting to control others. To allow to any human beings no existence of their own but what depends on others, is giving far too high a premium on bending others to their purposes. Where liberty cannot be hoped for, and power can, power becomes the grand object of human desire; those to whom others will not leave the undisturbed management of their own affairs, will compensate themselves, if they can, by meddling for their own purposes with the affairs of others. Hence also women's passion for personal beauty, and dress and display; and all the evils that flow from it, in the way of mischievous luxury and social immorality. The love of power and the love of liberty are in eternal antagonism. Where there is least liberty, the passion for power is the most ardent and unscrupulous. The desire of power over others can only cease to be a depraving agency among mankind, when each of them individually is able to do without it: which can only be where respect for liberty in the personal concerns of each is an established principle.

But it is not only through the sentiment of personal dignity, that the free direction and disposal of their own faculties is a source of individual happiness, and to be fettered and restricted in it, a source of unhappiness, to human beings, and not least to women. There is nothing, after disease, indigence, and guilt, so fatal to the pleasurable enjoyment of life as the want of a worthy outlet for the active faculties. Women who have the cares of a family, and while they have the cares of a family, have this outlet, and it generally suffices for them: but what of the greatly increasing number of women, who have had no opportunity of exercising the vocation which they are mocked by telling them is their proper one? What of the women whose children have been lost to them by death or distance, or have grown up, married, and formed homes of their own? There are abundant examples of men who, after a life engrossed by business, retire with a competency to the enjoyment, as they hope, of rest, but to whom, as they are unable to acquire new interests and excitements that can replace the old, the change to a life of inactivity brings ennui, melancholy, and premature death. Yet no one thinks of the parallel case of so many worthy and devoted women, who, having paid what they are told is their debt to society—having brought up a family blamelessly to manhood and womanhood—having kept a house as long as they had a house needing to be kept—are deserted by the sole occupation for which they have fitted themselves; and remain with undiminished activity but with no employment for it, unless perhaps a daughter or daughter-in-law is willing to abdicate in their favour the discharge of the same functions in her younger household. Surely a hard lot for the old age of those who have worthily discharged, as long as it was given to them to discharge, what the world accounts their only social duty. Of such women, and of those others to whom this duty has not been committed at all—many of whom pine through life with the consciousness of thwarted vocations, and activities which are not suffered to expand—the only resources, speaking generally, are religion and charity. But their religion, though it may be one of feeling, and ceremonial observance, cannot be a religion of action, unless in the form of charity. For charity many of them are by nature admirably fitted; but to practise it usefully, or even without doing mischief, requires the education, the manifold preparation, the knowledge and the thinking powers, of a skilful administrator. There are few of the administrative functions of government for which a person would not be fit, who is fit to bestow charity usefully. In this as in other cases (pre-eminently in that of the education of children), the duties permitted to women cannot be performed properly, without their being trained for duties which, to the great loss of society, are not permitted to them. And here let me notice the singular way in which the question of women's disabilities is frequently presented to view, by those who find it easier to draw a ludicrous picture of what they do not like, than to answer the arguments for it. When it is suggested that women's executive capacities and prudent counsels might sometimes be found valuable in affairs of State, these lovers of fun hold up to the ridicule of the world, as sitting in Parliament or in the Cabinet, girls in their teens, or young wives of two or three and twenty, transported bodily, exactly as they are, from the drawing-room to the House of Commons. They forget that males are not usually selected at this early age for a seat in Parliament, or for responsible political functions. Common sense would tell them that if such trusts were confided to women, it would be to such as having no special vocation for married life, or preferring another employment of their faculties (as many women even now prefer to marriage some of the few honourable occupations within their reach), have spent the best years of their youth in attempting to qualify themselves for the pursuits in which they desire to engage; or still more frequently perhaps, widows or wives of forty or fifty, by whom the knowledge of life and faculty of government which they have acquired in their families, could by the aid of appropriate studies be made available on a less contracted scale. There is no country of Europe in which the ablest men have not frequently experienced, and keenly appreciated, the value of the advice and help of clever and experienced women of the world, in the attainment both of private and of public objects; and there are important matters of public administration to which few men are equally competent with such women; among others, the detailed control of expenditure. But what we are now discussing is not the need which society has of the services of women in public business, but the dull and hopeless life to which it so often condemns them, by forbidding them to exercise the practical abilities which many of them are conscious of, in any wider field than one which to some of them never was, and to others is no longer, open. If there is anything vitally important to the happiness of human beings, it is that they should relish their habitual pursuit. This requisite of an enjoyable life is very imperfectly granted, or altogether denied, to a large part of mankind; and by its absence many a life is a failure, which is provided, in appearance, with every requisite of success. But if circumstances which society is not yet skilful enough to overcome, render such failures often for the present inevitable, society need not itself inflict them. The injudiciousness of parents, a youth's own inexperience, or the absence of external opportunities for the congenial vocation, and their presence for an uncongenial, condemn numbers of men to pass their lives in doing one thing reluctantly and ill, when there are other things which they could have done well and happily. But on women this sentence is imposed by actual law, and by customs equivalent to law. What, in unenlightened societies, color, race, religion, or in the case of a conquered country, nationality, are to some men, sex is to all women; a peremptory exclusion from almost all honorable occupations, but either such as cannot be fulfilled by others, or such as those others do not think worthy of their acceptance. Sufferings arising from causes of this nature usually meet with so little sympathy, that few persons are aware of the great amount of unhappiness even now produced by the feeling of a wasted life. The case will be even more frequent, as increased cultivation creates a greater and greater disproportion between the ideas and faculties of women, and the scope which society allows to their activity.

When we consider the positive evil caused to the disqualified half of the human race by their disqualification—first in the loss of the most inspiriting and elevating kind of personal enjoyment, and next in the weariness, disappointment, and profound dissatisfaction with life, which are so often the substitute for it; one feels that among all the lessons which men require for carrying on the struggle against the inevitable imperfections of their lot on earth, there is no lesson which they more need, than not to add to the evils which nature inflicts, by their jealous and prejudiced restrictions on one another. Their vain fears only substitute other and worse evils for those which they are idly apprehensive of: while every restraint on the freedom of conduct of any of their human fellow-creatures (otherwise than by making them responsible for any evil actually caused by it), dries up *pro tanto* the principal fountain of human happiness, and leaves the species less rich, to an inappreciable degree, in all that makes life valuable to the individual human being.

Henrik Ibsen/A Doll's House

In *A Doll's House* Ibsen (1828—1906) voiced his indignation over the virtual slavery of women in society. He felt that the idealist, in this case Nora Helmer, needs to free herself from the stifling indifference and stupidity of her environment. It is, however, very questionable that she will succeed, for the social unit in which she lives denies her any love. After years of married life, Nora discovers that her husband is a stranger to her, and when she walks out on him, he considers that act a worse offense than the lack of love between them.

A Doll's House (1879) takes place in a thoroughly middle-class environment where the most important values are money and surface respectability. Torvald Helmer's fortunes have taken a turn for the better since he has been appointed manager of a bank. As the play opens, he teases his coquettish songbird Nora about being a spendthrift. Little does he know that his featherbrained wife has borrowed a large sum of money from a rather shady character named Krogstad, who once was his boyhood friend but who is now about to be dismissed by Helmer from his post at the bank. Nora needed the money to enable her sick husband to travel south and regain his health. As security for the bond she required her father's signature, but since he was dying she forged the signature and carelessly dated the bond three days after her father's death.

Krogstad discovers the discrepancy, and when he is endangered at the bank he threatens Nora that he will reveal her secret to Helmer and that she will have to face the legal consequences of her act. Nora is unable to convince Helmer that Krogstad should retain his job. He is dismissed and Helmer receives a letter from him. Nora tells her friend Christine Linde that the inevitable confrontation will lead to a miracle: Helmer will take the burden upon himself and show Nora his true love. As she waits for the critical moment, Christine begs Krogstad to retract what he has written. He complies, partly because of his former love for her, which now promises to be renewed. Christine had rejected his offer for marriage once, because a more profitable suitor had appeared and she needed the money. Now she is a widow who has worked hard and tediously for several years. She grasps at the opportunity to make a more comfortable life for herself under the protection of a male provider.

The following confrontation takes place right after the Helmers have returned from a party. Helmer goes to the mail box to get his letters and says to Nora: "Do you know, Nora, I have often wished that you might be threatened by some great danger, so that I might risk my life's blood, and everything, for your sake." To which Nora replies decidedly: "Now you must read your letter, Torvald."

As the concluding scene reveals, Torvald does not fulfill his promise. When Nora slams the door behind her, in what became one of the great symbolic gestures of the nineteenth century, she walks into a world for which she is completely unprepared. Will she be able to support herself, she who has none of the practical views and experiences of her friend Christine? What kind of work can she do? She has been a "skylark," a charmer, a cunningly sweet female contributing to the weaving of an intricate circle of mutual deception. Will she be a secretary, a telegraph operator for a day, for a year? Will she take a lover? Will she return to Helmer after the first night out in the winter cold? Her grand and melodramatic gesture raises more questions than the play intends to answer. Ibsen does not encourage women to make such spectacular exits: instead, in his play he criticizes a society that forces women into roles that make them unfit for work and life.

Nora   (*hanging on his neck*) Good-night, Torvald—Good-night!
Helmer   (*kissing her on the forehead*) Good-night, my little singing-bird. Sleep sound, Nora. Now I will read my letters through.

[*He takes his letters and goes into his room, shutting the door after him.*]

Nora (*gropes distractedly about, seizes* Helmer's *domino, throws it round her, while she says in quick, hoarse, spasmodic whispers*) Never to see him again. Never! Never! (*Puts her shawl over her head.*) Never to see my children again either—never again. Never! Never!—Ah! the icy, black water—the unfathomable depths —If only it were over! He has got it now—now he is reading it. Good-bye, Torvald and my children!

[*She is about to rush out through the hall, when* Helmer *opens his door hurriedly and stands with an open letter in his hand.*]

Helmer   Nora!
Nora   Ah!——
Helmer   What is this? Do you know what is in this letter?

Nora	Yes, I know. Let me go! Let me get out!
Helmer	(*holding her back*) Where are you going?
Nora	(*trying to get free*) You shan't save me, Torvald!
Helmer	(*reeling*) True? Is this true, that I read here? Horrible! No, no— it is impossible that it can be true.
Nora	It is true. I have loved you above everything else in the world.
Helmer	Oh, don't let us have any silly excuses.
Nora	(*taking a step towards him*) Torvald——!
Helmer	Miserable creature—what have you done?
Nora	Let me go. You shall not suffer for my sake. You shall not take it upon yourself.
Helmer	No tragedy airs, please. (*Locks the hall door.*) Here you shall stay and give me an explanation. Do you understand what you have done? Answer me? Do you understand what you have done?
Nora	(*looks steadily at him and says with a growing look of coldness in her face*) Yes, now I am beginning to understand thoroughly.
Helmer	(*walking about the room*) What a horrible awakening! All these eight years—she who was my joy and pride—a hypocrite, a liar—worse, worse—a criminal! The unutterable ugliness of it all! For shame! For shame! (Nora *is silent and looks steadily at him. He stops in front of her.*) I ought to have suspected that something of the sort would happen. I ought to have foreseen it. All your father's want of principle—be silent!—all your father's want of principle has come out in you. No religion, no morality, no sense of duty—. How I am punished for having winked at what he did! I did it for your sake, and this is how you repay me.
Nora	Yes, that's just it.
Helmer	Now you have destroyed all my happiness. You have ruined all my future. It is horrible to think of! I am in the power of an unscrupulous man; he can do what he likes with me, ask anything he likes of me, give me any orders he pleases—I dare not refuse. And I must sink to such miserable depths because of a thoughtless woman!
Nora	When I am out of the way, you will be free.
Helmer	No fine speeches, please. Your father had always plenty of those ready, too. What good would it be to me if you were out of the way, as you say? Not the slightest. He can make the affair known everywhere; and if he does, I may be falsely suspected of having been a party to your criminal action.

Very likely people will think I was behind it all—that it was I who prompted you! And I have to thank you for all this—you whom I have cherished during the whole of our married life. Do you understand now what it is you have done for me?

Nora (*coldly and quietly*) Yes.

Helmer It is so incredible that I can't take it in. But we must come to some understanding. Take off that shawl. Take it off, I tell you. I must try and appease him some way or another. The matter must be hushed up at any cost. And as for you and me, it must appear as if everything between us were just as before—but naturally only in the eyes of the world. You will still remain in my house, that is a matter of course. But I shall not allow you to bring up the children; I dare not trust them to you. To think that I should be obliged to say so to one whom I have loved so dearly, and whom I still——. No, that is all over. From this moment happiness is not the question; all that concerns us is to save the remains, the fragments, the appearance——.

[*A ring is heard at the front-door bell.*]

Helmer (*with a start*) What is that? So late! Can the worst——? Can he——? Hide yourself, Nora. Say you are ill.

[Nora *stands motionless.* Helmer *goes and unlocks the hall door.*]

Maid (*half-dressed, comes to the door*) A letter for the mistress.

Helmer Give it to me. (*Takes the letter, and shuts the door.*) Yes, it is from him. You shall not have it; I will read it myself.

Nora Yes, read it.

Helmer (*standing by the lamp*) I scarcely have the courage to do it. It may mean ruin for both of us. No, I must know. (*Tears open the letter, runs his eye over a few lines, looks at a paper enclosed and gives a shout of joy.*) Nora! (*She looks at him questioningly.*) Nora!— No, I must read it once again——. Yes, it is true! I am saved! Nora, I am saved!

Nora And I?

Helmer You too, of course; we are both saved, both you and I. Look, he sends you your bond back. He says he regrets and repents— that a happy change in his life—never mind what he says! We are saved, Nora! No one can do anything to you. Oh, Nora, Nora!—no, first I must destroy these hateful things. Let me see——. (*Takes a look at the bond.*) No, no, I won't look at it.

The whole thing shall be nothing but a bad dream to me. (*Tears up the bond and both letters, throws them all into the stove, and watches them burn.*) There—now it doesn't exist any longer. He says that since Christmas Eve you———. These must have been three dreadful days for you, Nora.

Nora   I have fought a hard fight these three days.

Helmer   And suffered agonies, and seen no way out but———. No, we won't call any of the horrors to mind. We will only shout with joy, and keep saying, "It's all over! It's all over!" Listen to me, Nora. You don't seem to realize that it is all over. What is this?—such a cold, set face! My poor little Nora, I quite understand; you don't feel as if you could believe that I have forgiven you. But it is true, Nora, I swear it; I have forgiven you everything. I know that what you did, you did out of love for me.

Nora   That is true.

Helmer   You have loved me as a wife ought to love her husband. Only you had not sufficient knowledge to judge of the means you used. But do you suppose you are any the less dear to me, because you don't understand how to act on your own responsibility? No, no; only lean on me; I will advise you and direct you. I should not be a man if this womanly helplessness did not just give you a double attractiveness in my eyes. You must not think any more about the hard things I said in my first moment of consternation, when I thought everything was going to overwhelm me. I have forgiven you, Nora; I swear to you I have forgiven you.

Nora   Thank you for your forgiveness.

[*She goes out through the door to the right.*]

Helmer   No, don't go———. (*Looks in.*) What are you doing in there?

Nora   (*from within*) Taking off my fancy dress.

Helmer   (*standing at the open door*) Yes, do. Try and calm yourself, and make your mind easy again, my frightened little singing-bird. Be at rest, and feel secure; I have broad wings to shelter you under. (*Walks up and down by the door.*) How warm and cosy our home is, Nora. Here is shelter for you; here I will protect you like a hunted dove that I have saved from a hawk's claws. I will bring peace to your poor beating heart. It will come, little by little, Nora, believe me. Tomorrow morning you will look upon it all quite differently; soon everything will be just as it was before. Very soon you won't need me to assure you that I have forgiven you; you will yourself feel the certainty that I have done so. Can you suppose I should ever think of such a thing as repudiating you, or even reproaching you? You have no idea what a true man's heart is like, Nora. There is something so indescribably sweet and satisfying, to a man, in the knowledge that he has forgiven his wife——forgiven her freely, and with all his heart. It seems as if that had made her, as it were, doubly his own; he has given her a new life, so to speak; and she has in a way become both wife and child to him. So you shall be for me after this, my little scared, helpless darling. Have no anxiety about anything, Nora; only be frank and open with me, and I will serve as will and conscience both to you——. What is this? Not gone to bed? Have you changed your things?

Nora	(*in everyday dress*) Yes, Torvald, I have changed my things now.
Helmer	But what for?——so late as this.
Nora	I shall not sleep to-night.
Helmer	But, my dear Nora——.
Nora	(*looking at her watch*) It is not so very late. Sit down here, Torvald. You and I have much to say to one another.

[*She sits down at one side of the table.*]

Helmer	Nora——what is this?——this cold, set face?
Nora	Sit down. It will take some time; I have a lot to talk over with you.
Helmer	(*sits down at the opposite side of the table*) You alarm me, Nora!—— and I don't understand you.
Nora	No, that is just it. You don't understand me, and I have never understood you either—before to-night. No, you mustn't interrupt me. You must simply listen to what I say. Torvald, this is a settling of accounts.
Helmer	What do you mean by that?
Nora	(*after a short silence*) Isn't there one thing that strikes you as strange in our sitting here like this?
Helmer	What is that?
Nora	We have been married now eight years. Does it not occur to you that this is the first time we two, you and I, husband and wife, have had a serious conversation?
Helmer	What do you mean by serious?
Nora	In all these eight years—longer than that—from the very

beginning of our acquaintance, we have never exchanged a word on any serious subject.

Helmer. Was it likely that I would be continually and for ever telling you about worries that you could not help me to bear?

Nora I am not speaking about business matters. I say that we have never sat down in earnest together to try and get at the bottom of anything.

Helmer But, dearest Nora, would it have been any good to you?

Nora That is just it; you have never understood me. I have been greatly wronged, Torvald—first by papa and then by you.

Helmer What! By us two—by us two, who have loved you better than anyone else in the world?

Nora (*shaking her head*) You have never loved me. You have only thought it pleasant to be in love with me.

Helmer Nora, what do I hear you saying?

Nora It is perfectly true, Torvald. When I was at home with papa, he told me his opinion about everything, and so I had the same opinions; and if I differed from him I concealed the fact, because he would not have liked it. He called me his doll-child, and he played with me just as I used to play with my dolls. And when I came to live with you——

Helmer What sort of an expression is that to use about our marriage?

Nora (*undisturbed*) I mean that I was simply transferred from papa's hands into yours. You arranged everything according to your own taste, and so I got the same tastes as you—or else I pretended to, I am really not quite sure which—I think sometimes the one and sometimes the other. When I look back on it, it seems to me as if I had been living here like a poor woman—just from hand to mouth. I have existed merely to perform tricks for you, Torvald. But you would have it so. You and papa have committed a great sin against me. It is your fault that I have made nothing of my life.

Helmer How unreasonable and how ungrateful you are, Nora! Have you not been happy here?

Nora No, I have never been happy. I thought I was, but it has never really been so.

Helmer Not—not happy!

Nora No, only merry. And you have always been so kind to me. But our home has been nothing but a playroom. I have been your doll-wife, just as at home I was papa's doll-child; and here the children have been my dolls. I thought it great fun when you played with me, just as they thought it great fun when I played with them. That is what our marriage has been, Torvald.

Helmer	There is some truth in what you say—exaggerated and strained as your view of it is. But for the future it shall be different. Play-time shall be over, and lesson-time shall begin.
Nora	Whose lessons? Mine, or the children's?
Helmer	Both yours and the children's, my darling Nora.
Nora	Alas, Torvald, you are not the man to educate me into being a proper wife for you.
Helmer	And you can say that!
Nora	And I—how am I fitted to bring up the children?
Helmer	Nora!
Nora	Didn't you say so yourself a little while ago—that you dare not trust me to bring them up?
Helmer	In a moment of anger! Why do you pay any heed to that?
Nora	Indeed, you were perfectly right. I am not fit for the task. There is another task I must undertake first. I must try and educate myself—you are not the man to help me in that. I must do that for myself. And that is why I am going to leave you now.
Helmer	*(springing up)* What do you say?
Nora	I must stand quite alone, if I am to understand myself and everything about me. It is for that reason that I cannot remain with you any longer.
Helmer	Nora! Nora!
Nora	I am going away from here now, at once. I am sure Christine will take me in for the night——.
Helmer	You are out of your mind! I won't allow it! I forbid you!
Nora	It is no use forbidding me anything any longer. I will take with me what belongs to myself. I will take nothing from you, either now or later.
Helmer	What sort of madness is this!
Nora	To-morrow I shall go home——I mean, to my old home. It will be easiest for me to find something to do there.
Helmer	You blind, foolish woman!

Nora   I must try and get some sense, Torvald.

Helmer   To desert your home, your husband and your children! And you don't consider what people will say!

Nora   I cannot consider that at all. I only know that it is necessary for me.

Helmer   It's shocking. This is how you would neglect your most sacred duties.

Nora   What do you consider my most sacred duties?

Helmer   Do I need to tell you that? Are they not your duties to your husband and your children?

Nora   I have other duties just as sacred.

Helmer   That you have not. What duties could those be?

Nora   Duties to myself.

Helmer   Before all else, you are a wife and a mother.

Nora   I don't believe that any longer. I believe that before all else I am a reasonable human being, just as you are—or, at all events, that I must try and become one. I know quite well, Torvald, that most people would think you right, and that views of that kind are to be found in books; but I can no longer content myself with what most people say, or with what is found in books. I must think over things for myself and get to understand them.

Helmer   Can you not understand your place in your own home? Have you not a reliable guide in such matters as that?—have you no religion?

Nora   I am afraid, Torvald, I do not exactly know what religion is.

Helmer   What are you saying?

Nora   I know nothing but what the clergyman said, when I went to be confirmed. He told us that religion was this, and that, and the other. When I am away from all this, and am alone, I will look into that matter too. I will see if what the clergyman said is true, or at all events if it is true for me.

Helmer   This is unheard of in a girl of your age! But if religion cannot lead you aright, let me try and awaken your conscience. I suppose you have some moral sense? Or—answer me—am I to think you have none?

Nora   I assure you, Torvald, that is not an easy question to answer. I really don't know. The thing perplexes me altogether. I only know that you and I look at it in quite a different light. I am learning, too, that the law is quite another thing from what I

	supposed; but I find it impossible to convince myself that the law is right. According to it a woman has no right to spare her old dying father, or to save her husband's life. I can't believe that.
Helmer	You talk like a child. You don't understand the conditions of the world in which you live.
Nora	No, I don't. But now I am going to try. I am going to see if I can make out who is right, the world or I.
Helmer	You are ill, Nora; you are delirious; I almost think you are out of your mind.
Nora	I have never felt my mind so clear and certain as to-night.
Helmer	And is it with a clear and certain mind that you forsake your husband and your children?
Nora	Yes, it is.
Helmer	Then there is only one possible explanation.
Nora	What is that?
Helmer	You do not love me any more.
Nora	No, that is just it.
Helmer,	Nora!—and you can say that?
Nora	It gives me great pain, Torvald, for you have always been so kind to me, but I cannot help it. I do not love you any more.
Helmer	(*regaining his composure*) Is that a clear and certain conviction too?
Nora	Yes, absolutely clear and certain. That is the reason why I will not stay here any longer.
Helmer	And can you tell me what I have done to forfeit your love?
Nora	Yes, indeed I can. It was to-night, when the wonderful thing did not happen; then I saw you were not the man I had thought you.
Helmer	Explain yourself better—I don't understand you.
Nora	I have waited so patiently for eight years; for goodness knows, I knew very well that wonderful things don't happen every day. Then this horrible misfortune came upon me; and then I felt quite certain that the wonderful thing was going to happen at last. When Krogstad's letter was lying out there, never for a moment did I imagine that you would consent to accept this man's conditions. I was so absolutely certain that you would say to him: Publish the thing to the whole world. And when that was done——.

Helmer Yes, what then?—when I had exposed my wife to shame and disgrace?

Nora When that was done, I was so absolutely certain, you would come forward and take everything upon yourself, and say: I am the guilty one.

Helmer Nora——!

Nora You mean that I would never have accepted such a sacrifice on your part? No, of course not. But what would my assurances have been worth against yours? That was the wonderful thing which I hoped for and feared; and it was to prevent that, that I wanted to kill myself.

Helmer I would gladly work night and day for you, Nora—bear sorrow and want for your sake. But no man would sacrifice his honour for the one he loves.

Nora It is a thing hundreds of thousands of women have done.

Helmer Oh, you think and talk like a heedless child.

Nora Maybe. But you neither think nor talk like the man I could bind myself to. As soon as your fear was over—and it was not fear for what threatened me, but for what might happen to you—when the whole thing was past, as far as you were concerned it was exactly as if nothing at all had happened. Exactly as before, I was your little skylark, your doll, which you would in future treat with doubly gentle care, because it was so brittle and fragile. (*Getting up.*) Torvald—it was then it dawned upon me that for eight years I had been living here with a strange man, and had borne him three children——. Oh, I can't bear to think of it! I could tear myself into little bits!

Helmer (*sadly*) I see, I see. An abyss has opened between us—there is no denying it. But, Nora, would it not be possible to fill it up?

Nora As I am now, I am no wife for you.

Helmer I have it in me to become a different man.

Nora Perhaps—if your doll is taken away from you.

Helmer But to part!—to part from you! No, no Nora, I can't understand that idea.

Nora (*going out to the right*) That makes it all the more certain that if must be done.

[*She comes back with her cloak and hat and a small bag which she puts on a chair by the table.*]

Helmer Nora, Nora, not now! Wait till to-morrow.

Nora	(*putting on her cloak*) I cannot spend the night in a strange man's room.
Helmer	But can't we live here like brother and sister——?
Nora	(*putting on her hat*) You know very well that would not last long. (*Puts the shawl round her.*) Good-bye, Torvald. I won't see the little ones. I know they are in better hands than mine. As I am now, I can be of no use to them.
Helmer	But some day, Nora—some day?
Nora	How can I tell? I have no idea what is going to become of me.
Helmer	But you are my wife, whatever becomes of you.
Nora	Listen, Torvald. I have heard that when a wife deserts her husband's house, as I am doing now, he is legally freed from all obligations towards her. In any case I set you free from all your obligations. You are not to feel yourself bound in the slightest way, any more than I shall. There must be perfect freedom on both sides. See here is your ring back. Give me mine.
Helmer	That too?
Nora	That too.
Helmer	Here it is.
Nora	That's right. Now it is all over. I have put the keys here. The maids know all about everything in the house—better than I do. To-morrow, after I have left her, Christine will come here and pack up my own things that I brought with me from home. I will have them sent after me.
Helmer	All over! All over!—Nora, shall you never think of me again?
Nora	I know I shall often think of you and the children and this house.
Helmer	May I write to you, Nora?
Nora	No—never. You must not do that.
Helmer	But at least let me send you——.
Nora	Nothing—nothing——.
Helmer	Let me help you if you are in want.
Nora	No. I can receive nothing from a stranger.
Helmer	Nora—can I never be anything more than a stranger to you?
Nora	(*taking her bag*) Ah, Torvald, the most wonderful thing of all would have to happen.
Helmer	Tell me what that would be!
Nora	Both you and I would have to be so changed that——. Oh, Torvald, I don't believe any longer in wonderful things happening.

Helmer   But I will believe in it. Tell me? So changed that——?
Nora   That our life together would be a real wedlock. Good-bye.
     [*She goes out through the hall.*]
Helmer   (*sinks down on a chair at the door and buries his face in his hands*)
     Nora! Nora! (*Looks round, and rises.*) Empty. She is gone. (*A hope
     flashes across his mind.*) The most wonderful thing of all——?
     [*The sound of a door shutting is heard from below.*]

Leslie Fiedler / The Revenge on Women: Fitzgerald, Hemingway and Faulkner

In his book *Love and Death in the American Novel*, Leslie Fiedler discusses the various European influences as well as the indigenous forces that have made the American novel peculiarly American. Among the influences are the courtly love tradition, the sentimental novel of Samuel Richardson, the Gothic novel, and the historical romances of Sir Walter Scott, all transformed by and adjusted to the needs of an American milieu. Woman plays an important role in all forms of the novel. In nineteenth century American fiction she is either the good girl, the white Protestant virgin, or an ambiguous, dark-haired female who often has a strong sexual drive and is of Mediterranean or other "exotic" descent. Both types, however, are a threat. The fair maid wants to civilize the male, while the dark lady threatens to arouse his passion and thus destroy him.

To avoid this dilemma, several great American authors have rejected women altogether from their house of fiction. Fiedler feels that the American writer has not been able to portray a mature and fulfilling relationship between a man and a woman and as a result "our classic literature is a literature of horror for boys." Thus Huck and Jim, Ishmael and Queequeg, and most of all Natty Bumppo and Chingagook present, with variations, the following archetypal situation: "Two lonely men, one darkskinned, one white, bend together over a carefully guarded fire in the virgin heart of the American wilderness; they have forsaken all others for the sake of the austere, almost inarticulate, but unquestioned love which binds them to each other and to the world of nature which they have preferred over civilization." But the white and his darkskinned companion are kept at a distance from each other by the sameness of their sex and by the difference of their race. They are safe from each other. Thus racism and sexism in their various manifestations permeate America's fiction.

When we consider that Fitzgerald, Hemingway, and Faulkner are inevitably tied to nineteenth century fiction, and when we realize that their novels are widely read in the private world of the livingroom and the public world of the classroom, then we cannot help but wonder what vicious circle their fiction helps to perpetuate. Are the bitches of Fitzgerald, Hemingway, and Faulkner an imitation of "reality"? Does the avid reader find their counterpart in the world around him? Which comes first: the fictional bitch and then the real one, or the real bitch and then the fictional one? An enlightened reader will realize that these unquestionably great authors have created fictions that accurately reveal perhaps a personal neurosis, but also the deep neuroses that afflict our society and specifically the relationships between men and women. The perceptive reader will not confuse a symbol with a living woman, and he will agree with Fiedler's comment on the pernicious influence of the Clarissa symbol: "The imposition of the Clarissa-image on the young girl represents an insidious form of enslavement; all the idealizations of the female from the earliest days of courtly love had been in fact devices to deprive her of freedom and self-determination, but this last represents the final attempt to imprison woman within the myth of Woman. The demand that every woman act out an allegorical role of Womanhood is like the contemporary pressure on all Negroes to play The Negro; and the Clarissa-image, when degraded from archetype to stereotype, is analogous to the current image of Uncle Tom."

The first notable anti-virgin of our fiction, the prototype of the blasphemous portraits of the Fair Goddess as bitch in which our twentieth-century fiction abounds, is quite deliberately called Daisy—after James's misunderstood American Girl. She is, of course, the Daisy Fay Buchanan of Scott Fitzgerald's *The Great Gatsby*, the girl who lures her lovers on, like America itself, with a "voice . . . full of money." More like James's Maggie Verver, perhaps, than Daisy Miller in the potency of her charm, she is yet another Heiress of All the Ages: great-great-granddaughter of that priceless Pearl, who got the best of the Old World and the New. She is an odd inversion of Clarissa-Charlotte Temple-Maggie Verver; no longer the abused woman, who only by her suffering and death castrates her betrayer, but the abusing woman, symbol of an imperialist rather than a colonial America. The phallic woman with a phallus of gold, she remains still somehow the magic princess James had imagined as the heroine of *The Golden Bowl*: "High in a white palace the king's daughter, the golden girl." To Fitzgerald, however, her fairy glamour is illusory, and once approached the White Maiden is revealed as a White Witch, the golden girl as a golden idol. On his palette, white and gold make a dirty color; for wealth is no longer innocent, America no longer innocent, the Girl who is the soul of both turned destructive and corrupt.

There is only one story that Fitzgerald knows how to tell, and no matter how he thrashes about, he must tell it over and over. The penniless knight, poor stupid Hans, caddy or bootlegger or medical student, goes out to seek his fortune and unluckily finds it. His reward is, just as in the fairy tales, the golden girl in the white palace; but quite differently from the fairy tales, that is not a happy ending at all. He finds in his bed not the white bride but the Dark Destroyer; indeed, there is no White Bride, since Dark Lady and Fair, witch and redeemer have fallen together. But it is more complicated even than this. Possessed of the power of wealth, Fitzgerald's women, like their wealthy male compeers, who seem their twins rather than their mates, are rapists and aggressors. Of both Daisy and her husband Tom, Fitzgerald tells us, "they smashed up things and creatures and then retreated back into their money." In a real sense, not Daisy but Jay Gatz, the Great Gatsby, is the true descendant of Daisy Miller: the naïf out of the West destined to shock the upholders of decorum and to die of a love for which there is no worthy object.

In Fitzgerald's world, the distinction between sexes is fluid and shifting, precisely because he has transposed the mythic roles and values of male and female, remaking Clarissa in Lovelace's image, Lovelace in Clarissa's. With no difficulty at all and only a minimum of rewriting, the boy Francis, who was to be a center of vision in *The World's Fair*, becomes the girl Rosemary as that proposed novel turned into *Tender Is the Night*. Thematically, archetypally even such chief male protagonists as Gatsby and Dick Diver are females; at least, they occupy in their stories the position of Henry James's Nice American Girls. It is they who embody innocence and the American dream, taking up the role the flapper had contemptuously abandoned for what was called in the '20's "freedom"; but they do not know this, projecting the dream which survives only in themselves upon the rich young ladies whom they desire. Early in *Tender Is the Night*, Dick Diver comes upon Nicole in Europe, and, dazzled by her "cream-colored dress . . . her very blonde hair . . . her face lighting up like an angel's," thinks of her as "a scarcely saved waif of disaster bringing him the essence of a continent. . . ." He reads into her, that is to say, the conventional meanings of the Good American Girl. But before his marriage with her has finally unmanned him, he comes to see her as an "evil-eyed" destroyer, and longs "to grind her grinning mask into jelly."

It is he, however, who is ground into jelly, crushed and driven from the imaginary sentimental paradise of married love to the lonely male refuge, the counter-paradise of mindless drunkenness. We see him last making the sign of the cross, a priest of Sentimental Love, who has arrived in the empty temple after the abdication of his goddess. Nicole, the goddess who failed, is postulated in the novel as a schizophrenic, in an attempt to explain her double role as Fair Lady and Dark, her two faces, angelic and diabolic, the melting and the grinning mask. But the schizophrenia is really in Diver, which is to say, in Fitzgerald, which is finally to say, in the American mind itself. There are not, in fact, two orders of women, good and bad, nor is there even one which seems for a little while bad, only to prove in the end utterly unravished and pure. There are only two sets of expectations and a single imperfect kind of woman caught between them: only actual incomplete females, looking in vain for a satisfactory definition of their role in a land of artists who insist on treating them as goddesses or bitches. The dream role and the nightmare role alike deny the humanity of women, who, baffled, switch from playing out one to acting out the other. Fitzgerald apparently never managed to accommodate to the fact that he lived at the moment of a great switch-over in roles, though he recorded that revolution in the body of his work. His outrage and self-pity constantly break through the pattern of his fiction, make even an ambitious attempt like *Tender Is the Night* finally too sentimental and whining to endure.

Only in *The Great Gatsby* does Fitzgerald manage to transmute his pattern into an objective form, evade the self-pity which corrodes the significance and the very shape of his other work—and this is perhaps because Gatsby is the most distant of all his protagonists from his real self. To Gatsby, Daisy appears in the customary semblance of the Fair Maiden, however; he finds her quite simply "the first 'nice' girl he had ever known." It is Howells' genteel epithet which occurs to him, though by Fitzgerald's time the capital letters are gone and the apologetic quotation marks have insidiously intruded. Daisy, rich and elegant and clean and sweet-smelling, represents to her status-hungry provincial lover, not the corruption and death she really embodies, but Success—which is to say, America itself. In Fitzgerald, the same fable that informs James is replayed, subtly transformed, for like James he has written an anti-Western, an "Eastern": a drama in which back-trailers reverse their westward drive to seek in the world which their ancestors abandoned the dream of riches and glory that has somehow evaded them. Fitzgerald's young men go east even as far as Europe; though unlike James's young women, they are in quest not of art and experience and the shudder of guilt, but of an even more ultimate innocence, an absolute America: a happy ending complete with new car, big house, money, and the girl.

In the symbolic geography of *The Great Gatsby*, the two halves of a nation are compressed into the two settlements on Long Island of West Egg and East Egg, from the first of which the not-quite arrived look yearningly across the water at those who are already *in*, Jay Gatsby at Daisy Buchanan. There is no need for a symbolic Europe to complete the scene; and, indeed, even in *Tender Is the Night*, Europe is only a place where the East Eggians go to play, a transatlantic extension of East Egg itself. In a concluding passage of great beauty and conviction, Fitzgerald manages to convey the whole world of aspiration which Daisy has represented to Gatsby, and transforms the book from a lament over the fall of the Fair Woman to an elegy for the lapsed American dream of innocent success:

> And as the moon rose higher the inessential houses began to melt away until gradually I became aware of the old island here that flowered once for Dutch sailors' eyes—a fresh, green breast of the new world . . . the trees that had made way for Gatsby's house, had once pandered in whispers to the last and greatest of all human dreams; for a transitory enchanted moment man must have held his breath in the presence of this continent . . . face to face for the last time in history with something commensurate with his capacity for wonder.
>
> And as I sat there brooding on the old, unknown world, I thought of Gatsby's wonder when he first picked out the green light at the end of Daisy's dock. He had come a long way to this blue lawn, and his dream must have seemed so close that he could hardly fail to grasp it. He did not know that it was already behind him, somewhere back in the vast obscurity beyond the city, where the dark fields of the republic rolled on under the night.

For Fitzgerald, "love" was essentially yearning and frustration; and there is consequently little consummated genital love in his novels, though he identified himself with that sexual revolution which the '20's thought of as their special subject. The adolescent's "kiss" is the only climax his imagination can really encompass; and despite his occasionally telling us that one or another of his characters has "taken" a woman, it is the only climax he ever realizes in a scene. In his insufferable early books, the American institution of *coitus interruptus*, from bundling to necking a favorite national pastime, finds at last a laureate; and even in his more mature works, his women move from the kiss to the kill with only the barest suggestion of copulation between. Hemingway, on the other hand, is much addicted to describing the sex act. It is the symbolic center of his work: a scene to which he recurs when nostalgically evoking his boyhood as "Up in Michigan"; illustrating the virtues of the sturdy poor as in *To Have and Have Not;* reflecting on civil strife and heroism as in *For Whom the Bell Tolls;* or projecting the fantasies of a man facing old age as in *Across the River and Into the Trees.* There are, however, no *women* in his books! In his earlier fictions, Hemingway's descriptions of the sexual encounter are intentionally brutal, in his later ones unintentionally comic; for in no case, can he quite succeed in making his females human, and coitus performed with an animal, a thing, or a wet dream is either horrible or ridiculous. If in *For Whom the Bell Tolls* Hemingway has written the most absurd love scene in the history of the American novel, this is not because he lost momentarily his skill and authority; it is a give-away—a moment which illuminates the whole erotic content of his fiction.

Hemingway is only really comfortable in dealing with "men without women." The relations of father to son, of battle-companions, friends on a fishing trip, fellow inmates in a hospital, a couple of waiters preparing to close up shop, a bullfighter and his manager, a boy and a gangster: these move him to simplicity and truth. Perhaps he is best of all with men who stand alone—in night-time scenes when the solitary individual sweats in his bed on the verge of nightmare, or arises to confront himself in the glass; though he is at home, too, with the Rip Van Winkle archetype, with men in flight from women. Certainly, he returns again and again to the fishing trip and the journey to the war—those two traditional evasions of domesticity and civil life. Yet he feels an obligation to introduce women into his more ambitious fictions, though he does not know what to do with them beyond taking them to bed. All his life, he has been haunted by a sense of how simple it all was once, when he could take his Indian girl into the clean-smelling woods, stretch out beside her on the pine-needles (her brother standing guard), and rise to no obligations at all. In a story called "Fathers and Sons," he writes a tribute to that prototypical, mindless, undemanding, scarcely human girl: "Could you say she did first what no one has ever done better and mention plump brown legs, flat belly, hard little breasts, well holding arms, quick searching tongue, the flat eyes, the good taste of mouth . . . and hemlock needles stuck against your belly. . . . Long time ago good. Now no good."

In Hemingway the rejection of the sentimental happy ending of marriage involves the acceptance of the sentimental happy beginning of innocent and inconsequential sex, and camouflages the rejection of maturity and of fatherhood itself. The only story in which he portrays a major protagonist as having a child is the one in which he remembers with nostalgia his little Trudy of the "well holding arms, quick searching tongue," and looks forward to the time when his son will have a gun and they can pop off to the forest like two boys together. More typically he aspires to be not Father but "Papa," the Old Man of the girl-child with whom he is temporarily sleeping; and surely there is no writer to whom childbirth more customarily presents itself as the essential catastrophe. At best he portrays it as a plaguey sort of accident which forces a man to leave his buddies behind at the moment of greatest pleasure as in "Cross Country Snow"; at worst, it becomes in his fiction that horror which drives the tender-hearted husband of "Indian Camp" to suicide, or which takes Catherine away from Lieutenant Henry in *A Farewell to Arms*.

Poor things, all they wanted was innocent orgasm after orgasm on an island of peace in a world at war, love-making without end in a scarcely real country to which neither owed life or allegiance. But such relationship can, of course, never last, as Hemingway-Nick Adams-Lieutenant Henry has always known: "They all ended the same. Long time ago good. Now no good." Only the dead woman becomes neither a bore nor a mother; and before Catherine can quite become either she must die, killed not by Hemingway, of course, but by childbirth! It is all quite sad and lovely at the end: the last kiss bestowed on what was a woman and is now a statue, the walk home through the rain. Poe himself could not have done better, though he was haunted not by the memory of a plump little Indian on the hemlock needles but a fantasy of a high-born maiden "loved with a love that was more than love" and carried away by death.

Had Catherine lived, she could only have turned into a bitch; for this is the fate in Hemingway's imagination of all Anglo-Saxon women. In him, the cliché of Dark Lady and Fair survives, but stood on its head, exactly reversed. The Dark Lady, who is neither wife nor mother, blends with the image of Fayaway, the exotic servant-consort reconstructed by Melville in *Typee* out of memories of an eight-year-old Polynesian girl-child. In

Hemingway, such women are mindless, soft, subservient; painless devices for extracting seed without human engagement. The Fair Lady, on the other hand, who gets pregnant and wants a wedding, or uses her sexual allure to assert her power, is seen as a threat and a destroyer of men. But the seed-extractors are Indians or Latins, black-eyed and dusky in hue, while the castrators are at least Anglo-Saxon if not symbolically blond. Neither are permitted to be virgins; indeed, both are imagined as having been often possessed, though in the case of the Fair Woman promiscuity is used as a device for humiliating and unmanning the male foolish enough to have entered into a marriage with her. Through the Dark anti-virgin, on the other hand, a new lover enters into a blameless communion with the other uncommitted males who have possessed her and departed, as well as with those yet to come. It is a kind of homosexuality once-removed, the appeal of the whorehouse (Eden of the world of men without women) embodied in a single figure.

When Hemingway's bitches are Americans, they are hopeless and unmitigated bitches; symbols of Home and Mother as remembered by the boy who could never forgive Mama for having wantonly destroyed Papa's Indian collection! Mrs. Macomber, who, in "The Short Happy Life of Francis Macomber," kills her husband for having alienated the affections of the guide with whom she is having one of her spiteful little affairs, is a prime example of the type. And "the woman," in "The Snows of Kilimanjaro" another, who with her wealth has weaned her husband from all that sustained his virility, betrayed him to aimlessness and humiliation. Like Fitzgerald's betrayed men, he can choose only to die, swoon to the death he desires at the climax of a dream of escape.

The British bitch is for Hemingway only a demi-bitch, however, as the English are only, as it were, demi-Americans. Catherine is delivered from her doom by death; Brett Ashley in *The Sun Also Rises* (1926) is permitted, once at least, the gesture of herself rejecting her mythical role. But it is quite a feat at that, and Brett cannot leave off congratulating herself: "You know it makes one feel rather good deciding not to be a bitch." Yet Brett never becomes a woman really; she is mythicized rather than redeemed. And if she is the most satisfactory female character in all of Hemingway, this is because for once she is presented not as an animal or as a nightmare but quite audaciously as a goddess, the bitch-goddess with a boyish bob (Hemingway is rather fond of women who seem as much boy as girl), the Lilith of the '20's. No man embraces her without being in some sense castrated, except for Jake Barnes who is unmanned to begin with; no man approaches her without *wanting* to be castrated, except for Romero, who thinks naïvely that she is—or can easily become—a woman. Indeed, when Brett leaves that nineteen-year-old bullfighter, one suspects that, though she avows it is because she will not be "one of those bitches who ruins children," she is really running away because she thinks he might *make* her a woman. Certainly, Romero's insistence that she let her hair grow out has something to do with it: "He wanted me to grow my hair out. Me, with long hair. I'd look so like hell. . . . He said it would make me more womanly. I'd look a fright."

To yield up her cropped head would be to yield up her emancipation from female servitude, to become feminine rather than phallic; and this Brett cannot do. She thinks of herself as a flapper, though the word perhaps would not have occurred to her, as a member of the "Lost Generation"; but the Spaniards know her immediately as a terrible goddess, the avatar of an ancient archetype. She tries in vain to enter into the circle of Christian communion, but is always turned aside at the door; she changes her mind, she has forgotten her hat—the apparent reason never matters; she belongs to a world alien and prior to that of the Christian churches in which Jake finds a kind of peace. In Pamplona, Brett is surrounded by a group of *riau-riau* dancers, who desert a religious procession to follow her, set her up as a rival to Saint Fermin: "Some dancers formed a circle around Brett and started to dance. They wore big wreaths of white garlic around their necks. . . . They were all chanting. Brett wanted to dance but they did not want her to. They wanted her as an image to dance around." Incapable of love except as a moment in bed, Brett can bestow on her worshipers nothing more than the brief joy of a drunken ecstasy—followed by suffering and deprivation and regret. In the end, not only are her physical lovers unmanned and degraded, but even Jake, who is her priest and is protected by his terrible wound, is humiliated. For her service is a betrayal not only of his Catholic faith but of his pure passion for bullfighting and trout-fishing; and the priest of the bitch-goddess is, on the purely human level, a pimp.

In the work of William Faulkner, the fear of the castrating woman and the dis-ease with sexuality present in the novels of his contemporaries, Fitzgerald and Hemingway, attain their fullest and shrillest expression. Not content with merely projecting images of the anti-virgin, he insists upon editorializing against the woman he travesties in character and situation. No Jiggs and Maggie cliché of popular anti-feminism is too banal for him to use; he reminds us (again and again!) that men are help-less in the hands of their mothers, wives, and sisters; that females do not think but proceed from evidence to conclusions by paths too devious for males to follow; that they possess neither morality nor honor; that they are capable, therefore, of betrayal without qualm or quiver of guilt but also of inexplicable loyalty; that they enjoy an occasional beating at the hands of their men; that they are unforgiving and without charity to other members of their own sex; that they lose keys and other small useful articles with maddening regularity but are quite capable of finding things invisible to men; that they use their sexuality with cold calculation to achieve their inscrutable ends, etc., etc.

Until his last books, Faulkner treated with respect only females, white ladies or colored women, past the menopause. The elderly maiden or widowed aunt is the sole female figure in his fiction exempt from travesty and contempt. Up to the very verge of her climacteric, woman seems to Faulkner capable of the most shameless concupiscence, like Miss Burden in *Light in August*, cowering naked in the garden of the decaying house waiting to be captured and possessed in an obscene game of hide-and-seek. Faulkner sometimes gives the impression of the village misogynist swapping yarns with the boys at the bar in order to reveal a truth about women which shocks even himself. Like old Varner in *The Hamlet*, he keeps assuring his readers that he "cheerfully and robustly and un-deviatingly" declines to accept "any such theory as female chastity other than as a myth to hoodwink young husbands. . . ." But there is little robust or cheerful about his attitudes, however undeviatingly he may assert them; he is less like Varner fundamentally than like Hightower, the scared and stinking refugee from life in *Light in August*, who cries out in despair that "the husband of a mother, whether he be the father or not is already a cuckold . . . what woman has ever suffered from any brute as men have suffered from good women?"

Pubescent or nubile women, for Faulkner, fall into two classes, rough-ly corresponding to those of Hemingway, though for the former both are terrifying: great, sluggish, mindless daughters of peasants, whose fertility and allure are scarcely distinguishable from those of a beast in heat; and the febrile, almost fleshless but sexually insatiable daughters of the aristocracy. Not the women he observes but those he dreams inhabit Faulkner's novels, myths of masculine protest: the peasant wench as earth goddess (Lena Grove in *Light in August*, Dewey Dell in *As I Lay Dying*, Eula Varner in *The Hamlet*), or the coed as nymphomaniac Venus

(Cecily of *Soldiers' Pay*, Patricia in *Mosquitoes*, Temple Drake in *Sanctuary*). Their very names tend toward allegory, "Dewey Dell," for instance, suggesting both a natural setting and woman's sex, her sex as a fact of nature, while "Temple Drake" evokes both a ruined sanctuary and the sense of an unnatural usurpation: woman becomes a sexual aggressor—more drake than duck.

Unlike the natural women of Hemingway, Faulkner's dewiest dells turn out to be destroyers rather than redeemers, quicksands disguised as sacred groves. In his portrayal of Lena Grove, he relents for once into something like admiration; but his Eula Varner is more typical. Faulkner begins by describing Eula, the goddess who presides over the revels of *The Hamlet* and is married off in the end to its Devil, Flem Snopes, in terms of a pagan dithyramb to Aphrodite: "Her entire appearance suggested some symbology out of the old Dionysic Times, honey in sunlight and bursting grapes, the writhen bleeding of the crushed fecundated vine beneath the hard rapacious trampling goat-hoof." What begins as a pre-Christian eulogy to the inarticulate manifestation of sheer fertility imperceptibly slips over into a puritan cry of distress and distaste before unredeemed, burgeoning life.

When Faulkner abandons mythology for more direct physical description, his uneasiness before Eula's languor and inert lusciousness is even more clearly betrayed. "She simply did not move at all of her own volition, save to and from the table and to and from bed. She was late in learning to walk. . . . She remained in it [her perambulator] long after she had grown too large to straighten her legs out. . . . She did nothing. She might as well have been a foetus." If she is a foetus, however, Eula is an almost intolerably alluring one, a foetus-vampire, as it were; for hanging sluggishly in her mother's arms, she seems, Faulkner writes, even at the age of five or six, an "indisputably female burden like a bizarre and chaperoned Sabine rape." And after she begins to walk to school, men and boys gape, whistle, and howl in the unquenchable anguish and joy of pure desire. It is an absurd conceit, hysterical, a little mad—tolerable only because Faulkner so obviously believes in it, believes in the terror of mere inert female flesh not as a fact of life but as an article of faith!

Just as his Eula figures are all motionless, quivering, mammalian softness, Faulkner's Temple figures are sheer motion, a blur of dancing legs and wind blown hair in a speeding car: "sexless yet somehow troubling." It is the assertion of femaleness which upsets him in Eula Varner; and it is its denial which disturbs him in Temple Drake. Temple is disconcertingly almost a man, almost phallic; and, indeed, at the moment of her rape by Popeye, it is difficult to tell which one is the phallus bearer, to whom the bloody corncob really belongs. "Then I thought about being a man," Temple says later, "and as soon as I thought it, it happened. . . . It made a kind of plopping sound, like blowing a little rubber tube wrong-side outward. . . . I could feel it, and I lay right still to keep from laughing about how surprised he was going to be . . ." In *Sanctuary*, Faulkner's revulsion from woman's betrayal of her traditionally submissive role reaches so shrill a pitch that, in simple self-defense, he has felt it necessary to disavow that novel as a pot-boiler; yet it is obviously written in earnest though at white heat, a nightmare directly transcribed. Fortunately, it is not quite convincing enough to be unbearable, though it possesses enough hallucinatory vividness to give it the baleful appeal of a Dickensian or Dostoevskian grotesque. *Sanctuary* is, on the one hand, the darkest of all Faulkner's books, a brutal protest to the quality of American life written in the pit of the Great Depression; but on the other hand, it is the dirtiest of all the dirty jokes exchanged among men only at the expense of the abdicating Anglo-Saxon Virgin.

Temple is not only a lady, but the very image of all those Fair Ladies whose fall or resistance had been the central subject of genteel literature ever since *Charlotte Temple* was published in the United States. That her name is an inversion of that of the prototypical American heroine is, perhaps, only an accident, one of the more satisfactory jokes of history; and certainly Faulkner did not know that the original of Maggie Verver was Henry James's cousin Minny Temple, whose frailness, white skin, and red hair also distinguish Temple Drake. The title of his book, however, makes it clear that Faulkner is fully aware that he is dealing not with a mere change in mores but with the desecration of a cult object. Out of the "high delicate head" of Faulkner's Temple, at any rate, look eyes which are "cool, predatory, and discreet," but their discretion is belied by the "bold painted mouth." She fools no one; the wife of a gangster into whose hideout she has stumbled sees immediately that though Temple, like her illustrious prototypes, is still the Girl on the Run, she no longer means to run quite fast enough to get away. And even Gowan Stevens, Temple's escort and male opposite number, is not too drunk to understand what she really wants, though drunk enough not to be able to take advantage of his knowledge. "Don't think I don't see your name where it's written on that lavatory wall!" he tells her in impotent spite. It is the final degradation; the holy name on the lavatory wall!

Before Faulkner is through, we have been compelled to watch the ex-snow maiden, the former golden girl, not only raped (which is nothing new, of course, since she was born being raped, was Clarissa before she was Maggie Verver), but begging to be had, whimpering for the consummation she had once fled in terror. Beside Temple, pleading with Red, brutal thug and stud, to satisfy her, even Daisy Buchanan seems in retrospect a quasi-lady, Brett not really a bitch at all. Western literature before the coming of Sentimentalism is rich in images of destructive women—Thaïs and Cleopatra and Lilith herself; but Temple is more than a recrudescence of that rejected orthodox archetype. She represents a lust of the nerves rather than of the flesh, a *programmatic* concupiscence entered upon as a declaration of independence, is in short a queasy male image of the flapper—the New Woman of the 1920's. Not content to be violated, the woman becomes the violator and Faulkner responds with nausea:

> He came toward her. She did not move. Her eyes began to grow darker and darker, lifting into her skull above a half-moon of white, without a focus, with the blank rigidity of a statue's eyes. She began to say Ah-ah-ah-ah in an expiring voice, her body arching slowly backward as though forced by an exquisite torture. When he touched her she sprang like a bow, hurling herself upon him, her mouth gaped and ugly like that of a dying fish as she writhed her loins against him. . . . With her hips grinding against him, her mouth gaping in straining protrusion, bloodless, she began to speak. "Let's hurry. Anywhere. . . . Come on. What're you waiting for?" She strained her mouth toward him, dragging his head down, making a whimpering moan. "Please. Please. Please. Please. You've got to. I'm on fire, I tell you."

Toward the end of his life, Faulkner seems to have repented of his many blasphemies against woman and to have committed himself to redeeming one by one all his anti-virgins; but his attempts at redemption somehow do not touch the level of acceptance reached by his original travesties. In *Requiem for a Nun*, he portrays Temple as a mother, as married to Gowan Stevens, who once read her name on the lavatory wall. Insanely burning once more for a new Red, she is not permitted to abase herself again, but is redeemed by the self-sacrifice of a Negro girl, and is left at the play's end aching with a higher lust for religious belief, about to follow her husband home. In *The Town*, Faulkner carries Eula's refurbishing even further than he had Temple's, actually rewriting Eula's past history as he pretends to recapitulate it, and turning her into the very model of female courage and endurance. This time the former avatar of female corruption herself performs the act of self-sacrifice, dies to assure an honorable future for her daughter—an innocent young girl, who is left at the novel's end advancing, wide-eyed and pure, on Greenwich Village. The epitaph inscribed on Eula's grave by her impotent husband is, we are asked to believe, truer than that husband can guess or any decent citizen is prepared to grant:

> Eula Varner Snopes
> 1889   1927
> A Virtuous Wife is a Crown to her Husband
> Her Children Rise and Call Her Blessed

And even this is not the end. In *The Long Hot Summer*, a film which lists Faulkner's name among the credits, Eula is demythicized as well as redeemed: made into the customary Hollywood image of the sexy but sincere young wife, who begins wriggling like a taken fish in the arms of her new husband, while the boys wolf-call and wail in the stifling dusk. In the end, however, she helps to win that husband from weakness to strength, returns to his arms and legitimate bliss, when he has proved himself a true son to his father and a good citizen! Eula and Temple alike fade into the stereotype of the Good Bad Girl, who in turn gives birth to the sweet young thing, and the Protestant Virgin is restored to her shrine; but it makes no difference. Faulkner's art fails him when he turns from nausea and despair to sentimentality and maudlin pity; and even the popular mind rejects his attempts at converting his archetypes into the stereotypes of market-place culture.

The Social and Legal Status of Women

Bruno Bettelheim / Growing Up Female

While the women of America apparently have "done well" in education, finding jobs, and husbands, says Bruno Bettelheim, they are "touched with a sense of grievance too vivid to put them at rest." Early in his essay, Bettelheim states his purpose: "What I shall try to show in this article is that the grievance is very real, and very justifiable, although it is barely understood." Bettelheim contends that the manner in which American girls are brought up is responsible for the grievances which they later have as women. The goals set up for the women are often contradictory and bewildering. We need a change in our attitudes, writes Bettelheim, and "a reform in attitudes must take place among those who have anthing to do with bringing up the young. For until parents, teachers, and psychologists honestly perceive the prejudice in their assumptions about the proper role of growing girls, equal education of the sexes will continue to be a mockery, and we must expect the continuing disintegration of young marriages as emotional distance grows between immature couples." Our view of women "is still far from psychologically mature," and Bettelheim suggests that "a rational and psychologically balanced view would appreciate and enjoy the ways that women are truly different from men, but it would recognize that in *most* respects they have more in common with men than our society is now willing to grant."

Into what is a modern girl to grow? Many a psychologist or educator today will find few questions more recurrent, or more troubling than this one, if he stops to consider it. On every side he encounters growing girls and educated women who may seem to have followed out the respected modern formulas: they have "done well" at school, at finding jobs, at finding husbands, at running homes, at planning activities of all sorts. And yet they remain, as Veblen put it, *"touched with a sense of grievance too vivid to put them at rest."* They are frequently baffled by this and so, unhappily, are some of the psychologists they consult. In trying to help women—to "accept the womanly role," for example—they often seem to aggravate the grievance, rather than cure it.

What I shall try to show in this article is that the grievance is very real, and very justifiable, although it is barely understood. The ways in which we bring up many girls in America, and the goals we set for them are so strangely—and often painfully—contradictory that it is only too predictable that their expectations of love and work and marriage should frequently be confused, and that deep satisfactions should elude them. Very few human problems have been so transformed by the convulsive growth of modern society as those of women; but the parents and psychologists and educators who guide young women today have hardly begun to inquire into what a modern and satisfying female life might really be.

Of course it can be argued that many of the special difficulties of women—particularly their emotional difficulties—are timeless and practically inevitable, springing as they do from the distorted images of females which preoccupy so many men. Freud was probably right in thinking that the male infant's overattachment to his mother projects him into a continuing emotional predicament which is peculiarly difficult for most men to solve, and often warps the demands they make of women. Bound emotionally to the infantile image of his mother as unassailably pure, a man may seek out a superior woman he can worship. Or, trying to break the infantile bond, he may choose a woman who appears inferior to himself. The different kinds of emotional balm men seek from women are as various as their frustrations when they do not find it. But the female who needs and wants a man—and all women do—is often placed in a sadly absurd position: she must shape herself to please a complex male image of what she should be like—but alas it is often an image having little to do with her own real desires or potentialities; and these may well be stunted or concealed as she grows into womanhood.

Certainly such irrational demands on women are nothing new, as we can learn from the Bible. In the purely psychological sphere, relations between the sexes have always been difficult. But we often forget that until the modern industrial era, the great majority of people had little time or energy to devote to purely emotional "satisfaction" and "relationships." Life was still taken up with the basic necessities of food, clothing, and shelter. To secure them, most men and women and their children worked extremely hard—and often worked together—in their homes and shops and fields. If the family was to survive and prosper, the women and girls simply had to do their heavy share, and this earned them a certain respect. It would seem from the available evidence that enough good feeling existed between the sexes to make their emotional difficulties manageable—especially if their sex relations were satisfying. What we today call "psychological satisfactions" were frosting on the cake—the cake of economic survival, and simple sex.

Now the technological revolution has brought us to precisely the opposite condition. Most women no longer need be bound to men by economic necessity, they rarely share any work with their husbands, and their time is often their own. Reluctant as they are to face it, women are at least reaching that stage where they can shape their own personal relations if they choose. What choices are they making, and how successful are they?

Most women claim to base their relations on what they conceive to be "love"—on "emotional satisfaction." In this, they are clearly the children of modern technology and the easy life it brings. So too is psychoanalysis itself, which aims to make emotional satisfaction more possible. But now a savage paradox is slowly—all too slowly—dawning on the psychoanalysts and their crowds of female patients: it appears that relations entered into chiefly to gain psychological satisfaction more often than not end in psychological despair. "*Love*," as Saint-Exupéry put it, "*does not consist in gazing at each other, but in looking outward in the same direction.*" For what kind of love, and what kind of life, are we preparing our girls today?

Education for Failure

Paul Goodman has suggested that boys today are growing up in ways he calls "absurd." But how much more absurd are the ways in which we raise our daughters! We tell them early that they are very different from little boys and make them play with dolls instead of baseballs; but then, from kindergarten on through college, we provide them with exactly the same education given to boys—an education clearly designed to prepare boys for a life of competition and independent responsibility.

Consider the contradictions which are thus thrust upon the growing girl. For fifteen years or more she is officially encouraged to compete with boys in the schoolroom, to develop her mind and her initiative, to be second to none. She may study the same physics and history as her boyfriends, work at jobs not too different from theirs, share many of the same political and social interests. And then our curious system insists she "fall in love" with a potential husband: she is in fact expected to love giving up what she may have loved until then, and suddenly find deep fulfillment in taking care of a child, a home, a mate. Her life is to be filled with what are, to her husband, after-hours occupations, and the training of her youth is seemingly intended to fall away like an afterbirth. After years of apparent equality, it is made clear that males are *more* equal, and some females resent this. And they should. Our educational system has ostensibly prepared them for a kind of liberated marital and occupational life that in fact rarely exists in our society; at the same time it celebrates the values of an antiquated form of marriage inherited from a time when wives were prepared for little else.

If many girls seem to accept these hypocrisies calmly, perhaps it is because they have been made aware, quite early in the game, that their role in society will in fact be very different from that of the boys sitting next to them in the class room. The boys have no doubt that their schooling is intended, at least, to help them make a *success* in their mature life, to enable them to accomplish something in the outside world. But the girl is made to feel that she must undergo precisely the same training only because she may need it if she is a *failure*—an unfortunate who somehow cannot gain admission to the haven of marriage and motherhood where she properly belongs. Surely this is absurd.

Actually, the gravest damage is done long before this. The little girl's first storybooks and primers, for example, hardly ever show a woman as working or active outside the home. It makes no difference that over five million American children under twelve have full-time working mothers. The little girl is expected to shape herself in the image of the maternal housekeeping women in these stories, and never mind what certain unfortunate mothers may be obliged to do. And emphasizing society's ambivalence, this image of the stay-at-home woman is presented by her female teacher, who may well be a working mother. In these early years, it is rare indeed for girls to hear the slightest suggestion that they might one day do the interesting work of this world quite as well as many men, or even better.

It is little wonder then that, as adolescence approaches in the last year of grade school, many girls are already quite convinced that what *really* counts is not any commitment to their studies—although they may be conscientious—but their ability to carry on social, emotional, and sexual relations that will make them popular and ultimately attract the right boys. And here matters are made more difficult by the fact that young girls tend to mature faster physically and emotionally than boys, although the boys may do better academically. The girls soon perceive that they are ahead of the boys in the maturity and sophistication of their desires. The boys seem more childish, less grown up, less certain about their ability to cope with the other sex. What is more, they often come from homes where mother knows best, and now they find themselves ruled by female teachers who day after day impress upon them their authority and competence. In this situation it is not easy for a boy to gain confidence in his maleness, to say the least. (Later on, of course, both sexes are exposed to male teachers in high school and college, but by then it is often too late to undo the damage.)*

Thus the high-school and college girl must face a frequently awful predicament. She—and her mother—feel she must be popular with boys. And to get the dates she wants, she must try to reassure the boys that they are really superior to her; but deep down she cannot believe in this pretense, and she may well resent the necessity for it. Once she has gained the ultimate objective and is safely married, she will, as likely as not, drop the mask and begin to assert in her home what she is convinced is a superior maturity. By then, however, it may no longer exist, for boys typically catch up with girls in this respect during their mid-twenties. And in the meantime the boys are generally given a good deal more freedom to experiment—to "sow their wild oats."

A good many young men, for example, may skirt marriage until they are into their thirties—and they are allowed to go their way, suffering no

---

*Many boys drop out of school before they are given male teachers: if they are to protect their male image of themselves, they cannot take the domination of females any longer. Similarly, the aggressive delinquency which gets boys into trouble is often no more than a desperate attempt to assert their maleness. Since the girls in school are often more mature socially and sexually, the boys find that they can clearly assert male superiority only in aggressive and competitive sports. Having learned this, they choose aggressive ways to prove themselves male when outside the school.

more than a mild nagging and some teasing from their friends. It is tacitly acknowledged that they need more time to find themselves in their work before they settle down, and they remain popular in both married and unmarried circles. They will be considered failures only when they cannot support themselves, or make headway in their careers. By contrast, the situation of an unmarried girl is altogether different, often cruelly so. No matter how gifted she may be in her work—or how brilliantly she has put her education to use—a young woman bears an odor of failure if she does not marry soon.

Indeed, the pressures upon the young girl to marry safely and quickly may seem inexorable just when she is trying to embark on her own path; and they are exerted in ways that are quite unfamiliar to boys. During his first years at college, for example, a boy is likely to undergo a "crisis of identity," exposed as he is to conflicting new ideas and ways of acting and chances to experiment. As a junior or senior, however, he may start to find himself through serious academic work. A girl may undergo a parallel experience, only to discover that her new dedication to scholarship may rule her out of the marriage market. Fearing that her single-minded absorption will allow her chances to slip by, she stops herself dead in her tracks; or worse, she cannot make up her mind about what she wants, and she may suffer a college-girl "break-down."

Nor does this happen only in colleges. Many a girl emerges from high school with a vague feeling that she can, she should, make something of herself. But everyone around her insists that she will find fulfillment only through marriage—and her friends are getting married. So she buckles down to a brief course in beauty culture or secretarial work. Later, as the wife of a clerk or skilled worker, she is as restless and bewildered as the college girl who gave up an interest that was becoming "too absorbing" so that she could marry off into the suburbs. Neither girl can quite understand what has gone wrong—she is after all an undoubted success in the eyes of others.

Wed to Ceremonial Futility

And what in fact *has* gone wrong? What happens when the young bride at last enters the home she has been taught to think of as her true domain? In truth, she may find that the much-touted labors and pleasures of the hearth are among the sad delusions of our times. For if it is hard for male youth nowadays to find meaningful work, as Paul Goodman has argued, the fate of the home-bound wife is surely harder.

Of course, modern labor-saving devices have abolished most of the backbreaking housework of the past—and good riddance; but at the same time they are doing away with the real satisfactions this work once yielded. Using her husband's money to buy machine-made clothes for her family involves no unique or essential labors of her own. Much the same can be said about cooking with highly prepared ingredients. What remains, apart from child rearing, are the most stultifying mechanical tasks—dusting, making beds, washing, and picking up. And beyond these lie chiefly the petty refinements of "homemaking"—what Veblen described as the occupation of ceremonial futility.

The very people who sell women products to enhance the home are shrewdly aware of this futility. A close study by the sociologist Florence Kluckhohn has shown that advertising aimed at the housewife often describes the home as a kind of penal colony from which she should escape as quickly and for as long as possible. Typically, the ad for an automatic stove shows a woman putting on her hat, leaving, and coming back hours later to find the dinner all cooked. The advertiser, as Mrs. Kluckhohn points out, does not say *where* she has been; just to get away, he implies, is a blessing.

Since work around the house is now less than interesting, children are the natural target for the young wife's energies. Here at least she feels considerably more sophisticated than her mother. After all she has had extensive schooling, and has perhaps worked briefly at a demanding job, and motherhood has been depicted to her as another tremendous and enlarging experience—the climax, somehow, to what has gone before. Yet in fact the care of an infant forces her to give up most of her old interests, and unless she is fascinated by the minute developments of the baby, she will seldom find that any new and different enrichment has entered her life to replace them.

This impoverishment is particularly acute when she has her first child. Later on, the concerns of her older children may enliven her days while she cares for a newcomer. However, I believe the current trend toward larger middle-class families reflects not merely a greater prosperity but also the needs of the middle-class mother who finds existence empty without small children to care for. Reluctant to return to the outer world—or perhaps lacking confidence in her ability to do so—she must find something to occupy her which seems vital and demanding of her concentration.

But things change once her children are of school age—and even more so in their teens. They certainly need a mother, but they actually *need* far less of her than she may devote to them. Chauffeuring children around the suburbs, for example, takes time and requires someone who drives a car, but this person need not be a mother. The children themselves would prefer to be free of it and the tight scheduling it imposes. The same goes for arranging the children's social life, which again they would much prefer to do themselves.

Of course the professed concern of many mothers is to watch over their children's educational life, and help them with their psychological problems. But in these things too, the children would often rather be on their own, except for those occasional crises where the parents are needed for support. And sadly enough the modern mother is often in a poor position to give support when her child is doing badly in school or is not very popular and hence feels defeated. Having invested so much emotionally in her child's achievement, her pride suffers at his failure and as likely as not she administers a bawling out when understanding and compassion are needed. Thus, she may fail as a mother because her inner needs make her work at it too hard. The children of women who are doing interesting work of their own during the day will often find more sensible and sympathetic mothers to help them with their studies and problems in the evening. On the other hand, the mother who urges her girl on toward intellectual achievement while staying at home herself poses a contradiction which probably is not lost on the girl.

Where motherhood does not bring satisfaction, the woman turns to her husband with the demand, spoken or unspoken, that he somehow make up to her for what she is missing in life. She waits for him to come home with word of the outer world and its happenings. At the same time, she may work hard at being a wife, trying to advance his career, plotting to get him ahead socially. But even if this sort of thing works, he may resent it—it will not be his success but hers.

Sometimes a wife will spend her husband's money heedlessly and egg him on to achieve higher earnings and status, thus blindly demanding things to make up for her empty feelings of failure as a woman. Other wives simply nag, or they repress their resentment altogether and accept the prospect of a stultifying life. The husband begins in turn to resent his nagging wife and even his family life; or he may resent her for her passive dreariness. In either case they both suffer, often without in the least knowing why. Living with such parents, a growing girl may well absorb, and keep for life, a distorted view of what a man is for, and how he can be used.

No doubt it will be argued that there is more to a modern woman's life than this—that laborsaving devices have so freed housewives from their chores that they can undertake useful and interesting activities of all sorts without actually taking jobs. Such claims seem questionable. Undeniably, a good many housewives do find time for activities outside the home, but all too often the activities themselves are really frivolous or make-work, and their experiences of them are futile and unrewarding. I refer not merely to gardening—which replaces the conspicuous embroidery of an earlier age—or to the ubiquitous bridge circle and country-club life. I also mean activities like the PTA, the League of Women Voters, and charity work which pass as "constructive" and "valuable." Examined closely, these are often used to cover up a void of really serious and interesting involvement. And according to a recent study, "Volunteer workers are increasingly being assigned to fund-raising or low-level routine, from which little achievement satisfaction is possible."

In short, to quote Veblen again, "Woman is endowed with her share—which there is reason to believe is more than an even share—of the instinct of workmanship, to which futility of life or of expenditure is obnoxious." And it is when this impulse is denied expression that she feels the sense of grievance which runs like a vivid current through the lives of so many women today.

Competition in Bed

If the instincts for workmanship in modern women are widely frustrated, so are her sexual instincts. Of course sexual difficulties are neither a recent curse of the young, nor limited to girls. But the way we prepare our children for sexual life has burdened girls far more than boys.

In Latin countries, as in many other lands, girls are prepared from early childhood to accept a yielding and passive role, not only in sexual relations, but in the life of the family, where the man traditionally dominates. But the American girl is raised in contradiction. On the one hand, she is told that to be feminine means to be yielding and courted, and that she must respect this norm. She certainly cannot, for example, ask a boy she likes for a date, nor can she pay the expenses when she goes out with him (although she may sometimes "go dutch"). She may feel most reluctant simply to call up a boy to talk with him or to ask him to take a walk with her.

Yet at the same time she has been taught from childhood to think and act for herself where it counts most emotionally—she should strive for success, and compete equally with boys at school. What she has *not* been taught is that men and women are neither wholly equal, nor wholly opposite, but complementary. She has never been encouraged to quietly consider the ways she and the boys she knows are alike, in the talents and aspirations they could build up together and in the emotional needs they share; and the ways they are not, as in their sexual and maternal functions. As a result she does not know where and when to be "feminine" and where and when to be "equal."

The adult world leads her to think that the "active woman" is necessarily an unfeminine and sexually inadequate woman—something which is patently untrue. Women who strive to "wear the pants" do so for defensive and neurotic reasons, just as the very need to be dominant, whether in man or woman, is due to feelings of inferiority or to thwarted desires. But it is quite a different thing for a girl to do purposeful work, *not* because of some twisted drive, but because she wants to realize her own potentials. Unless we distinguish clearly between the two kinds of striving we stifle the healthy growth of girls by labeling them unfeminine.

At the same time, girls are led into an equally dangerous misunderstanding about the sexual act itself. While men and women need not be so different in their personal aspirations as our society now pretends, they *are* different in the way they experience sex. Here much confusion was created by the psychiatrist Wilhelm Reich and his rather too-facile following among the intelligentsia. For their effect has been to lead both partners to expect that they can and should have a parallel orgastic experience. Too often, the parallel is mistakenly thought to mean a similar if not identical experience, and the desire for orgasm may lead to frustration in both man and woman.

This problem is very different in some societies where modern technology has not affected the lives of women and their expectations. It is still sufficient for a woman if her lover or husband enjoys sex with her. Since his enjoyment proves her a good woman, she too can enjoy herself; she does not worry whether she is frigid or torrid, and as likely as not she achieves total release. Her lover is not obliged by any conscious code to provide her with orgasm; he can enjoy himself, experience orgasm, and thus help her to feel fully satisfied herself.

In our own society, boys need as much as ever to have their virility attested by their sexual partners; and girls have a parallel need. But today the boy wants his girl to prove him a man by her so-called "orgastic experience," and the girl is even worse off. She not only has to prove him a man by making him experience orgasm; she must also prove her femininity in some way or else fear she is frigid.

She is now quite used to performing with males on equal grounds, but she has little sense of how to complement them. She cannot suddenly learn this in bed. Trying to make sure that the man has an orgastic experience, and also wondering if she can have one herself, she becomes so worried that she truly experiences little satisfaction, and ends up pretending. Sexual intercourse cannot often bear the burden of proving so many things in additon to being enjoyable. It becomes another competition between man and woman: who can make whom have an orgastic experience? And the lovers cannot even enjoy their mutual desire or the forgetting of self in the act.

With both sex and household work often less than satisfying, it is not surprising that so many modern marriages turn sour, and that the phenomenon of homosexuality looms as importantly as it does today.

Many young wives soon realize that their husbands are neither willing nor able to complement them in their motherly tasks in any satisfying way. Resentful in many cases of her husband's fuller life, a young wife nevertheless may try to force him to share motherhood with her; but he can seldom do this in present-day society without suffering emotional damage. And try as she will, she cannot find compensation in the marriage itself for her own thwarted aspirations.

The results are often men who want women, but don't know what to do with them when they get them; and women who get men, but who are disappointed in them and in themselves when they live together. Mutually disappointed, it is natural that each sex seek out its own company; for only then can they really be themselves on a truly equal basis, freed of anxiety, disappointment, or inferiority feeling. Who has not observed the tendency of the sexes to segregate themselves in certain married circles? However, when relations between the sexes are so plagued, then a kind of homosexuality may also become rampant. And indeed, psychiatrists have recently been noting an alarming rise in both female and male homosexuality.

However, if I can trust my experience, female homosexuality is not increasing so much as the number of women who are unwilling to pretend they enjoy having a role forced on them that frustrates their aspirations; and so they seek the company of a partner who can share them. Sometimes two such women find it convenient to live together, and slowly, as in a good marriage, the partners blend their lives.

In some cases—but much less often than is sometimes assumed—this leads to a desire for sexual relations. But unlike most male homosexuals, such women can often switch their affections to the other sex if they can find a male who really wants and needs to "look outward with them" (and I would add inward) in the same direction. (This, of course, does not hold true for a hard core of female homosexuals.)

The upbringing of most girls today also fosters something resembling female homosexuality. The old intimacy between mothers and daughters who actually worked together for the survival of the family has now practically vanished. As we have seen, many women now feel compelled to prove themselves good mothers by making sure their daughters are "successes" in life, and so it is difficult for warm confidence to grow between them. Such a girl naturally longs for real affection, for closeness to another woman who will give her what she wanted from her mother, and never got. After knowing such a rewarding experience—which need not, and preferably should not, be of a gross sexual nature—some young women are enriched by it, and are more able to move on to a successful heterosexual relation.

Miss Buck's "Solution"

At this point the prospects of the young female for a satisfying marriage may seem fairly hopeless. Whether marriage as we know it is obsolete, I do not know, but frankly I doubt it. Despite its shortcomings, it is still the best institution we have developed to combat loneliness and to provide a structure within which two adults can find intimate satisfaction and continue to grow.

But no institution can make for intimacy or anything else; it can at best provide a framework, and this framework itself cannot insure that youthful love will be transmuted into two fulfilled lives, as young people today so widely and so fruitlessly hope. To make marriage work today, our children must be prepared for it by a very different kind of upbringing than the one they are getting. They must expect far less of the institution itself and much more of themselves in the way of hard work to help each other live interesting and satisfying lives. They must not compulsively marry so early that they peg each other to permanent immaturity. And they must recognize that woman's place cannot be confined simply to the home.

Fortunately, there are more than a few mature marriages to be found, but in these the partners have come to see that the feelings of love—and the affection for idiosyncrasies of personality—which lie between them can count for very little by themselves in making their relations work. The crucial questions for a married couple concern the kinds of world in which they can actively interest themselves as men and women and as parents—and their connections to their work as well as to each other. If these connections act to bring the members of the family together, the marriage has a strong chance of survival.

But of course this is not easy. Often the husband's work may split him off from his wife instead of bringing them together. Not long ago a rather extreme form of this dilemma was presented in a novel called *Command the Morning* by Pearl Buck. She told of several wives of scientists working on the secret atomic project at Los Alamos during the war, tiresomely caught up in the usual, antiquated variety of American marriage. They could live a lonely life with secretive husbands, who could not share with them the excitement of their work. Or they could look for some secret excitement of their own in promiscuous adventure. Only the heroine, a female physicist, is shown to have a complete life, for she shares the creative suspense of the scientists. And as she and one of the scientists become involved in work together, they inevitably fall in love. Now Miss Buck is unable to conceive any outcome for this affair except a conventional home-bound marriage, or no marriage at all. It was apparently beyond her to imagine a marriage where both partners still love each other and remain part of the same working world. And so, of course, she has her female physicist reject her lover and the prospect of imprisonment in domesticity, because she can't give up her science.

Obviously I do not think these are the only choices to be made. But I have no doubt that Miss Buck speaks for a great many people who do think so. When such choices do arise, how do we advise young girls to deal with them?

Recently I discussed this problem with some psychoanalytic friends, many of them particularly concerned with the problem of women. The majority of the analysts still embraced a nineteenth-century solution to the problem similar to Miss Buck's. Woman belongs in the home and should be satisfied to live in a subordinate relation to her dominant husband. Her life can be made more bearable if she is helped to gain some meaning from her after-hours community activities, from aesthetic pursuits; and from her sexual life with her husband—or, if need be, from some extramarital sexual adventures.

Some analysts are more sensitive to the predicaments of their women patients. They advise a woman to seek meaningful work until the time she gets married or pregnant. Then, she should make an about-face in her way of life, if not also in her emotions. She should then accept the so-called womanly role, stay at home, and raise her children for a decade or longer, during the very years when she is in the prime of life. During this period she must be helped not to be too frustrated a wife, or too inextricably involved in the lives of her children. Then, when the children are at last in grade or high school, she should make another about-face, recognize the limitations of the PTA life, and return to the more satisfying occupations she knew before.

The latter solution is actually the one that the vast majority of working mothers—voluntarily or involuntarily—have chosen to follow. But one result of this sudden switching back and forth in their commitments is that many women resentfully feel that they lived a meaningful life only before they got married—a feeling that can have disastrous effects on them, their marriages, and their children. Their solution, in short, leaves the conflict between career and child care unexamined.

I am convinced that modern women will have to confront this conflict, and solve it. It might mean adopting the system found in some other societies where women work—i.e., entrusting part of infant care to the older children, or sharing it with relatives. It might well mean more arrangements whereby young children are entrusted to the care of well-qualified professional people, at least for part of the time.

Some kind of change along such lines is badly needed, but it will not be an easy reform to make, given the resistance that may be expected. And in trying to bring it about, women unfortunately will not be able to count on much support from the psychoanalysts. For, as we have seen, the preconceptions of psychoanalysts about the proper feminine role prevent them from really helping a girl successfully to grow up female—that is, to become female in her sexual relations and in child-rearing, and yet to develop as fully as a male does in all other respects.

This inability stems from the very nature of psychoanalysis as a method essentially concerned with exploring the recesses of the mind, with little regard for the shape of the society in which the mind must function. For the same reason, psychoanalysis has little to offer when it comes to reforming education; for education prepares the child to live in society and so must concern itself with what society ought to be. Psychoanalysis as such has very little to say about what society ought to be; its proper task is to help the individual solve some problem which prevents him from being what *he* wants to be.

This is why psychoanalysis is so often ineffective in helping a girl to find herself. It may help her greatly in dealing with problems of sexual repression, just as it may help a young student overcome his inability to study—these are problems of *personal* self-realization. But it cannot help her to decide what kind of woman she wants to be or what role she wants to play in the community, any more than it can help a student decide on a *course* of study toward a career. These are problems of *social* self-realization, and to deal with them as personal psychoanalytic problems may only serve to muddle and aggravate them.

Can Adults Grow Up?

Clearly we cannot look to the psychoanalysts for leadership in opening up new social opportunities for women. But, paradoxically enough, hope for a more rational approach to the problems of women can be found in the discoveries of Freud himself.

Freud felt rather uneasy in discussing the psychology of women. Basically he remained caught up in his own nineteenth-century middle-class background with his typical overesteem for his mother and his compensatory feeling that he should dominate his wife. He accepted this view as part of the "natural order of things," and, as we have seen, its shadow still hovers over today's psychoanalysts, and our society generally.

But it is worth noting that Freud himself, while always the courteous gentleman when with his wife, often turned for companionship to intellectually active women who, according to his own view, had chosen the unfeminine role in life. He lived domestically as superior male, but in his work sought the company of women he treated as equals.

Freud thus stood at the threshold of a new era in the relations of man and woman, and was not able to cross it. But he did forge the tools that might now enable us to take the steps impossible for him. He was able to demonstrate that the repressive sex taboos of his time were in fact a counterpart of the Victorian overvaluation of the forbidden woman. And by showing us how to uncover these repressions, he opened a way for healthier and more satisfying sexual relations to develop in the years that followed.

Like most great reforms in man's thinking, this one grew from the most honest and most searching kind of examination of what people glibly profess, anxiously evade, and blindly do. We should by now be capable to extending a similar self-examination to the contradictions in our attitudes toward women.

If we do this, I suggest we shall find that although women have been accorded votes and education and jobs over the years, our view of them and their potentials is still far from psychologically mature. Indeed it is in many ways still biased in the unhappy limitations it imposes on the possibilities of women to make the most of their capacities. A rational and psychologically balanced view would appreciate and enjoy the ways that women are truly different from men, but it would recognize that in *most* respects they have far more in common with men than our society is now willing to grant.

Above all, such a reform in attitudes must take place among those who have anything whatever to do with bringing up the young. For until parents, teachers, and psychologists honestly perceive the prejudice in their assumptions about the proper role of growing girls, equal education of the sexes will continue to be a mockery, and we must expect the continuing disintegration of young marriages as emotional distance grows between immature couples. Only a thorough effort by their elders to grow up in their thinking will enable our boys to become adults so secure in their masculinity that they are afraid neither of fulfillment in women, nor of taking their male place in the home. And only such an effort will enable our girls to accept marriage and motherhood as an important part of their future, but a part that will not waste—in desperation, resignation, or boredom—the best of their lives and possibilities.

Gunnar Myrdal / A Parallel to the Negro Problem

When Swedish sociologist Gunnar Myrdal published his *An American Dilemma* in 1944, he included an Appendix titled "A Parallel to the Negro Problem" which described and analyzed the similarities between the treatment of blacks and women in our society. Myrdal contends that the close relationship between the fight for the rights of blacks and the fight for the rights of women is no accident, and that "the ideological and economic factors behind the two movements—the emancipation of women and children and the emancipation of Negroes—have much in common and are closely interrelated." The similarities between the two groups are exemplified by the beliefs that blacks and women both have inferior endowments and both are "contented" and really do not want more civil rights and equal opportunities. Further, both have come to believe in their inferior status and endowments; both have accepted their "place" in society; in both cases those persons defining their "place" believed they were acting in the interests of the subordinate group. Myrdal discusses these similarities and also the forces in our society which have contributed to those two emancipation struggles being similar.

There is, however, one linguistic difference which reflects attitudinal differences towards blacks and women. While Myrdal continually refers to "the Negro problem," he does not refer to "the woman problem"; instead, he speaks of "the women's problem." The phrase "the Negro problem" carries with it the connotation that the Negro is the problem, when in fact the bigoted white is the problem. The fact that we do not speak about "the woman problem," but instead refer to the "woman question" or "the women's problem," indicates that there are some attitudinal differences which the parallel that Myrdal draws between blacks and women does not take into account.

For a further treatment of the similarities between the status and treatment of blacks and women in America, see Chapter Six, "The Negro Parallel," in Caroline Bird, *Born Female* (New York, 1969).

In every society there are at least two groups of people, besides the Negroes, who are characterized by high social visibility expressed in physical

Appendix 5 in *An American Dilemma*, by Gunnar Myrdal. Copyright © 1944, 1962 by Harper & Row, Publishers, Inc. Reprinted by permission of the publishers.

appearance, dress, and patterns of behavior, and who have been "suppressed." We refer to women and children. Their present status, as well as their history and their problems in society, reveal striking similarities to those of the Negroes. In studying a special problem like the Negro problem, there is always a danger that one will develop a quite incorrect idea of its uniqueness. It will, therefore, give perspective to the Negro problem and prevent faulty interpretations to sketch some of the important similarities between the Negro problem and the women's problem.

In the historical development of these problem groups in America there have been much closer relations than is now ordinarily recorded. In the earlier common law, women and children were placed under the jurisdiction of the paternal power. When a legal status had to be found for the imported Negro servants in the seventeenth century, the nearest and most natural analogy was the status of women and children. The ninth commandment—linking together women, servants, mules, and other property—could be invoked, as well as a great number of other passages of Holy Scripture. We do not intend to follow here the interesting developments of the institution of slavery in America through the centuries, but merely wish to point out the paternalistic idea which held the slave to be a sort of family member and in some way—in spite of all differences—placed him beside women and children under the power of the *paterfamilias*.

There was, of course, even in the beginning, a tremendous difference both in actual status of these different groups and in the tone of sentiment in the respective relations. In the decades before the Civil War, in the conservative and increasingly antiquarian ideology of the American South, woman was elevated as an ornament and looked upon with pride, while the Negro slave became increasingly a chattel and a ward. The paternalistic construction came, however, to good service when the South had to build up a moral defense for slavery, and it is found everywhere in the apologetic literature up to the beginning of the Civil War. For illustration, some passages from George Fitzhugh's *Sociology for the South*, published in 1854, may be quoted as typical:

> The kind of slavery is adapted to the men enslaved. Wives and apprentices are slaves; not in theory only, but often in fact. Children are slaves to their parents, guardians and teachers. Imprisoned culprits are slaves. Lunatics and idiots are slaves also.[1]
>
> A beautiful example and illustration of this kind of communism, is found in the instance of the Patriarch Abraham. His wives and his children,

his men servants and his maid servants, his camels and his cattle, were all equally his property. He could sacrifice Isaac or a ram, just as he pleased. He loved and protected all, and all shared, if not equally, at least fairly, in the products of their light labour. Who would not desire to have been a slave of that old Patriarch, stern and despotic as he was?... Pride, affection, self-interest, moved Abraham to protect, love and take care of his slaves. The same motives operate on all masters, and secure comfort, competency and protection to the slave. A man's wife and children are his slaves, and do they not enjoy, in common with himself, his property?[2]

Other protagonists of slavery resort to the same argument:

In this country we believe that the general good requires us to deprive the whole female sex of the right of self-government. They have no voice in the formation of the laws which dispose of their persons and property.... We treat all minors much in the same way.... Our plea for all this is, that the good of the whole is thereby most effectually promoted....[3]

Significant manifestations of the result of this disposition [on the part of the Abolitionists] to consider their own light a surer guide than the word of God, are visible in the anarchical opinions about human governments, civil and ecclesiastical, and on the rights of women, which have found appropriate advocates in the abolition publications.... If our women are to be emancipated from subjection to the law which God has imposed upon them, if they are to quit the retirement of domestic life, where they preside in stillness over the character and destiny of society;... if, in studied insult to the authority of God, we are to renounce in the marriage contract all claim to obedience, we shall soon have a country over which the genius of Mary Wolstonecraft would delight to preside, but from which all order and all virtue would speedily be banished. There is no form of human excellence before which we bow with profounder deference than that which appears in a delicate woman,... and there is no deformity of human character from which we turn with deeper loathing than from a woman forgetful of her nature, and clamourous for the vocation and rights of men.[4]

...Hence her [Miss Martineau's] wild chapter about the "Rights of Women," her groans and invectives because of their exclusion from the offices of the state, the right of suffrage, the exercise of political authority. In all this, the error of the declaimer consists in the very first movement of the mind. "The Rights of *Women*" may all be conceded to the sex, yet the rights of *men* withheld from them.[5]

The parallel goes, however, considerably deeper than being only a structural part in the defense ideology built up around slavery. Women at that time lacked a number of rights otherwise belonging to all free white citizens of full age.

So chivalrous, indeed, was the ante-bellum South that its women were granted scarcely any rights at all. Everywhere they were subjected to political, legal, educational, and social and economic restrictions. They took no part in governmental affairs, were without legal rights over their property or the guardianship of their children, were denied adequate educational facilities, and were excluded from business and the professions.[6]

The same was very much true of the rest of the country and of the rest of the world. But there was an especially close relation in the South between the subordination of women and that of Negroes. This is perhaps best expressed in a comment attributed to Dolly Madison, that the Southern wife was "the chief slave of the harem."[7]

From the very beginning, the fight in America for the liberation of the Negro slaves was, therefore, closely coordinated with the fight for women's emancipation. It is interesting to note that the Southern states, in the early beginning of the political emancipation of women during the first decades of the nineteenth century, had led in the granting of legal rights to women. This was the time when the South was still the stronghold of liberal thinking in the period leading up to and following the Revolution. During the same period the South was also the region where Abolitionist societies flourished, while the North was uninterested in the Negro problem. Thereafter the two movements developed in close interrelation and were both gradually driven out of the South.

The women suffragists received their political education from the Abolitionist movement. Women like Angelina Grimke, Sarah Grimke, and Abby Kelly began their public careers by speaking for Negro emancipation and only gradually came to fight for women's rights. The three great suffragists of the nineteenth century—Lucretia Mott, Elizabeth Cady Stanton, and Susan B. Anthony—first attracted attention as ardent campaigners for the emancipation of the Negro and the prohibition of liquor. The women's movement got much of its public support by reason of its affiliation with the Abolitionist movement: the leading male advocates of woman suffrage before the Civil War were such Abolitionists as William Lloyd Garrison, Henry Ward Beecher, Wendell Phillips, Horace Greeley and Frederick Douglass. The women had nearly achieved their aims, when the Civil War induced them to suppress all tendencies distracting the federal government from the prosecution of the War. They were apparently fully convinced that victory would bring the suffrage to them as well as to the Negroes.[8]

The Union's victory, however, brought disappointment to the women suffragists. The arguments "the Negro's hour" and "a political necessity" met and swept aside all their arguments for leaving the word "male" out of the 14th Amendment and putting "sex" alongside "race" and "color" in the 15th Amendment.[9] Even their Abolitionist friends turned on them, and the Republican party shied away from them. A few Democrats, really not in favor of the extension of the suffrage to anyone, sought to make political capital out of the women's demands, and said with Senator Cowan of Pennsylvania, "If I have no reason to offer why a Negro man shall not vote, I have no reason why a white woman shall not vote." Charges of being Democrats and traitors were heaped on the women leaders. Even a few Negroes, invited to the women's convention of January, 1869, denounced the women for jeopardizing the black man's chances for the vote. The War and Reconstruction Amendments had thus sharply divided the women's problem from the Negro problem in actual politics.[10] The deeper relation between the two will, however, be recognized up till this day. Du Bois' famous ideological manifesto *The Souls of Black Folk*[11] is, to mention only one example, an ardent appeal on behalf of women's interests as well as those of the Negro.

This close relation is no accident. The ideological and economic forces behind the two movements—the emancipation of women and children and the emancipation of Negroes—have much in common and are closely interrelated. Paternalism was a preindustrial scheme of life, and was gradually becoming broken in the nineteenth century. Negroes and women, both of whom had been under the yoke of the paternalistic system, were both strongly and fatefully influenced by the Industrial Revolution. For neither group is the readjustment process yet consummated. Both are still problem groups. The women's problem is the center of the whole complex of problems of how to reorganize the institution of the family to fit the new economic and ideological basis, a problem which is not solved in any part of the Western world unless it be in the Soviet Union or Palestine. The family problem in the Negro group, as we find when analyzing the Negro family, has its special complications, centering in the tension and conflict between the external patriarchal system in which the Negro was confined as a slave and his own family structure.

As in the Negro problem, most men have accepted as self-evident, until recently, the doctrine that women had inferior endowments in most of those respects which carry prestige, power, and advantages in society, but that they were, at the same time, superior in some other respects. The arguments, when arguments were used, have been about the same: smaller brains, scarcity of geniuses and so on. The study of women's intelligence and personality has had broadly the same history as the one we record for Negroes. As in the case of the Negro, women themselves have often been brought to believe in their inferiority of endowment. As the Negro was awarded his "place" in society, so there was a "woman's place." In both cases the rationalization was strongly believed that men, in confining them to this place, did not act against the true interest of the subordinate groups. The myth of "contented women," who did not want to have suffrage or other civil rights and equal opportunities, had the same social function as the myth of the "contented Negro." In both cases there was probably— in a static sense—often some truth behind the myth.

As to the character of the deprivations, upheld by law or by social conventions and the pressure of public opinion, no elaboration will here be made. As important and illustrative in the comparison, we shall, however, stress the conventions governing woman's education. There was a time when the most common idea was that she was better off with little education. Later the doctrine developed that she should not be denied education, but that her education should be of a special type, fitting her for her "place" in society and usually directed more on training her hands than her brains.

Political franchise was not granted to women until recently. Even now there are, in all countries, great difficulties for a woman to attain public office. The most important disabilities still affecting her status are those barring her attempt to earn a living and to attain promotion in her work. As in the Negro's case, there are certain "women's jobs," tradition-ally monopolized by women. They are regularly in the low salary bracket and do not offer much of a career. All over the world men have used the trade unions to keep women out of competition. Woman's competition has, like the Negro's, been particularly obnoxious and dreaded by men because of the low wages women, with their few earning outlets, are prepared to work for. Men often dislike the very idea of having women on an equal plane as co-workers and competitors, and usually they find it even more "unnatural" to work under women. White people generally hold similar attitudes toward Negroes. On the other hand, it is said about women that they prefer men as bosses and do not want to work under another woman. Negroes often feel the same way about working under other Negroes.

In personal relations with both women and Negroes, white men generally prefer a less professional and more human relation, actually a more paternalistic and protective position—somewhat in the nature of patron to client in Roman times, and like the corresponding strongly paternalistic relation of later feudalism. As in Germany it is said that every gentile has his pet Jew, so it is said in the South that every white has his "pet nigger," or—in the upper strata—several of them. We sometimes marry the pet woman, carrying out the paternalistic scheme. But even if we do not, we tend to deal kindly with her as a client and a ward, not as a competitor and an equal.

In drawing a parallel between the position of, and feeling toward, women and Negroes we are uncovering a fundamental basis of our culture. Although it is changing, atavistic elements sometimes unexpectedly break through even in the most emancipated individuals. The similarities in the women's and the Negroes' problems are not accidental. They were, as we have pointed out, originally determined in a paternalistic order of society. The problems remain, even though paternalism is gradually declining as an ideal and is losing its economic basis. In the final analysis, women are still hindered in their competition by the function of procreation; Negroes are laboring under the yoke of the doctrine of unassimilability which has remained although slavery is abolished. The second barrier is actually much stronger than the first in America today. But the first is more eternally inexorable.[12]

Notes

1. P. 86.

2. *Ibid.*, p. 297.

3. Charles Hodge, "The Bible Argument of Slavery," in E. N. Elliott (editor), *Cotton Is King*, and *Pro-Slavery Arguments* (1860), pp. 859—860.

4. Albert T. Bledsoe, *An Essay on Liberty and Slavery* (1857), pp. 223—225.

5. W. Gilmore Simms, "The Morals of Slavery," in *The Pro-Slavery Argument* (1853), p. 248. See also Simms' "Address on the Occasion of the Inauguration of the Spartanburg Female College," August 12, 1855.

6. Virginius Dabney, *Liberalism in the South* (1932), p. 361.

7. Cited in Harriet Martineau, *Society in America* (1842, first edition 1837), Vol. II, p. 81.

8. Carrie Chapman Catt and Nettie Rogers Shuler, *Woman Suffrage and Politics* (1923), pp. 32 ff.

9. The relevant sections of the 14th and 15th Amendments to the Constitution are (italics ours):

    14th Amendment

    > *Section 2.* Representatives shall be apportioned among the several States according to their respective numbers, counting the whole number of persons in each State, excluding Indians not taxed. But when the right to vote at any election for the choice of Electors for President and Vice President of the United States, Representatives in Congress, the executive and judicial officers of a State, or the members of the Legislature thereof, is denied to any of the *male* inhabitants of such State, being twenty-one years of age, and citizens of the United States, or in any way abridged, except for participation in rebellion, or other crime, the basis of representation therein shall be reduced in the proportion which the number of such *male* citizens shall bear to the whole number of *male* citizens twenty-one years of age in such State.

    15th Amendment

    > *Section 1.* The right of citizens of the United States to vote shall not be denied or abridged by the United States or by any State on account of *race, color or previous condition of servitude.*

10. While there was a definite affinity between the Abolitionist movement and the woman suffrage movement, there was also competition and, perhaps, antipathy, between them that widened with the years. As early as 1833, when Oberlin College opened its doors to women—the first college to do so—the Negro men students joined other men students in protesting (Catt and Shuler, *op. cit.*, p. 13). The Anti-Slavery Convention held in London in 1840 refused to seat the women delegates from America, and it was on this instigation that the first women's rights convention was called (*ibid.*, p. 17). After the passage of the 13th, 14th, and 15th Amendments, which gave legal rights to Negroes but not to women, the women's movement split off completely from the Negroes' movement, except for such a thing as the support of both movements by the rare old liberal, Frederick Douglass. An expression of how far the two movements had separated by 1903 was given by one of the leaders of the women's movement at that time, Anna Howard Shaw, in answer to a question posed to her at a convention in New Orleans:

    > "'What is your purpose in bringing your convention to the South? Is it the desire of suffragists to force upon us the social equality of black and white women? Political equality lays the foundation for social equality. If you give the ballot to women, won't you make the black and white woman equal politically and therefore lay the foundation for a future claim of social equality?'...

"I read the question aloud. Then the audience called for the answer, and I gave it in these words, quoted as accurately as I can remember them.

"'If political equality is the basis of social equality, and if by granting political equality you lay the foundation for a claim of social equality, I can only answer that you have already laid that claim. You did not wait for woman suffrage, but disfranchised both your black and white women, thus making them politically equal. But you have done more than that. You have put the ballot into the hands of your black men, thus making them the political superiors of your white women. Never before in the history of the world have men made former slaves the political masters of their former mistresses!'" (*The Story of a Pioneer* [1915], pp. 311–312.)

11. 1903.

12. Alva Myrdal, *Nation and Family* (1941), Chapter 22, "One Sex a Social Problem," pp. 398–426.

Helen Mayer Hacker / Women as a Minority Group

To the question "Can it be said that women have a minority group status in our society?" Professor Hacker answers: "If we assume that there are no differences attributable to sex membership as such that would justify casting men and women in different social roles, it can readily be shown that women do occupy a minority group status in our society." While she recognizes and discusses the similarities between the treatment and status of blacks and women in our society, Professor Hacker also takes into account the differences. She discusses the various kinds of competition between men and women and how that competition is similar to and different from the competition between blacks and whites. Professor Hacker concludes her article with a section titled "The Marginal Woman," in which she says: "Arising out of the present contravention of the sexes is the marginal woman, torn between rejection and acceptance of traditional roles and attributes. Uncertain of the ground on which she stands, subjected to conflicting cultural expectations, the marginal woman suffers the psychological ravages of instability, conflict, self-hate, anxiety, and resentment." "Women as a

Hacker, "Women as a Minority Group," *Social Forces*, October 1951, pp. 60–69. Reprinted by permission of the publisher.

Minority Group" has been highly recommended by various contemporary women's liberation spokeswomen and has had wide circulation through reprinting.

Although sociological literature reveals scattered references to women as a minority group, comparable in certain respects to racial, ethnic, and national minorities, no systematic investigation has been undertaken as to what extent the term "minority group" is applicable to women. That there has been little serious consideration of women as a minority group among sociologists is manifested in the recently issued index to *The American Journal of Sociology* wherein under the heading of "Minority Groups" there appears: "See Jews; Morale; Negro; Races and Nationalities; Religious Groups; Sects." There is no cross-reference to women, but such reference is found under the heading "Family."

Yet it may well be that regarding women as a minority group may be productive of fresh insights and suggest leads for further research. The purpose of this paper is to apply to women some portion of that body of sociological theory and methodology customarily used for investigating such minority groups as Negroes, Jews, immigrants, etc. It may be anticipated that not only will principles already established in the field of intergroup relations contribute to our understanding of women, but that in the process of modifying traditional concepts and theories to fit the special case of women new viewpoints for the fruitful reexamination of other minority groups will emerge.

In defining the term "minority group," the presence of discrimination is the identifying factor. As Louis Wirth[1] has pointed out, "minority group" is not a statistical concept, nor need it denote an alien group. Indeed for the present discussion I have adopted his definition: "A minority group is any group of people who because of their physical or cultural character-istics, are singled out from the others in the society in which they live for differential and unequal treatment, and who therefore regard themselves as objects of collective discrimination." It is apparent that this definition includes both objective and subjective characteristics of a minority group: the fact of discrimination and the awareness of discrimination, with attendant reactions to that awareness. A person who on the basis of his group affiliation is denied full participation in those opportunities which the value system of his culture extends to all members of the society satisfies the objective criterion, but there are various circumstances which may prevent him from fulfilling the subjective criterion.

In the first place, a person may be unaware of the extent to which his group membership influences the way others treat him. He may have formally dissolved all ties with the group in question and fondly imagine his identity is different from what others hold it to be. Consequently, he interprets their behavior toward him solely in terms of his individual characteristics. Or, less likely, he may be conscious of his membership in a certain group but not be aware of the general disesteem with which the group is regarded. A final possibility is that he may belong in a category which he does not realize has group significance. An example here might be a speech peculiarity which has come to have unpleasant connotations in the minds of others. Or a lower class child with no conception of "class as culture" may not understand how his manners act as cues in eliciting the dislike of his middle class teacher. The foregoing cases all assume that the person believes in equal opportunities for all in the sense that one's group affiliation should not affect his role in the larger society. We turn now to a consideration of situations in which this assumption is not made.

It is frequently the case that a person knows that because of his group affiliation he receives differential treatment, but feels that this treatment is warranted by the distinctive characteristics of his group. A Negro may believe that there are significant differences between whites and Negroes which justify a different role in life for the Negro. A child may accept the fact that physical differences between him and an adult require his going to bed earlier than they do. A Sudra knows that his lot in life has been cast by divine fiat, and he does not expect the perquisites of a Brahmin. A woman does not wish for the rights and duties of men. In all these situations, clearly, the person does not regard himself as an "object of collective discrimination."

For the two types presented above: (1) those who do not know that they are being discriminated against on a group basis; and (2) those who acknowledge the propriety of differential treatment on a group basis, the subjective attributes of a minority group member are lacking. They feel no minority group consciousness, harbor no resentment, and, hence, cannot properly be said to belong in a minority group. Although the term "minority group" is inapplicable to both types, the term "minority group status" may be substituted. This term is used to categorize persons who are denied rights to which they are entitled according to the value system of the observer. An observer, who is a firm adherent of the democratic ideology, will often consider persons to occupy a minority group status who are well accommodated to their subordinate roles.

No empirical study of the frequency of minority group feelings among women has yet been made, but common observation would suggest that consciously at least, few women believe themselves to be members of a minority group in the way in which some Negroes, Jews, Italians, etc., may so conceive themselves. There are, of course, many sex-conscious women, known to a past generation as feminists, who are filled with re-sentment at the discriminations they fancy are directed against their sex. Today some of these may be found in the National Woman's Party which since 1923 has been carrying on a campaign for the passage of the Equal Rights Amendment. This amendment, in contrast to the com-promise bill recently passed by Congress, would at one stroke wipe out all existing legislation which differentiates in any way between men and women, even when such legislation is designed for the special pro-tection of women. The proponents of the Equal Rights Amendment hold the position that women will never achieve equal rights until they abjure all privileges based on what they consider to be only presumptive sex differences.

Then there are women enrolled in women's clubs, women's auxiliaries of men's organizations, women's professional and educational associations who seemingly believe that women have special interests to follow or unique contributions to make. These latter might reject the appellation of minority group, but their behavior testifies to their aware-ness of women as a distinct group in our society, either overriding dif-ferences of class, occupation, religion, or ethnic identification, or special-ized within these categories. Yet the number of women who participate in "women's affairs" even in the United States, the classic land of associa-tions, is so small that one cannot easily say that the majority of women display minority group consciousness. However, documentation, as well as a measuring instrument, is likewise lacking for minority consciousness in other groups.

Still women often manifest many of the psychological characteristics which have been imputed to self-conscious minority groups. Kurt Lewin[2] has pointed to group self-hatred as a frequent reaction of the minority group member to his group affiliation. This feeling is exhibited in the person's tendency to denigrate other members of the group, to accept the dominant group's stereotyped conception of them, and to indulge in "mea culpa" breast-beating. He may seek to exclude himself from the average of his group, or he may point the finger of scorn at himself. Since a person's conception of himself is based on the defining gestures of others, it is unlikely that members of a minority group can wholly escape personality distortion. Constant reiteration of one's inferiority must often lead to its acceptance as a fact.

Certainly women have not been immune to the formulations of the "female character" throughout the ages. From those, to us, deluded creatures who confessed to witchcraft to modern sophisticates who speak disparagingly of the cattiness and disloyalty of women, women reveal their introjection of prevailing attitudes toward them. Like those minority groups whose self-castigation outdoes dominant group derision of them, women frequently exceed men in the violence of their vituperations of their sex. They are more severe in moral judgments, especially in sexual matters. A line of self-criticism may be traced from Hannah More, a blue-stocking herself, to Dr. Marynia Farnham, who lays most of the world's ills at women's door. Women express themselves as disliking other women, as preferring to work under men, and as finding exclusively female gatherings repugnant. The *Fortune* polls conducted in 1946 show that women, more than men, have misgivings concerning women's participation in industry, the professions, and civic life. And more than one-fourth of women wish they had been born in the opposite sex![3]

Militating against a feeling of group identification on the part of women is a differential factor in their socialization. Members of a minority group are frequently socialized within their own group. Personality development is more largely a resultant of intra- than inter-group interaction. The conception of his role formed by a Negro or a Jew or a second-generation immigrant is greatly dependent upon the definitions offered by members of his own group, on their attitudes and behavior toward him. Ignoring for the moment class differences within the group, the minority group person does not suffer discrimination from members of his own group. But only rarely does a woman experience this type of group belongingness. Her interactions with members of the opposite sex may be as frequent as her relationships with members of her own sex. Women's conceptions of themselves, therefore, spring as much from their intimate relationships with men as with women. Although this consideration might seem to limit the applicability to women of research findings on minority groups, conversely, it may suggest investigation to seek out useful parallels in the socialization of women, on the one hand, and the

socialization of ethnics living in neighborhoods of hetereogeneous population, on the other.

Even though the sense of group identification is not so conspicuous
in women as in racial and ethnic minorities, they, like these others, tend to
develop a separate sub-culture. Women have their own language, comparable to the argot of the underworld and professional groups. It may
not extend to a completely separate dialect as has been discovered in
some preliterate groups, but there are words and idioms employed
chiefly by women. Only the acculturated male can enter into the conversation of the beauty parlor, the exclusive shop, the bridge table, or
the kitchen. In contrast to men's interest in physical health, safety, money,
and sex, women attach greater importance to attractiveness, personality,
home, family, and other people.[4] How much of the "woman's world" is
predicated on their relationship to men is too difficult a question to discuss here. It is still a controversial point whether the values and behavior
patterns of other minority groups, such as the Negroes, represent an im-
manent development, or are oriented chiefly toward the rejecting world.
A content analysis contrasting the speech of "housewives" and "career
women," for example, or a comparative analysis of the speech of men and
women of similar occupational status might be one test of this hypothesis.

We must return now to the original question of the aptness of the
designation of minority group for women. It has been indicated that
women fail to present in full force the subjective attributes commonly
associated with minority groups. That is, they lack a sense of group
identification and do not harbor feelings of being treated unfairly because
of their sex membership. Can it then be said that women have a minority
group status in our society? The answer to this question depends upon the
values of the observer whether within or outside the group—just as is
true in the case of any group of persons who, on the basis of putative
differential characteristics are denied access to some statuses in the
social system of their society. If we assume that there are no differences
attributable to sex membership as such that would justify casting men
and women in different social roles, it can readily be shown that women
do occupy a minority group status in our society.

Minority Group Status of Women

Formal discriminations against women are too well-known for any but
the most summary description. In general they take the form of being

barred from certain activities or, if admitted, being treated unequally. Discriminations against women may be viewed as arising from the generally ascribed status "female" and from the specially ascribed statuses of "wife," "mother," and "sister." (To meet the possible objection that "wife" and "mother" represent assumed, rather than ascribed, statuses, may I point out that what is important here is that these statuses carry ascribed expectations which are only ancillary in the minds of those who assume them.)

As female, in the economic sphere, women are largely confined to sedentary, monotonous work under the supervision of men, and are treated unequally with regard to pay, promotion, and responsibility. With the exceptions of teaching, nursing, social service, and library work, in which they do not hold a proportionate number of supervisory positions and are often occupationally segregated from men, they make a poor showing in the professions. Although they own 80 percent of the nation's wealth, they do not sit on the boards of directors of great corporations. Educational opportunities are likewise unequal. Professional schools, such as architecture and medicine, apply quotas. Women's colleges are frequently inferior to men's. In co-educational schools women's participation in campus activities is limited. As citizens, women are often barred from jury service and public office. Even when they are admitted to the apparatus of political parties, they are subordinated to men. Socially, women have less freedom of movement, and are permitted fewer deviations in the proprieties of dress, speech, manners. In social intercourse they are confined to a narrower range of personality expression.

In the specially ascribed status of wife, a woman—in several States— has no exclusive right to her earnings, is discriminated against in employment, must take the domicile of her husband, and in general must meet the social expectation of subordination to her husband's interests. As a mother, she may not have the guardianship of her children, bears the chief stigma in the case of an illegitimate child, is rarely given leave of absence for pregnancy. As a sister, she frequently suffers unequal distribution of domestic duties between herself and her brother, must yield preference to him in obtaining an education, and in such other psychic and material gratifications as cars, trips, and living away from home.

If it is conceded that women have a minority group status, what may be learned from applying to women various theoretical constructs in the field of intergroup relations?

Social Distance Between Men and Women

One instrument of diagnostic value is the measurement of social distance between dominant and minority groups. But we have seen that one important difference between women and other minorities is that women's attitudes and self-conceptions are conditioned more largely by interaction with both minority and dominant group members. Before measuring social distance, therefore, a continuum might be constructed of the frequency and extent of women's interaction with men, with the poles conceptualized as ideal types. One extreme would represent a complete "ghetto" status, the women whose contacts with men were of the most secondary kind. At the other extreme shall we put the woman who has prolonged and repeated associations with men, but only in those situations in which sex-awareness plays a prominent role or the woman who enters into a variety of relationships with men in which her sex identity is to a large extent irrelevant? The decision would depend on the type of scale used.

This question raises the problem of the criterion of social distance to be employed in such a scale. Is it more profitable to use we-feeling, felt interdependence, degree of communication, or degrees of separation in status? Social distance tests as applied to relationships between other dominant and minority groups have for the most part adopted prestige criteria as their basis. The assumption is that the type of situation into which one is willing to enter with average members of another group reflects one's estimate of the status of the group relative to one's own. When the tested group is a sex-group rather than a racial, national, religious, or economic one, several important differences in the use and interpretation of the scale must be noted:

1. Only two groups are involved: men and women. Thus, the test indicates the amount of homogeneity of we-feeling only according to the attribute of sex. If men are a primary group, there are not many groups to be ranked secondary, tertiary, etc. with respect to them, but only one group, women, whose social distance cannot be calculated relative to other groups.

2. Lundberg[5] suggests the possibility of a group of Catholics registering a smaller social distance to Moslems than to Catholics. In such an event the group of Catholics, from any sociological viewpoint, would be classified as Moslems. If women expressed less social distance to men than to women,

should they then be classified sociologically as men? Perhaps no more so than the legendary Negro who, when requested to move to the colored section of the train, replied, "Boss, I'se done resigned from the colored race," should be classified as white. It is likely, however, that the group identification of many women in our society is with men. The feminists were charged with wanting to be men, since they associated male physical characteristics with masculine social privileges. A similar statement can be made about men who show greater social distance to other men than to women.

Social distance may be measured from the standpoint of the minority group or the dominant group with different results. In point of fact, tension often arises when one group feels less social distance than the other. A type case here is the persistent suitor who underestimates his desired sweetheart's feeling of social distance toward him.

3. In social distance tests the assumption is made of an orderly progression—although not necessarily by equal intervals—in the scale. That is, it is not likely that a person would express willingness to have members of a given group as his neighbors, while simultaneously voicing the desire to have them excluded from his country. On all scales marriage represents the minimum social distance, and implies willingness for associations on all levels of lesser intimacy. May the customary scale be applied to men and women? If we take the expressed attitude of many men and women not to marry, we may say that they have feelings of social distance toward the opposite sex, and in this situation the usual order of the scale may be preserved.

In our culture, however, men who wish to marry, must perforce marry women, and even if they accept this relationship, they may still wish to limit their association with women in other situations. The male physician may not care for the addition of female physicians to his hospital staff. The male poker player may be thrown off his game if women participate. A damper may be put upon the hunting expedition if women come along. The average man may not wish to consult a woman lawyer. And so on. In these cases it seems apparent that the steps in the social distance scale must be reversed. Men will accept women at the supposed level of greatest intimacy while rejecting them at lower levels.

But before concluding that a different scale must be constructed when the dominant group attitude toward a minority group which is being tested is that of men toward women, the question may be raised as to whether marriage in fact represents the point of minimum social distance. It may not imply anything but physical intimacy and work accommodation, as was frequently true in non-individuated societies, such as preliterate groups and the household economy of the Middle Ages, or marriages of convenience in the European upper class. Even in our own democratic society where marriage is supposedly based on romantic love there may be little communication between the partners in marriage. The Lynds[6] report the absence of real companionship between husband and wife in Middletown. Women have been known to say that although they have been married for twenty years, their husband is still a stranger to them. There is a quatrain of Thoreau's that goes:

> Each moment as we drew nearer to each
> A stern respect withheld us farther yet
> So that we seemed beyond each other's reach
> And less acquainted than when first we met.

Part of the explanation may be found in the subordination of wives to husbands in our culture, which is expressed in the separate spheres of activity for men and women. A recent advertisement in a magazine of national circulation depicts a pensive husband seated by his knitting wife, with the caption, "Sometimes a man has moods his wife cannot understand." In this case the husband is worried about a pension plan for his employees. The assumption is that the wife, knowing nothing of the business world, cannot take the role of her husband in this matter.

The presence of love does not in itself argue for either equality of status nor fullness of communication. We may love those who are either inferior or superior to us, and we may love persons whom we do not understand. The supreme literary examples of passion without communication are found in Proust's portrayal of Swann's obsession with Odette, the narrator's infatuation with the elusive Albertine, and, of course, Dante's longing for Beatrice.

In the light of these considerations concerning the relationships between men and women, some doubt may be cast on the propriety of placing marriage on the positive extreme of the social distance scale with respect to ethnic and religious minority groups. Since inequalities of status are preserved in marriage, a dominant group member may be willing to marry a member of a group which, in general, he would not wish admitted to his club. The social distance scale which uses marriage as a sign of an extreme degree of acceptance is inadequate for appreciating the position of women, and perhaps for other minority groups as well. The relationships among similarity of status, communication as a measure of intimacy, and love must be clarified before social distance tests can be applied usefully to attitudes between men and women.

Caste-Class Conflict

Is the separation between males and females in our society a caste line? Folsom[7] suggests that it is, and Myrdal[8] in his well-known Appendix 5 considers the parallel between the position of and feelings toward women and Negroes in our society. The relation between women and Negroes is historical, as well as analogical. In the seventeenth century the legal status of Negro servants was borrowed from that of women and children, who were under the patria potestas, and until the Civil War there was considerable cooperation between the Abolitionist and woman suffrage movements. According to Myrdal, the problems of both groups are resultants of the transition from a pre-industrial, paternalistic scheme of life to individualistic, industrial capitalism. Obvious similarities in the status of women and Negroes are indicated in Chart 1.

While these similarities in the situation of women and Negroes may lead to increased understanding of their social roles, account must also be taken of differences which impose qualifications on the comparison of the two groups. Most importantly, the influence of marriage as a social elevator for women, but not for Negroes, must be considered. Obvious, too, is the greater importance of women to the dominant group, despite the economic, sexual, and prestige gains which Negroes afford the white South. Ambivalence is probably more marked in the attitude of white males toward women than toward Negroes. The "war of the sexes" is only an expression of men's and women's vital need of each other. Again, there is greater polarization in the relationship between men and women. Negroes, although they have borne the brunt of anti-minority group feeling in this country, do not constitute the only racial or ethnic minority, but there are only two sexes. And, although we have seen that social distance exists between men and women, it is not to be compared with the social segregation of Negroes.

At the present time, of course, Negroes suffer far greater discrimination than women, but since the latter's problems are rooted in a biological reality less susceptible to cultural manipulation, they prove more lasting.

Chart 1.   Castelike status of women and Negroes

Negroes	*Women*
1. *High social visibility*	
a. Skin color, other "racial" characteristics	a. Secondary sex characteristics
b. (Sometimes) distinctive dress—bandana, flashy clothes	b. Distinctive dress, skirts, etc.
2. *Ascribed attributes*	
a. Inferior intelligence, smaller brain, less convoluted, scarcity of geniuses	a. Ditto
b. More free in instinctual gratifications. More emotional, "primitive" and childlike. Imagined sexual prowess envied.	b. Irresponsible, inconsistent, emotionally unstable. Lack strong super-ego. Women as "temptresses"
c. Common stereotype "inferior"	c. "Weaker"
3. *Rationalizations of status*	
a. Thought all right in his place	a. Woman's place is in the home
b. Myth of contented Negro	b. Myth of contented woman—"feminine" woman is happy in subordinate role
4. *Accommodation attitudes*	
a. Supplicatory whining intonation of voice	a. Rising inflection, smiles, laughs, downward glances
b. Deferential manner	b. Flattering manner
c. Concealment of real feelings	c. "Feminine wiles"
d. Outwit "white folks"	d. Outwit "menfolk"
e. Careful study of points at which dominant group is susceptible to influence	e. Ditto
f. Fake appeals for directives; show of ignorance	f. Appearance of helplessness
5. *Discriminations*	
a. Limitations on education—should fit "place" in society	a. Ditto
b. Confined to traditional jobs—barred from supervisory positions Their competition feared No family precedents for new aspirations	b. Ditto

Chart 1. (*continued*)

Negroes	*Women*
c. Deprived of political importance	c. Ditto
d. Social and professional segregation	d. Ditto
e. More vulnerable to criticism	e. e.g. conduct in bars.

6. *Similar problems*
   a. Roles not clearly defined, but in flux as result of social change
      Conflict between achieved status and ascribed status

Women's privileges exceed those of Negroes. Protective attitudes toward Negroes have faded into abeyance, even in the South, but most boys are still taught to take care of girls, and many evidences of male chivalry remain. The factor of class introduces variations here. The middle class Negro endures frustrations largely without the rewards of his white class peer, but the lower class Negro is still absolved from many responsibilities. The reverse holds true for women. Notwithstanding these and other differences between the position of women and Negroes, the similarities are sufficient to render research on either group applicable in some fashion to the other.

Exemplary of the possible usefulness of applying the caste principle to women is viewing some of the confusion surrounding women's roles as reflecting a conflict between class and caste status. Such a conflict is present in the thinking and feeling of both dominant and minority groups toward upper class Negroes and educated women. Should a woman judge be treated with the respect due a judge or the gallantry accorded a woman? The extent to which the rights and duties of one role permeate other roles so as to cause a role conflict has been treated elsewhere by the writer.[9] Lower class Negroes who have acquired dominant group attitudes toward the Negro resent upper class Negro pretensions to superiority. Similarly, domestic women may feel the career woman is neglecting the duties of her proper station.

Parallels in adjustment of women and Negroes to the class-caste conflict may also be noted. Point 4 "Accommodation Attitudes" of the foregoing chart indicates the kinds of behavior displayed by members of both groups who accept their caste status. Many "sophisticated" women are retreating from emancipation with the support of psychoanalytic derivations.[10] David Riesman has recently provided an interesting discussion of changes "in the denigration by American women of their own sex" in which he explains their new submissiveness as in part a reaction to the weakness of men in the contemporary world.[11] "Parallelism" and "Negroidism" which accept a racially-restricted economy reflect allied tendencies in the Negro group.

Role segmentation as a mode of adjustment is illustrated by Negroes who indulge in occasional passing and women who vary their behavior according to their definition of the situation. An example of the latter is the case of the woman lawyer who, after losing a case before a judge who was also her husband, said she would appeal the case, and added, "The judge can lay down the law at home, but I'll argue with him in court."

A third type of reaction is to fight for recognition of class status. Negro race leaders seek greater prerogatives for Negroes. Feminist women, acting either through organizations or as individuals, push for public disavowal of any differential treatment of men and women.

Race Relations Cycle

The "race relations cycle," as defined by Robert E. Park,[12] describes the social processes of reduction in tension and increase of communication in the relations between two or more groups who are living in a common territory under a single political or economic system. The sequence of competition, conflict, accommodation, and assimilation may also occur when social change introduces dissociative forces into an assimilated group or causes accommodated groups to seek new definitions of the situation.[13] The ethnic or nationality characteristics of the groups involved are not essential to the cycle. In a complex industrialized society groups are constantly forming and re-forming on the basis of new interests and new identities. Women, of course, have always possessed a sex-identification though perhaps not a group awareness. Today they represent a previously accommodated group which is endeavoring to modify the relationships between the sexes in the home, in work, and in the community.

The sex relations cycle bears important similarities to the race relations cycle. In the wake of the Industrial Revolution, as women acquired industrial, business, and professional skills, they increasingly sought employment in competition with men. Men were quick to perceive them as a rival group and made use of economic, legal, and ideological weapons to eliminate or reduce their competition. They excluded women from the trade unions, made contracts with employers to prevent their hiring women, passed laws restricting the employment of married women, caricatured the working woman, and carried on ceaseless propaganda to return women to the home or keep them there. Since the days of the suffragettes there has been no overt conflict between men and women on a group basis. Rather than conflict, the dissociative process between the sexes is that of contravention,[14] a type of opposition intermediate between competition and conflict. According to Wiese and Becker, it includes rebuffing, repulsing, working against, hindering, protesting, obstructing, restraining, and upsetting another's plans.

The present contravention of the sexes, arising from women's competition with men, is manifested in the discriminations against women, as well as in the doubts and uncertainties expressed concerning women's character, abilities, motives. The processes of competition and contravention are continually giving way to accommodation in the realtionships between men and women. Like other minority groups, women have sought a protected position, a niche in the economy which they could occupy, and, like other minority groups, they have found these positions in new occupations in which dominant group members had not yet established themselves and in old occupations which they no longer wanted. When women entered fields which represented an extension of services in the home (except medicine!), they encountered least opposition. Evidence is accumulating, however, that women are becoming dissatisfied with the employment conditions of the great women-employing occupations and present accommodations are threatened.

What would assimilation of men and women mean? Park and Burgess in their classic text define assimilation as "a process of interpenetration and fusion in which persons and groups acquire the memories, sentiments, and attitudes of other persons or groups, and, by sharing their experiences and history, are incorporated with them in a cultural life." If accommodation is characterized by secondary contacts, assimilation holds the promise of primary contacts. If men and women were truly assimilated, we would find no cleavages of interest along sex lines. The special provinces of men and women would be abolished. Women's pages would disappear from the newspaper and women's magazines from the stands. All special women's organizations would pass into limbo. The sports page and racing news would be read indifferently by men and women. Interest in cookery and interior decoration would follow individual rather than sex lines. Women's talk would be no different from men's talk, and frank and full communication would obtain between the sexes.

The Marginal Woman

Group relationships are reflected in personal adjustments. Arising out of the present contravention of the sexes is the marginal woman, torn between rejection and acceptance of traditional roles and attributes. Uncertain of the ground on which she stands, subjected to conflicting cultural expectations, the marginal woman suffers the psychological ravages of instability, conflict, self-hate, anxiety, and resentment.

In applying the concept of marginality to women, the term "role" must be substituted for that of "group."[15] Many of the traditional devices for creating role differentiation among boys and girls, such as dress, manners, activities, have been de-emphasized in modern urban middle class homes. The small girl who wears a play suit, plays games with boys and girls together, attends a co-educational school, may have little awareness of sexual differentiation until the approach of adolescence. Parental expectations in the matters of scholarship, conduct toward others, duties in the home may have differed little for herself and her brother. But in high school or perhaps not until college she finds herself called upon to play a new role. Benedict[16] has called attention to discontinuities in the life cycle, and the fact that these continuities in cultural conditioning take a greater toll of girls than of boys is revealed in test scores showing neuroticism and introversion.[17] In adolescence girls find the frank, spontaneous behavior toward the neighboring sex no longer rewarding. High grades are more likely to elicit anxiety than praise from parents, especially mothers, who seem more pleased if male callers are frequent. There are subtle indications that to remain home with a good book on a Saturday night is a fate worse than death. But even if the die is successfully cast for popularity, all problems are not solved. Girls are encouraged to heighten their sexual attractiveness, but to abjure sexual expression.

Assuming new roles in adolescence does not mean the complete relinquishing of old ones. Scholarship, while not so vital as for the boy, is still important, but must be maintained discreetly and without obvious effort. Mirra Komarovsky[18] has supplied statements of Barnard College girls of the conflicting expectations of their elders. Even more than to the boy is the "all-round" ideal held up to girls, and it is not always possible to integrate the roles of good date, good daughter, good sorority sister, good student, good friends, and good citizen. The superior achievements of college men over college women bear witness to the crippling division of energies among women. Part of the explanation may lie in women's having interiorized cultural notions of feminine inferiority in certain fields, and even the most self-confident or most defensive woman may be filled with doubt as to whether she can do productive work.

It may be expected that as differences in privileges between men and women decrease, the frequency of marginal women will increase. Widening opportunities for women will call forth a growing number of women capable of performing roles formerly reserved for men, but whose acceptance in these new roles may well remain uncertain and problematic. This hypothesis is in accord with Arnold Green's[19] recent critical re-examination of the marginal man concept in which he points out that it is those Negroes and second-generation immigrants whose values and behavior most approximate those of the dominant majority who experience the most severe personal crises. He believes that the classical marginal man symptoms appear only when a person striving to leave the racial or ethnic group into which he was born is deeply identified with the family of orientation and is met with grudging, uncertain, and unpredictable acceptance, rather than with absolute rejection, by the group he is attempting to join, and also that he is committed to success-careerism. Analogically, one would expect to find that women who display marginal symptoms are psychologically bound to the family of orientation in which they experienced the imperatives of both the traditional and new feminine roles, and are seeking to expand the occupational (or other) areas open to women rather than those who content themselves with established fields. Concretely, one might suppose women engineers to have greater personality problems than women librarians.

Other avenues of investigation suggested by the minority group approach can only be mentioned. What social types arise as personal adjustments to sex status? What can be done in the way of experimental modification of the attitudes of men and women toward each other and themselves? What hypotheses of inter-group relations may be tested in regard to men and women? For example, is it true that as women approach the cultural standards of men, they are perceived as a threat and tensions increase? Of what significance are regional and community variations in the treatment of and degree of participation permitted women, mindful here that women share responsibility with men for the perpetuation of attitudes toward women? This paper is exploratory in suggesting the enhanced possibilities of fruitful analysis, if women are included in the minority group corpus, particularly with reference to such concepts and techniques as group belongingness, socialization of the minority group child, cultural differences, social distance tests, conflict between class and caste status, race relations cycle, and marginality. I believe that the concept of the marginal woman should be especially productive, and am now engaged in an empirical study of role conflicts in professional women.

Notes

1. Louis Wirth, "The Problem of Minority Groups," *The Science of Man in the World Crisis*, ed. by Ralph Linton (1945), p. 347.

2. Kurt Lewin, "Self-Hatred Among Jews," *Contemporary Jewish Record*, IV (1941), 219—232.

3. *Fortune*, September, 1946, p. 5.

4. P. M. Symonds, "Changes in Sex Differences in Problems and Interests of Adolescents with Increasing Age," *Journal of Genetic Psychology*, 50 (1937), pp. 83—89, as referred to by Georgene H. Seward, *Sex and the Social Order* (1946), pp. 237—238.

5. George A. Lundberg, *Foundations of Sociology* (1939), p. 319.

6. Robert S. and Helen Merrell Lynd, *Middletown* (1929), p. 120, and *Middletown in Transition* (1937), p. 176.

7. Joseph Kirk Folsom, *The Family and Democratic Society* (1943), pp. 623—624.

8. Gunnar Myrdal, *An American Dilemma* (1944), pp. 1073—1078.

9. Helen M. Hacker, Towards a Definition of Role Conflict in Modern Women (unpublished manuscript).

10. As furnished by such books as Helene Deutsch, *The Psychology of Women* (1944—1945) and Ferdinand Lundberg and Marynia F. Farnham, *Modern Woman: The Lost Sex* (1947).

11. David Riesman, "The Saving Remnant: An Examination of Character Structure," *Years of the Modern: An American Appraisal*, ed. by John W. Chase (1949), pp. 139—140.

12. Robert E. Park, "Our Racial Frontier on the Pacific," *The Survey Graphic*, 56 (May 1, 1926), pp. 192—196.

13. William Ogburn and Meyer Nimkoff, *Sociology* (2d ed., 1950), p. 187.

14. Howard Becker, *Systematic Sociology on the Basis of the "Beziehungslehre" and "Gebildelehre" of Leopold von Wiese* (1932), pp. 263—268.

15. Kurt Lewin, *Resolving Social Conflicts* (1948), p. 181.

16. Ruth Benedict, "Continuities and Discontinuities in Cultural Conditioning," *Psychiatry*, 1 (1938), pp. 161—167.

17.   Georgene H. Seward, *op. cit.*, pp. 239–240.

18.   Mirra Komarovsky, "Cultural Contradictions and Sex Roles," *The American Journal of Sociology*, LII (November 1946), 184–189.

19.   Arnold Green, "A Re-Examination of the Marginal Man Concept," *Social Forces*, 26 (December 1947), pp. 167–171.

Dean D. Knudsen / The Declining Status of Women: Popular Myths and the Failure of Functionalist Thought

While it is widely believed that in the middle of the twentieth century, the status of American women has improved and there has developed more equality between the status of men and women, the following selection presents evidence to the contrary. Professor Dean Knudsen, through an examination of the United States census data from 1940–1964, indicates that in terms of women's occupational, economic, and educational achievements, women have suffered a loss in status. Professor Knudsen also discusses the self-fulfilling prophecy element in job discrimination and the social scientist's role in perpetuating the discrimination against women: "... given the conviction that women should not pursue occupations in competition with men, women and employers together develop a self-fulfilling prophecy. ... Women, ambivalent about careers and convinced that they will face discrimination, make lesser efforts than men, permitting employers to justify discrimination by appealing to evidence of lower achievement and commitment to employment. The effect is the perpetuation of a belief that sexual equality exists and that only effort is lacking, to which social scientists have offered their support." Although Professor Knudsen does not discuss the self-fulfilling prophecy as a factor generally at work in the subjegation of other groups, it is clear that in this respect, as in so many others, women face the same problems as the Blacks. If one were to substitute "black" for "woman" and "white" for "men" in the above quote from Knudsen's article, the comparison becomes apparent. The answer to the argument is, of course, to break the vicious cycle of the self-fulfilling prophecy.

Knudsen, "The Declining Status of Women: Popular Myths and the Failure of Functionalist Thought," *Social Forces*, December 1969, pp. 183–193. Reprinted by permission of the publisher.

Abstract

Despite frequent claims of equality of status for women and men, U.S. Census data from 1940—64 suggest a gradual but persistent decline in women's occupational, economic, and educational achievements, compared to those of men. These findings suggest that women have suffered a loss in status, as measured by the variables usually used to determine social status. In the discussion of these findings the normative nature of the functional definition of sex roles is identified as a justification for discrimination against women.

A common theme of much literature in the social sciences has developed the idea of a gradual but persistent equalization of statuses of men and women. It often has been assumed that the battle for women's rights is won, and whatever inequity still persists derives entirely from a failure of women to exercise their legal, educational, occupational, and social prerogatives.[1]

It is the purpose of this paper to challenge some current conceptions of the status of women, especially in contrast to their status of earlier years, and to make some assessment of the sources of the increasing inequality that has developed in the United States. Further, the institutionalization of this inequality will be used to illustrate the conservative nature of much modern social science research.

The Modern Context of Sex-Defined Statuses

While the modern industrial society has effectively destroyed the narrow definition of appropriate female roles that persisted throughout most of the early Hebrew-Christian era and into Colonial America, the idea of complete legal and social equality did not finally emerge as a viable ideal for the majority of the population until the early twentieth century. However, even during this recent period such equality has not been accepted without contest, despite legal sanctions. Enactment of *Title VII* of the Civil Rights Act of 1964 resulted in 2,031 complaints of discrimination against women, about one-third of the total number presented to the Equal Employment Opportunity Commission during its first year of operation (Interdepartmental Committee, 1966:43). Such numerous complaints offer significant evidence of a continuing antifemale discrimination in employment.

However, both professional and popular publications have frequently assumed that discrimination has ceased, and that the trend is toward equality of opportunity and equality of fact. Thus it is stated that "The status discrepancy has narrowed considerably in recent years yet men remain dominant in many spheres. Initiative in dating and proposing marriage, the double sex standard and a broader field of occupational choice for males are illustrative" (Babchuck and Bates, 1963:377).

Similar optimistic interpretations emerge from an investigation of publications of U.S. Government agencies, as is evident from the following statements:

> Women's Gains, 1950—60. During the 1950s, the professions in which women made their most significant employment *gains*—either in terms of percentage increases or number of workers—were those relating to service and social needs of society.... Challenging careers for qualified college women have never before existed in such variety—*nor offered so many rewards* (U.S. Department of Labor, 1964:71, italics added).

Dimensions of Female Status

To effectively judge the nature of the current status of women, it is necessary to indicate a common misuse of status-related concepts and the significance such abuse has for disguising status discrepancy. Status, though ambiguous in sociological usage, refers to *relative* prestige, esteem, power or recognition of two or more categories within the same general classification. As Laswell (1965:42—43) states it, "In all definitions and uses of the term 'status,' factual comparison is implicit. Labeling Methodists implies the existence of non-Methodists; elite implies that non-elite also exist" (see also Gordon, 1963:245—248). Thus, status of women is always relative to men, and the attempt at measurement of status for women or men which involves historical comparisons only within rather than between sex categories is inappropriate at best and grossly misleading at worst. For example, when it is claimed that in 1960, "nearly $2\frac{3}{4}$ million women had a professional, technical or kindred position—a 41 percent increase in ten years" (U.S. Department of Labor, 1964:71), the statistic is impressive until comparable figures for men are provided—nearly $4\frac{1}{2}$ million and an increase of 51 percent in ten years (U.S. Bureau of the Census, 1960, computed).

Comparisons of historical data between the sexes are thus crucial to an understanding of the status of women.[2] Only by examining the

Table 1. Percent of employed women and men in each occupational category for 1940, 1950, 1960, and 1966

Occupational categories*	Female				Male			
	1940[1]	1950[1]	1960[1]	1966[2]	1940[1]	1950[1]	1960[1]	1966[2]
Professional, technical and kindred	13.4	12.4	13.0	14.0	6.1	7.3	10.3	12.6
Managers, officials and proprietors	3.5	4.3	3.7	4.4	9.6	10.7	10.7	13.6
Clerical and kindred	21.1	27.3	29.7	32.5	6.0	6.5	6.9	7.2
Sales workers	7.3	8.5	7.8	7.0	6.7	6.3	6.9	6.0
Craftsmen, foremen and kindred	1.2	1.5	1.2	0.9	14.9	18.6	19.5	19.3
Operatives and kindred	18.1	19.2	15.4	15.8	17.9	20.1	19.9	21.1
Laborers, except farm and mine	1.0	0.7	0.5	0.4	9.0	8.1	6.9	7.0
Private household workers	17.7	8.5	7.9	7.5	0.3	0.2	0.1	0.0
Service workers	11.0	12.2	13.4	15.6	5.8	5.8	6.0	7.0
Farmers and farm managers	1.4	0.7	0.6	0.5	14.7	10.4	5.5	4.3
Farm laborers	2.9	2.9	1.1	1.4	8.3	14.9	2.8	2.0
Not reported	1.0	0.7	0.5	—	0.7	1.1	4.6	—
Total	100.0	100.0	100.0	100.0	100.0	100.0	100.0	100.0
Number employed (thousands)	11,178	15,772	21,172	25,236	33,892	40,662	43,467	45,847

[1] Source: U.S. Bureau of Census *U.S. Census of Population: 1960: Vol. 1* (Washington, D.C.: Government Printing Office, 1964), Table 89, p. 1–219.

[2] Source: U.S. Bureau of Census, *Statistical Abstract of the United States, 1967* (Washington, D.C.: Government Printing Office, 1967), computed.

* Slightly different totals and percentage figures are obtained for 1940 and 1950 if "Experienced Labor Force" or "Economically Active" are used as the basis of computation. However only for the "operatives" category in 1940 is the difference greater than 1 percent (−1.4) and greater than 0.5 percent for "professional, technical, and kindred" in 1940 (− 0.6 percent) and for "operatives" in 1950 (− .8 percent). If data in the 1967 *Statistical Abstract* are used to compute 1960 figures there are four changes: professional, technical and kindred, −0.08 percent; managers, officials and proprietors, + 1.3 percent; private household workers, + 1.9 percent; service workers, + 0.7 percent. These differences may be due to definitions and also to date of data collections.

position of women relative to men in 1940, 1950, and 1960 can an adequate assessment begin. In an effort to make statuses comparable, male and female achievements will be examined in the three most commonly operationalized measures of social class and status: occupation, income, and education.[3]

Occupation as a measure of status

Probably no aspect of feminine behavior has received the attention that has been focused since World War II upon the employment of women, especially mothers of young children. Though there has been a substantial amount of research, there is no agreement about empirical findings concerning the supposed negative effects that out-of-home work by married women has upon family life in any aspect—themselves, their marital relationships, or their children (e.g., Nye and Hoffman, 1963). Increases in the percentage of the labor force that is female suggest an increased interest in work-for-pay outside of the home, whatever the motivation, though the majority of positions filled by women can hardly be classified as creative and intellectually demanding.

Table 1 shows the within-sex occupational distribution of both female and male workers, 1940–66, a period during which the relative size of the clerical and kindred category for women increased by over 50 percent, drawn largely from private household workers and operatives. It should be noted that during the 25-year period there has been only a slight change in the relative sizes of the two highest-status categories, the professional and managerial positions for women, though considerable increases for men.

Additional information is provided by an examination of the percentage in each occupational category that was female during the same period, in Table 2. Several complementary patterns emerge from a consideration of trends. There has been a slight but persistent decline in the proportions of professional, technical and kindred workers that were female, while either a definite increase or a leveling occurred for every other category. For clerical and kindred workers, sales, service and farm workers, the increase was substantial—a shift of over 10 percent from male to female workers in every instance. Thus, while there are now more women professionals than in earlier years, their proportion of the total number of professionals has declined, from about two-fifths to slightly over one-third during the past 25 years.

Further consideration of professional workers shows only slight

Table 2.   Employed persons: percent female for occupational categories for 1940, 1950, 1960 and 1966

Occupational categories*	1940[1]	1950[1]	1960[2]	1966[3]
Professional, technical and kindred	41.6	39.5	38.1	37.9
Managers, officials and proprietors	11.2	13.5	14.4	15.3
Clerical and kindred	53.9	62.3	67.6	71.3
Sales workers	26.1	33.9	35.8	39.5
Craftsmen, foremen and kindred	1.9	3.0	2.9	2.5
Operatives and kindred	25.3	27.1	27.4	29.1
Laborers, except farm and mine	3.3	3.7	5.4	3.0
Private household workers	94.4	94.8	96.5	98.0
Service workers	38.4	44.6	52.3	55.0
Farmers and farm managers	3.0	2.7	4.7	6.0
Farm laborers	10.3	18.7	16.8	28.8

[1]   Source: U.S. Bureau of Census, *Census of Population, 1950:* Vol. 2 (Washington, D.C.: Government Printing Office, 1953), computed from Table 124, pp. 1–261 to 1–266.

[2]   Source: U.S. Bureau of Census, *U.S. Census of Population: 1960:* Vol. 1 (Washington, D.C.: Government Printing Office, 1964), computed from Table 202, pp. 1–528 to 1–533.

[3]   Source: U.S. Bureau of Census, *Statistical Abstract of the United States: 1967* (Washington, D.C.: Government Printing Office, 1967), No. 327, p. 230 (computed).

*   Some slight differences are obtained if "Experienced Labor Force" or "Economically Active" are used as the basis of computation.

gains for women, as illustrated by the data in Table 3. All specific professional categories involving 5,000 or more women in 1960 are included. It is significant that the Women's Bureau publication (U.S. Department of Labor, 1964) used these categories to provide evidence of employment gains by females during the 1950 decade. However, an assessment of the changes suggests no great increase in professional occupations by women when compared to men, but rather a modest decline. In twelve of the twenty-one categories listed, the percentage increase for males exceeded that of females, and the overall increase for males was greater, despite a much larger base of population in 1950. Further, in only two of the nine cases where the female percentage increase was greater did the number of women exceed that of men, those of musicians and therapists and healers. In six of the twelve cases where the male increase was greater, however, the number of men was at least twice that of women.

Such data suggest several conclusions regarding female participation in professional employment during the past quarter century. First, while

Table 3. Number of employed persons in 1960 and percentage change 1950—60 in specific professional categories by sex

Occupational category	Female[1]		Male[2]	
	Number 1960	Percent change: 1950—60	Number 1960	Percent change: 1950—60
Total employed	2,753,052	+ 41	4,479,358	+ 51
Teachers*	1,196,526	+ 43	475,388	+ 66
Nurses, professional	567,884	+ 45	14,495	+ 51
Musicians, music teachers	109,638	+ 40	82,246	+ 8
Accountants, auditors	79,045	+ 41	392,257	+ 22
Librarians	71,836	+ 46	12,045	+ 90
Social welfare, recreation workers	60,667	+ 15	36,029	+ 54
College presidents, professors, instructors	38,850	+ 30	138,889	+ 45
Editors, reporters	37,438	+ 40	63,279	+ 43
Religious workers	35,099	+ 21	21,239	+ 66
Personnel, labor relations workers	30,215	+ 100	67,957	+ 81
Sports instructors, officials	24,931	+ 123	51,957	+ 53
Dietitians, nutritionists	24,237	+ 15	1,882	+ 40
Therapists, healers	19,752	+ 62	16,902	+ 18
Physicians, surgeons	15,513	+ 32	213,413	+ 18
Recreation, group workers	15,497	+ 129	20,858	+ 121
Natural scientists	14,738	+ 10	134,592	+ 30
Social scientists	14,177	+ 24	42,403	+ 77
Lawyers, judges	7,434	+ 19	204,974	+ 13
Engineers, technical	7,211	+ 11	853,738	+ 62
Pharmacists	7,129	− 2	85,026	+ 5
Public relations workers, publicity workers	7,005	+ 258	23,358	+ 41

[1]   Source: U.S. Department of Labor, Woman's Bureau, *Job Horizons for College Women in the 1960s* (Washington, D.C.: Government Printing Office, 1964), Table 2, p. 67.

[2]   Source: U.S. Bureau of Census. *U.S. Census of Population:* Vol. 1 (Washington, D.C.: Government Printing Office, 1960). Table 202, pp. 1—528 to 1—533 (computed).

*   Category does not include art, music, dancing, or physical education teachers who are classified elsewhere.

there has been an increase in the number of women employed in professions, the percentage increase is considerably less than that of men, and the female has neither displaced nor seriously challenged the American male's dominance in professional positions. Second, greatest relative female increases occurred primarily in those specific categories which already had an overwhelming majority of men—auditors and accountants, personnel and labor relations workers, sports instructors and officials, physicians and surgeons, lawyers and judges, and public relations workers and publicity writers. Third, in the remaining categories of relatively greater female increase are those occupations uniquely compatible with homemaking responsibilities, and thus lend themselves to part-time or irregular patterns of work involvement, especially in the case of musicians and music teachers. Finally, the frequently mentioned claim of increased varieties of work and rewards can be validated only if placed in the context of historical comparisons rather than in relation to male opportunities, since the growth in numbers of women employed has occurred predominantly in the lower-status occupations.

Income as a measure of status

Income provides another basis for relative evaluation of the recipient's status, by focusing upon the economic rewards offered and may be especially meaningful in terms of filling the more repetitive and less creative positions that have often been assigned to women. In terms of historical data, incremental rewards for women relative to men may be interpreted as evidence of an increasing status, while increased inequality of reward suggests a relative loss if occupational levels are similar in status ranking.[4]

In Table 4, the median salaries for only those women who were full-time year-round workers within various occupational classifications during the past quarter century are presented. The 1939 data are for the prewar end-of-depression period and in comparison to that income level, the 1966 incomes indicate an increase of at least 400 percent in nearly every case. Of greater significance, however, is the proportion of male income that was received by females within the various categories. In only one instance was the proportion greater in 1966 than in 1939, that of professional, technical, and kindred workers, but even this difference was less than 5 percent.

When occupation and income are considered simultaneously, however, even this apparent gain is minimized. Since the professional, tech-

Table 4. Median wage or salary income in dollars of year-round full-time female workers, and percent of male income earned by females in specific years by occupational category

Occupational category	1939[1] Median income	1939[1] Percent	1949[2] Median income	1949[2] Percent	1959[3] Median income	1959[3] Percent	1966[1] Median income	1966[1] Percent
Professional, technical and kindred	$1277	60.8	$2615	60.6	$4385	64.2	$5826	65.1
Managers, officials and proprietors	$1218	54.0	$2382	57.3	$3934	56.9	$4919	54.0
Clerical and kindred	$1072	78.5	$2255	70.2	$3493	68.1	$4316	66.5
Sales workers	$745	51.3	$1658	49.3	$2340	42.2	$3103	41.0
Craftsmen, foremen and kindred	$995	63.7	$2280	67.2	—	—	$4345	60.4
Operatives and kindred	$742	58.5	$1926	64.9	$2916	63.3	$3416	55.9
Laborers except farm and mine	$738	74.5	$1912	79.9	*	—	*	—
Private household workers	$339	61.7	$799	53.1	$1146	—	$1297	—
Service workers	$607	59.6	$1455	58.2	$2241	56.0	$2815	55.4
Farmers and farm managers	$403	93.7	$854	51.6	—	—	—	—
Farm laborers	$245	67.1	$474	42.0	—	—	—	—

[1] Source: U.S. Department of Commerce, *Current Population Reports: Consumer Income*, Series P-60, No. 53 (Washington, D.C.: Government Printing Office, December 28, 1967), Table 34, p. 51 (computed).

[2] Source: David L. Kaplan and M. Claire Casey. "*Occupational Trends in the U.S., 1900 to 1960*," U.S. Department of Commerce, *Current Population Reports: Consumer Income*, Series P-60, No. 35 (Washington, D.C.: Government Printing Office, January 5, 1961), Table 38, p. 52 (computed).

[3] Source: U.S. Department of Commerce, *Current Population Reports: Consumer Income*, Series P-60, No. 35 (Washington, D.C.: Government Printing Office, January 5, 1961), Table 38, p. 52 (computed).

* Data for comparison not available for year-round full-time workers due to insufficient numbers of women or men in the category.

nical, and kindred category contained relatively fewer women in 1965 than in 1940, the apparent gain was achieved by relatively few women. Further, clerical and kindred workers, that category with the greatest relative numerical increase in employment, was subject to the largest relative loss in income, a decrease of 12 percent.

For women, the relationship between levels of income and numbers employed in any occupational category is clearly a negative one: as the proportion of workers being female in any occupational category increased, the relative income of women has declined over the past quarter century. It is a strong, if not perfect, negative correlation with the greatest gains in one measure offset by the greatest losses in the other.[5]

To account for such losses of relative income, it could be argued that women have gradually shifted from a broadly dispersed distribution throughout each occupational category toward a concentration at the lower income levels of each classification. Data in Table 3 offer no support for such an interpretation, at least among professional workers. Even this suggestion, however, assumes that women either have demonstrated a gradual but persistent loss of motivation for competitive positions or have been systematically discriminated against by employers. Either of these choices tacitly recognizes the pattern of incremental inequality in relative income at given occupational levels.

Perhaps it should be noted that the well-publicized but only occasionally successful professional woman often is idealized much as the self-made man was through the "American dream" of earlier years. The myth of female equality rests in some measure upon the glamorization of these exceptional cases, making it appear that individual effort is the lacking ingredient in success, rather than a lack of equal opportunity.

Education as a measure of status

Education is the third generally used measure of social status. Because education is highly correlated with both occupation and income, it was expected that data regarding educational achievement would also indicate a relatively disadvantaged situation for women. In addition, since education is the primary means by which women can effectively enter the competitive market, it may reflect most clearly the normative expectations of females and their parents in occupational achievements.

In Table 5 median educational achievements are presented for males and females at various ages under age 40, when most formal education has ceased. Females at all ages in 1940 had higher grade levels of completion

Table 5. Median educational achievements for males and females by age for 1940, 1950, and 1960, and percent increase by sex

Age	1940[1]		1950[2]		1960[2]		Percent Increase 1940–60	
	Male	Female	Male	Female	Male	Female	Male	Female
17	10.2	10.7	10.4	10.8	10.8	11.1	6	4
18	10.7	11.3	11.2	11.7	11.6	11.9	8	5
19	11.0	11.8	11.9	12.2	12.2	12.3	11	4
20	11.0	11.7	12.1	12.2	12.3	12.4	12	6
21	11.0	11.8	12.0	12.2	12.3	12.4	12	5
22	10.9	11.6	11.9	12.2	12.3	12.4	13	7
23	10.8	11.3	11.8	12.1	12.3	12.3	14	9
24	10.7	11.1	11.8	12.1	12.3	12.3	15	11
25–29	—	—	12.0	12.1	12.3	12.3	2*	2*
30–34	—	—	11.4	11.8	12.1	12.2	6*	3*
35–39	—	—	10.3	10.7	12.1	12.2	17*	14*

[1]   Source: U.S. Bureau of the Census. *U.S. Census of Population: 1950:* Volume 2 (Washington, D.C.: Government Printing Office, 1953), Table 114, pp. 1–223 to 235 and Table 115 pp. 1–236 to 243.

[2]   Source: U.S. Bureau of the Census. *U.S. Census of Population: 1960:* Volume 1 (Washington, D.C.: U.S. Government Printing Office, 1964), Table 173, pp. 1–404 to 410.

*   1950–60 comparisons.

than males, with most differences involving a half grade or more. In 1950, these differences had declined in size, and had practically been eliminated by 1960. For college age persons, 19–24, median male achievement was practically identical to that of females in 1960, in spite of military service, work responsibilities and other demands which interrupt educational efforts for males. This fact is particularly important in terms of competing in the modern work force, since inadequate education leads to employment with less rewards, both in economic and in prestige terms.

The columns at the right in Table 5 further illustrate the recent trends in education. In every instance, median education of males increased more rapidly than that of females, and twice as rapidly at several age levels. The same trend exists for those ages with equal educational achievement in 1960, suggesting that males will receive more education than females in the coming years.

Additional data in Table 6, concerning various aspects of educational participation offer further evidence of greater male achievements. As the

Table 6.   Comparisons of educational participation for 1940, 1950, 1960 and 1964, and percent change by sex

Educational participation	1940	1950	1960	1964	Percent Change 1940–64
Instructional staffs[1]					
Percent female	77.8	78.7	71.0	68.9	− 14.9
Mean salary (1964 dollars)	3182	3922	5434	6240	+ 96.1
Enrolled in school, aged 20–24[2]					
Percent female	7.5	4.6	7.4	12.4*	+ 65.3*
Percent male	9.3	14.2	19.9	29.2*	+214.0*
Students enrolled for degree credit[3]					
Percent female	40.2	30.3	35.3	38.0	− 5.5
Faculties in institutions of higher education[3]					
Percent female	27.6	24.5	22.0	22.1	− 19.9

1   Source: U.S. Bureau of Census, *Statistical Abstract of the United States, 1967* (Washington, D.C.: Government Printing Office, 1967), No. 166, p. 120 (computed).

2   *Ibid.*, No. 151, p. 112 (computed).

3   *Ibid.*, No. 189, p. 133 (computed).

*   Data used are for 1966.

average salaries for elementary and secondary teachers have increased, the proportions of teachers that are female have declined. Despite a sizeable increase in school enrollment for females aged 20–24, the percentage increase for men for the 1940–66 period is over three times that for women. From 1940 to 1950, the data indicate that there was a sizeable relative and absolute loss for women in terms of enrollment, probably due to the postwar demands for education on the part of male veterans and the limited facilities available. However, the special deference to males during that period—to the later detriment of females—reflected a general perspective about women as being less worthy or beneficial to society than men if resources permit only one to be educated. Thus, only after a partial solution of the postwar space limitations did enrollment by women increase, though the percentage increase figures from 1950–66 mask a persistent pattern of greater relative and absolute enrollment by males.

Consistent with these interpretations, the data show a slight loss in the percentage of degree students who are females from 1940 to the present, though a gradual increase since 1950 has occurred. Finally, in terms of the faculties of institutions of higher education, females comprised a somewhat smaller proportion in 1964 than in 1940, despite the demand for teachers.

The data on education support and illustrate the earlier findings regarding the status of women. There appears to be considerable evidence that not only have women failed to achieve equality in terms of occupation and income, but in education—the one area of historic superiority— women are relatively less well off now than 25 years ago. Regardless of the type of data examined, it appears that the effects of lower educational participation, especially during the late 1940s and 1950s are currently reflected in occupational and income data. The emphasis on education for men, however, has had the effect of creating a higher level of education precisely in those areas related to greatest rewards in occupational status and income—graduate training toward professional employment.

Thus, while women presently comprise an increased proportion of college enrollments, it appears that men are becoming better educated, especially beyond the baccalaureate, making the educational data more significant for future activities. The ultimate effect is the perpetuation of the system of employment which places women in low-level occupational positions. Their earlier educational superiority eliminated, women will increasingly be forced to create alternative channels to effect meaningful

competition in the occupational sphere, or to accept the relative deprivation deriving from inferior education if out-of-home employment is
desired. This situation exists despite some current evidence which suggests
that already women are better educated, more experienced, and better
qualified than men of equal levels (Harrison, 1964. See Simon *et al.*, 1967
for an alternative view).

Discussion

Data have been presented concerning the occupational, income, and
educational levels of women compared to those of men over the past
twenty-five years. In general women's status, as defined by such measures,
appears to have declined. In the face of an official equalitarian normative
structure, and the later reinforcements of legal sanctions, what explanations can be offered to account for this evidence of apparent incremental
inequality? Further, how does one account for the persistent failure of
social science to reveal this trend?

Discrimination on the basis of sex undoubtedly does exist in the
occupational market, often motivated by the presumed rational economic
concern over the marriage-pregnancy-maternity cycle and its accompanying absenteeism, though evidence does not support this concern (Harrison,
1964; Isambert-Jamati, 1962). Married women, faced with the choice of
either accepting a position of lower skill than her preparation would
permit or pursuing her legal rights by challenging the discriminatory
employment practices encountered may seek to avoid the trouble of
prolonged suits for the smaller relative gain over not working, particularly if she is working for personal self-satisfaction rather than from
economic necessity. It is probable also that the successful professional
woman who is devoted to her career and who holds a responsible position
will consider more carefully her work relations than will the avocational,
part-time worker, and thus compensate for anticipated discrimination
by increased effort. In another sense, given the fact of marital homogamy,
the potentially successful career woman is likely to have a professional
husband, and is therefore more likely, due to income levels, to work by
choice rather than by necessity. In short, those who are most capable of
succeeding are most likely to be involved by choice, while the less well-
trained are employed by necessity. This fact mitigates against women in
the competitive milieu, and probably explains the relative increase in income for professional women with a relative loss in numbers.

Though a variety of other explanations might be offered to explain the findings and the justification for both the sources and perpetuations of this institutionalized inequality, the conservative nature of modern social science also has contributed significantly to this development, through the use of an individualistic perspective and the dominance of functionalist interpretations. By detailing sex-based social roles appropriate to the marital relationship, the family is consigned the function of reproduction and early socialization in the total scheme of a hypothetical social integration. Further, in terms of reproduction and socialization functions the family is seen largely as an agency for assuring the persistence of social patterns by socializing children to class-based age and sex roles. The significance of the family then derives from its capacity to assist the integration of society by producing persons willing to accept and adequately fill traditionally defined sex roles (the classic statement is that of Parsons and Bales, 1955. See also Mead, 1949, and for an opposing view Gilman, 1898).

This neat system of analytic categories negatively defines nontraditional behaviors, particularly as these impinge upon the perceived family function and thus the normatively defined female role is that of childbearing and childrearing. As one author (Erikson, 1964:6, italics added) recently stated it: "... since a woman is never not-a-woman, she can see her long-range goals *only* in those modes of activity which include and integrate *her natural disposition.*"

This statement may be seen as typical of those to which Alice Rossi (1964:111) referred in criticizing the use of

> selective findings in social anthropology and psychoanalytic theory (which) ... have pronounced sex to be a universally necessary basis for role differentiation in the family. By extension, in the larger society women are seen as predominantly fulfilling nurturant, expressive functions ... (and) intellectually aggressive women ... are seen as deviants showing signs of "role conflict," "role confusion," or neurotic disturbance.

As a result of the preconceptions regarding appropriate sex roles, sociologists have asserted the value and necessity of certain family structures, which, if changed, would precipitate dysfunctional consequences for the total society. The traditional family is thus justified by appeals to a normative order which defines females as complementary to males. Fulfilling maternal roles is therefore the primary and highest order if not the only appropriate behavior. Many social scientists have echoed the sentiments expressed by Pope Pius XII: "... a woman's function, a woman's way, a woman's natural bent, is motherhood. Every woman is called to be a mother" (quoted by Cervantes, 1965:361).

In general, relative to the male's exercise of wide choices, the female's alternatives to maternity and homemaking have declined in appeal and significance. Given the emphasis in our society, and especially in "scientific" marriage courses in schools and colleges upon traditionally defined sex roles and the sanctions associated with them, it is not surprising that women are ambivalent, since increased labor outside the home has been largely the consequence of an expanding demand for female labor (Oppenheimer, 1966:261). This ambivalence, however natural in the face of contradictory pressures, permits rationalization of both one's choice and one's failure to adequately prepare for either work or motherhood (Kenniston and Kenniston, 1964; Friedan, 1963; Gavron, 1966).

It is not surprising then that women generally have lower levels of educational, occupational and financial achievement. Faced with normative definitions of sex roles, buttressed by "scientific" data and the threat of dysfunctional consequences, most women pursue educational goals with less dedication than men, are thus less well prepared for the competitive market and receive lower levels of economic rewards. However, even if women were dedicated to educational goals, socialization through the educational process may effect adherence to traditional roles (Davis and Olesen, 1965). Beyond their relatively inadequate preparation, the discrimination of employers, legitimated in some measure by the normative sex-role definition, in some circumstances has forced greater efforts by women than men to achieve comparable levels of social recognition as well as occupation and even education (Harrison, 1964; Simon *et al.*, 1967).

What of the future? Given the close correlation of occupation and income with educational achievement it appears likely that women will remain in an inferior position for the next generation. Perhaps the process of achieving social equality for women is similar to that of minority groups as some authors have suggested (cf. Kirkpatrick, 1963: 163–165; Hacker, 1951). Citizenship in full then rests upon the accomplishment of rights in civil, political and social relationships, and in that order (Marshall, 1965:105). Women, having achieved some degree of equality in civil rights earlier in this century, and political rights in recent years may ultimately utilize the schools to achieve complete social equality. However, this equality is neither immediately ahead nor easily accomplished.

Summary

Data have been presented which indicate that women have experienced a gradual but persistent decline in status as measured by occupation, income, and education. The sources of this lowered status include diminished efforts by women and institutionalized discrimination, both of which derive from a normative definition of sex roles based upon functionalist assumptions and presuppositions about the nature of society and of reality. Thus, given the conviction that women should not pursue occupations in competition with men, women and employers together develop a self-fulfilling prophecy (Hodges, 1964). Women, ambivalent about careers and convinced that they will face discrimination, make lesser efforts than men, permitting employers to justify discrimination by appealing to evidence of lower achievement and commitment to employment. The effect is that perpetuation of a belief that sexual equality exists and that only effort is lacking, to which social scientists have offered their support.

References

Anonymous
    1940   Victory, How Women Won It. New York: Wilson.
Babchuck, Nicholas, and Alan P. Bates
    1963   "The Primary Relations of Middle-Class Couples: A Study in Male Dominance." American Sociological Review 28(June): 377—384.
Cervantes, Lucius
    1965   "Woman's Changing Role in Society." Thought 60 (Autumn): 325—368.
Davis, Fred, and Virginia L. Olesen
    1965   "The Career Outlook of Professionally Educated Women." Psychiatry 28(November): 335—345.
Erikson, Erik H.
    1964   "Inner and Outer Space: Reflections on Womanhood." Daedalus 93(Spring): 1:26.
Friedan, Betty
    1963   The Feminine Mystique. New York: Dell.
Gavron, Hannah
    1966   The Captive Wife. London: Routledge & Kegan Paul.
Gilman, Charlotte P.
    1898   Women and Economics. Small, Maynard; republished. New York: Harper & Row, 1966.
Gordon, Milton M.
    1963   Social Class in American Sociology. New York: McGraw-Hill.

Hacker, Helen
  1951   "Women as a Minority Group." *Social Forces* 30(October): 60—69.
Harrison, Evelyn
  1964   "The Working Woman: Barriers in Employment." *Public Administration Review* 24(June): 78—85.
Hodges, Harold M.
  1964   *Social Stratification.* Cambridge: Schenkman.
Interdepartmental Committee on the Status of Women
  1966   *Report on Progress in 1966 on the Status of Women.* Washington, D.C.: Government Printing Office.
Isambert-Jamati, Vivian
  1962   "Absenteeism Among Women Workers in Industry." *International Labor Review* 85(March): 248—261.
Kenniston, Kenneth, and Ellen Kenniston
  1964   "An American Anachronism: The Image of Women and Men." *American Scholar* 33(Summer): 355—375.
Kirkpatrick, Clifford
  1963   *The Family.* 2d ed.; New York: Ronald Press.
Laswell, Thomas
  1965   *Class and Stratum.* Boston: Houghton Mifflin.
Marshall, T. H.
  1965   *Class, Citizenship and Social Development.* New York: Anchor Books.
Mead, Margaret
  1949   *Male and Female.* New York: Morrow.
Nye, F. Ivan, and Lois W. Hoffman
  1963   *Employed Women in America.* Chicago: Rand McNally.
Oppenheimer, Valerie Kincade
  1966   "The Female Labor Force in the United States: Factors Governing Its Growth and Changing Composition." Unpublished Ph.D. dissertation, University of California, Berkeley.
Parsons, Talcott, and Robert Bales
  1955   *Family, Socialization and Interaction Process.* Glencoe: Free Press.
Rossi, Alice M.
  1964   "Equality Between the Sexes: An Immodest Proposal." *Daedalus* 93(Spring): 98—143.
Simon, Rita J., *et al.*
  1967   "The Woman Ph.D.: A Recent Profile." *Social Problems* 15(Fall): 221—236.
U.S. Department of Commerce. Bureau of Census
  1960   *Characteristics of the Population.* Washington, D.C.: Government Printing Office: Table 202:1—528.
U.S. Department of Labor, Women's Bureau
  1964   *Job Horizons for College Women in the 1960s.* Bulletin 288.

1. An example of assumed near equality over 20 years ago is contained in the volume *Victory, How Women Won It* (Anonymous, 1940). In the foreword it is stated: "The Century from 1840 to 1940 may appropriately be called the Woman's Century.... In 1840 for the first time women proposed to unite, organize and to remove their grievances. In 1940 this aim with slight exceptions has been eliminated."

2. While the argument may be offered that status for women is based on noncomparable factors, such as effectiveness in childbearing, homemaking and other "feminine" capacities, such interpretations overlook several dimensions of the concept of status or prestige. First, as discussed above, status is not an appropriate term for such concerns, since the term itself implies comparability and relative evaluation. Second, neither professional nor popular literature typically refers to such behaviors as the basis for determining status in discussions of status changes. Third, such interpretations often are associated with efforts to obscure or justify the low status of women by an appeal to a natural predisposition or biological determinism.

3. Of necessity status is operationally defined in this paper in terms of the three easily measured variables usually associated with social class—occupation, income, and education. At issue in this discussion is the nature of changes in the general position of women relative to men, in the opportunity structure of our society and in the relative number and range of alternatives for life choices. Thus status, while conceptually including prestige, esteem, honor, and deference, frequently is empirically equated with social class because of the difficulty in measurement of such variables. No recent studies which compare males and females in terms of prestige or esteem, e.g., relative proportions which would have preferred to be born the opposite sex, etc., are known to the author. Consequently, status-related variables—not status itself—are being discussed in an effort to identify the process of change.

4. No effort here is being made to justify greater rewards for more important work in the society in terms of the functionalist argument. However, the rather close correlation of education, occupation and income is evidence that in general greater rewards accrue to higher-status occupations which are related to greater education.

5. An alternative approach to employment by occupation is that of industrial categories. When data are examined by industry, only two categories show a relatively greater female income in 1965 compared to 1940. Personal services had a net gain of slightly over 1 percent and public administration had an increase of $\frac{1}{2}$ or 1 percent. All others showed sizeable decreases, from 5 to 15 percent. The negative correlation is strong here as well, with those industries having the largest relative increase in numbers having the greatest relative loss in income.

Elizabeth Fisher/The Second Sex, Junior Division

Since most of the attitudes we hold as adults are formed during our childhood, it is relevant to examine here how females are portrayed in children's
books, especially the picture books. Elizabeth Fisher compares children's
books in terms of the portrayed characteristics, rights, and duties of males
as compared to those of the female. The argument she sets out to develop
and prove is that children are conditioned, through children's books, into
accepting the idea that men are superior to women, that boys are brought
up to express themselves and girls to please; that men have specified roles
which are different from the roles of women. Miss Fisher contends that
"the task of bringing women up to full human status is not going to be
easy. To start here, however, at the earliest years, should bring results."

We live in a sexist society. Almost from birth we are indoctrinated with
the notion of male superiority and female inferiority, male rights and
female duties. It is in the earliest years that children form images of their
worth, their future roles, the conscious and unconscious expectations
placed upon them. Investigating books for young children in book stores
and libraries I found an almost incredible conspiracy of conditioning.
Boys' achievement drive is encouraged; girls' is cut off. Boys are brought
up to express themselves; girls to please. The general image of the female
ranges from dull to degrading to invisible.

Since females comprise 51 per cent of the population of the United
States, one would expect them to be equally represented in the world of
picture books. On the contrary they vary between 20 and 30 percent. There
were five times as many males in the titles as there were females, four
times as many boys, men, or male animals pictured as there were females.
In special displays the situation was even worse. The fantasy worlds of
Maurice Sendak and Dr. Seuss are almost entirely male. The three major
prizewinners for this year, displayed together on a table at Brentano's,
were all about males: "Sounder" about a black boy by William Armstrong,
"A Day of Pleasure" by I. B. Singer, and "Sylvester and the Magic Pebble"
by William Steig. Where are all the missing females? Have they been

exposed to the elements, as with primitive tribes? Or are they sequestered behind walls, as in Southern Italy or the Near East?

This preponderance of males is not limited to humans. Animals in books are male for the most part. Elephants, bears, lions, tigers are males or, as in the Babar books, isolated females are shown in the company of a majority of males. In the veld it is the female lion who does all the work; in the picture-book world she doesn't exist. There are some books about female animals, and an occasional reference to the female of the species. Cows, obviously, are female. Hens, too. In "Rosie's Walk" by Pat Hutchins a hen walks unscathed and unnoticing through all kinds of dangers—re-enforcing the stereotype that nothing ever happens to she's. Sylvia the Sloth is the heroine of a not unpleasing book. Somehow the female animals tend to be those whose names are synonyms of derogation. Petunia the Goose, Frances the Badger—I suspect the choice of these animals reflects the low esteem in which women are held. A rhinoceros is male, a hippopotamus female. Leo Lionni's snail in "The Biggest House in the World" is a he who has a father but no mother, in clear controversion of biology.

Only in Noah's Ark does Biblical authority enforce equal representation for males and females. Except for Random House's "Pop-up Noah," which has eliminated Mrs. Noah and does not show the animals in equal distribution on the cover—males have a slight edge of course. The wives of Ham, Shem and Japheth, present in the Old Testament, were missing from all three children's versions I examined. Things have come to a pretty pass when one has to go to the Old Testament for an upgrading of the female.

It should be mentioned that folk tales tend to treat women somewhat better than do books with contemporary settings. Possibly this is because the former are often based on themes of come-uppance and vindication of the underdog, spontaneous products of wish fulfillment and the unconscious, while the latter are written to please or to sell. After all, although Hansel comes up with the device of dropping pebbles so that he and Gretel can find their way home, it is Gretel who disposes of the witch by pushing her into the oven. Wives are smarter than their husbands, and women make fools of the powerful. The folk tales reflect a pre-industrial culture where, though women may not have had equality, they did play vital functioning roles. They were not consuming or sexual objects, justified only by motherhood, as today's world all too often defines them. They were producers who functioned in agriculture and home industries such as spinning and weaving, who worked side by side with their men. Evidently the folk tales survive because they have certain psychological validities.

In the more modern downgrading of the female, not only are animals generally male, but personifications of the inanimate—machines, boats, engines, tractors, trains, automobiles—are almost invariably so. In life, ships are she's; in picture books—Little Toot, Max's boat Max in "Where the Wild Things Are"—I have yet to come across one that was not a he. Automobiles, at least in France where the Citroen D. S. 19 (*déesse*—goddess) is highly admired, are often thought of as feminine, but not by picture-book authors and illustrators. One exception to the masculinity of machines was written back in 1939 when Virginia Lee Burton created Mike Mulligan and his steam shovel Mary Anne.

This marked absence of the female applies even more strongly to books about blacks. Analogies between racism and sexism date back before the 19th century: both Mary Wollstonecraft and Thomas Paine compare black slavery to female slavery. In this country the woman's rights movement of the 19th century grew out of the Abolitionist movement, as today's Women's Liberation Movement relates to the Civil Rights Movement. History repeats itself. Just as black men achieved enfranchisement long before black or white women, so in the picture-book world have blacks achieved integration with whites and representation for themselves without a corresponding integration for the female, black or white. One of the earliest efforts in this direction was Jerrold Beim's "Swimming Hole" about black and white boys swimming together, and since then there have been a spate of books about blacks and whites and about blacks alone. But the only picture book I found about a black girl was Jacob Lawrence's "Harriet and the Promised Land" based on Harriet Tubman's life. Ezra Jack Keats has done several picture books about small boys, and a recent one of his, "A Letter to Amy," does bring in a girl, but in a token and not altogether flattering way. Peter is bringing Amy a letter to invite her, the only girl, to his birthday party, when he bumps into her accidentally. Amy runs away in tears. Later, the other boys say, "Ugh! A girl at the party!" but she comes anyway. One little girl can make it in a group of boys, from Robin Hood's Maid Marian on down through the centuries, but she'd better know her place.

Virginia Woolf pointed out that throughout literature women were generally shown only in relation to men, and this is still true in the picture-book world. Friendship between boys is much touted; friendship between boys and girls is frequent; but friendship between girls gets less attention, though surely this is a norm in life. The frequent depiction of one girl in a group of boys would seem to represent wish fulfillment for girls as well as boys. A boy is considered unmanly in a group of females, but a girl who achieves acceptance in a group of boys has evidently raised herself, the exception that proves the rule of general female inferiority.

Since there are so few females in the picture-book world, one would think they'd be very busy, but such is not the case. What they do is highly limited; more to the point is the sheer unreality of what they do not do. They do not drive cars. Though children see their mothers driving all the time, not a single description or picture of a woman driver could I find. In the world today women are executives, jockeys, stockbrokers, taxi-drivers, steelworkers, in picture books these are nonexistent.

Little girls in picture books tend to be passive, though sometimes manipulative. They walk, read, or dream. They seldom ride bicycles; if they do, it is seated behind a boy as in Dr. Seuss's "One Fish, Two Fish, Red Fish, Blue Fish." When I came across a little girl sailing paper boats in a book by Uri Shulevitz, I was overwhelmed with gratefulness. And the same might be said for my responses to Suzuki Beane and Eloise, both of whom are presented as highly exceptional.

Though there have been women doctors in this country for over a hundred years, and pediatrics is one of their preferred specialties, there is not a single woman doctor to be found. Women are nurses, librarians, teachers—but the principal is always male. They have emotions; they get angry; they disagree; they smile; they approve or disapprove; they want to please. What they do not do is act. Boys do; girls are—a highly artificial and unsatisfactory dichotomy.

In a country where over 40 percent of the women work, I know of only one picture book about working mothers, Eve Merriam's "Mommies at Work." But it wasn't in stock in any of the book stores I visited. However, while commendable—there are Mommies who split atoms, build bridges, direct TV shows, who are dancers, teachers, writers and doctors— it is also highly apologetic. The end, "all Mommies loving *the best of all* to be your very own Mommy and coming home to you," (my italics) gives it away. We don't feel the need to say about Daddy that he loves his children more than his work. Couldn't Mommy matter-of-factly like working and baby, too, as I'm sure many do?

No boys and girls must get the message—it's all right to work, but only if your work is subordinated to your role as mother. What does it matter that that will last twenty years and the rest of your life may well be spent as supernumerary, doing some kind of busy work? Or semitrained and at the bottom of the labor heap? This is the kind of contradiction that produces guilt and neurotic conflicts in mothers, fathers, and children, instead of the simple sharing we could achieve if men and women were taught to expand their roles.

A few other books, selected not entirely at random, will show some of the methods by which children are indoctrinated at an early age with stereotypes about male activity and female passivity, male involvement with things, women's with emotions, male dominance and female subordination. "A Tree Is Nice" by Janice Udry, illustrated by Marc Simont, seemingly innocent, is actually devastating when analyzed with an aware eye: a boy is high up in a tree balancing while a girl is on the ground watching. Successive pages show a boy fishing, a boy rolling in leaves, and another holding a rake, while a big girl leading a small boy walks by. Then a double-page spread with a huge tree in the center pictures seven boys and three girls. One of the latter is on the ground, helping a little boy up into the tree; the other two are on low limbs close in to the main trunk. The boys are shown adventuring, one hanging from a rope, the other five climbing way out or high up. Other pictures show a boy drawing in the sand, a boy in a tree, and boys planting trees. Note that there are 19 boys pictured to eight girls.

Another seemingly innocent book is William Steig's "CDB," a clever pun-puzzle book with pictures captioned by dialogue in letters. This is a funny book but implicit attitudes about girls and women are revealed. There are twice as many pictures of boys as girls in the book, and the girls tend to be passive or helpers. When they do anything, they do it badly or are discomfitted. A boy is shown on skates; the girl has fallen down. A girl turns a somersault, but it doesn't agree with her, she is dizzy. A girl dancing in a field of flowers is an exception and, giddy from the unusual activity, she is in ecstacy. There are angry females, several of them, but no angry males. Male work is respected; a boy tells a man writing at a desk, "If you're busy, I'll run away." Women are never shown in this context; they are at everybody's service. A woman tells fortunes—the supernatural has offered one of the few exciting outlets for women down through the ages, and witches are still making it, in and out of the Women's Liberation Movement.

One of the worst offenders in this brainwashing about roles and expectations has, perhaps, the most influence—Richard Scarry. His "Best

Word Book Ever" is a big illustrated dictionary with the Scarry trademark, humanized animals, demonstrating meanings and activities. Scarry's male-female divisions are scarifying: many more males, naturally, but they *really* do get to do everything. Toys, for example, are defined by showing 13 male animals playing with exciting toys—a tricycle, blocks, castle, scooter and rocking horse, as well as the traditional toy soldiers and electric trains. Two female animals play with a tea set and a doll! In the Scarry orchestra, out of 28 animals playing instruments, the two females were assigned those drawing-room clichés, the piano and the harp. The percentage in the New York Philharmonic is no better, but at least there the women play cello and bass viol. Many pages had only males as pro-tagonists, but the one page which showed only women was . . . what else? "In the Kitchen." The most infuriating page was entitled "Things We Do." Males in Scarry's book world dig, build, break, push, pull and do 15 other active things, including eat. The only two things females do are watch and sit.

What kind of world will a little girl educated on Scarry expect to grow into? It's a meager, thankless, and unrewarding prospect. No wonder both boys and girls identify with the boy's role in life.

Particularly sad is the realization that these books are perpetrated by women as well as men—women authors, illustrators and children's book editors. There are very good reasons why women so often "fawn like the spaniel"—the phrase is Mary Wollstonecraft's—but isn't it about time we stopped? It's true that till now men have had all the power, and in a world steeped in patriarchy, women internalize the notion of female inferiority and transmit it to the next generation, perpetuating the cycle. But aware-ness is upon us. The task of bringing women up to full human status is not going to be easy. To start here, however, at the earliest years, should bring results.

Protests about the retrograde situation have already risen in the Women's Liberation Movement, including an article in the first issue of Women: A Journal of Liberation. Women active in the movement are writing new children's books. A conference is planned to educate children's book editors. Several groups have protested primary-school textbooks and "Sesame Street" to some effect. The quarterly Aphra dedicates part of each issue to feminist criticism of various aspects of our culture, with articles on child-care books and children's television in prospect. As the move-ment grows, so will the protests. Editors and authors take note. Better meet change now, head on, than be forced into it or bypassed later on.

Faith A. Seidenberg / The Submissive Majority: Modern Trends in the Law Concerning Women's Rights

In the following selection, Faith Seidenberg reviews some of the laws which have discriminated against women. The article demonstrates how women have systematically been denied equal protection of the laws and at the same time indicates that within the past few years there has been "a small beginning towards equal rights." The laws regarding the rights and duties of women have not only led to institutionalized sexism, but "the law, it seems, has done little but perpetuate the myth of the helpless female best kept on her pedestal. In truth, however, that pedestal is a cage bound by a constricting social system and hemmed in by layers of archaic and antifeminist laws." Leo Kanowitz's *Women and the Law* (University of New Mexico Press, 1969) is recommended for a much longer treatment of the legal discriminations against women and the history and development of the discriminatory laws.

The popular assumption that the law is even-handed does not hold true in the area of women's rights. Under the guise of paternalism (and you notice the word refers to a father), women have systematically been denied the equal protection of laws. Recently, however, there has been an upsurge of the feminist movement, and men are being forced to take a second look at some of the paternalistic laws they have propounded. Although challenge to the laws adversely affecting women is presently at about the same stage that civil rights movement occupied in the 1930s, in the last few years there has nevertheless been a small beginning towards equal rights.

I / Criminal Law

The idea that a "bad" woman is much worse than a "bad" man probably can be traced to the witch hunts that took place in the early days of the American Colonies; however, it survives to the present day. For example, it is a crime for a woman to engage in prostitution[1] but not for her customer

Seidenberg, "The Submissive Majority: Modern Trends in the Law Concerning Women's Rights," 55 *Cornell Law Review* 262 (1970). Copyright 1970 by Cornell University. Reprinted by permission of the author and publisher.

to use her services. She is breaking the law, it seems, while he is only doing what comes naturally. However, in *City of Portland v. Sherill*[2] a city ordinance that punished women but not men who offered themselves for immoral purposes was held unconstitutional.

In addition, in several states higher penalties are imposed on a woman who commits a crime than on a man who commits the same crime.[3] The constitutionality of greater penalties for women was recently challenged in two cases. In *Commonwealth v. Daniels*[4] a woman was first sentenced to a term of from one to four years for the crime of robbery; one month later the sentence was vacated and the defendant resentenced to up to ten years under Pennsylvania's Muncy Act.[5] The Muncy Act provided that a woman imprisoned for a crime "punishable by imprisonment for more than a year" should be sentenced to an indeterminate period of up to three years except when the crime for which she was sentenced had a maximum of more than three years, in which case she had to receive the maximum sentence. That is, for a crime carrying a sentence of one to ten years, a man might have been sentenced to one to four years, but a woman could only be sentenced to an indefinite term of up to ten years. The discretion of the trial judge to set a maximum term for a woman of less than the maximum for the crime involved was thereby eliminated. The Superior Court of Pennsylvania affirmed the trial court's action, holding that longer incarceration for women is justifiable because of "the physiological and psychological make-up of women ... their roles in society [and] their unique vocational skills and pursuits...."[6] Whatever their significance, these characteristics did not convince the Pennsylvania Supreme Court that the Muncy Act's classification was reasonable. The court held that women are entitled to the protection afforded by the equal protection clause of the United States Constitution and, since the maximum sentence is the real sentence, that a sentence of ten years for women as opposed to four years for men is unconstitutional.[7] In *United States ex rel. Robinson v. York*[8] a federal district court held a Connecticut statute[9] similar to the Muncy Act unconstitutional. The decision was appealed by the state's Attorney General, but he withdrew the appeal after the decision came down in the *Daniels* case. Sixteen women, who had already served more time than a man's maximum sentence, were released.[10]

Criminal abortion statutes[11] are another example of the law's discrimination against women. That a woman has a right to control her own body is perhaps an idea whose time has yet to come, but there is at least a glimmering in some legal minds. Most lawyers and legislators, if they are talking about the subject at all, are still talking in terms of abortion reform instead of abortion repeal.[12] They discuss a need for change, but they sound a cautious note.[13] One case moving against the prevailing winds, however, is *People v. Belous*,[14] recently decided in the Supreme Court of California. The defendant was convicted for performing an abortion, and an amicus curiae counsel argued that

> [t]he right of reproductive autonomy sought to be protected here is clearly more basic and essential to a woman's dignity, self-respect and personal freedom than those personal rights . . . for which Constitutional protection has already been afforded. Probably, nothing except death itself can affect a woman's life more seriously than enforced bearing of children and enforced responsibility for them for perhaps the remainder of her and their lives. The choice must be that of the woman unless some overwhelming state interest requires otherwise, and those state interests generally adverted to will be shown below to be significantly, for constitutional purposes, less important than the interest of the woman herself. That right should be protected to the fullest by a holding that no state interest can control this field.[15]

In New York two bills, one for reform of abortion[16] and one for repeal,[17] were before the state legislature in the spring of 1969. Only the former had any chance of passing. Had it not been for the National Organization for Women's coming out strongly in 1968 for abortion repeal,[18] followed by agreement by the State Council of Churches[19] and the American Civil Liberties Union[20] on this position, the bills would probably not have been considered at all. However, as is beginning to be seen in California, where the abortion laws were just reformed,[21] abortion reform is worse from the standpoint of freedom of choice for the woman than no reform at all.[22]

II / Civil Rights

For untold years there have been so-called "protective" laws regulating the working conditions of women. Necessary changes are beginning to be made, but the progress is slow; even legal experts do not always recognize the full dimensions of the problem. One commentator, for example, has remarked of women's working laws:

> With regard to social policy, the initial reaction is that the modern woman should not be subjected to state protective restrictions on her right to work should she choose to experience the conditions from which she is being protected. However, it is clear that the extent to which sex differences con-

stitute "discrimination" is a question of degree, depending upon what social mores it seems desirable to perpetuate.... [Here], *considerations of preserving femininity and motherhood appear.*[23]

Unfortunately, this misses the point. The net effect of these laws is to limit the advancement of women in industry and, since women are everywhere the majority, to ensure that there is always a large supply of poorly-paid persons.

California has a particularly stringent system of governing women's employment. Section 1350 of the California Labor Code[24] for example, prohibits an employer from employing women workers for more than eight hours a day or forty-eight hours a week. The effect of this restriction is to prevent women, solely because of their sex, from pursuing certain better-paid occupations, such as running test equipment, doing final assembly work, and working as supervisors, and from earning overtime pay in the positions they now hold. In addition, paragraph 17 of the California Industrial Welfare Commission's Order No. 9—68[25] not only regulates wages, hours, and working conditions of women and minors in the transportation industry but also limits the number of pounds a woman may lift to twenty-five.

This regulatory system was recently challenged. In *Mengelkoch v. Industrial Welfare Commission*[26] plaintiffs asked that a three-judge court be convened because the constitutionality of section 1350 was an important constitutional issue to be resolved. The request was denied. However, in a similar case, *Rosenfeld v. Southern Pacific Co.*,[27] the judge ruled in favor of plaintiff. This case concerned both section 1350 and paragraph 17. In it, plaintiff, a woman, applied for a job that had just opened up at the defendant company's facilities at Thermal, California. Although she was the most senior employee bidding for the position and was fully qualified, the company assigned a male with less seniority than plaintiff. The company never tested or evaluated plaintiff's ability to perform the work required, but argued that the appointment was within its discretion as an employer and, since plaintiff was a woman, that her assignment to the position would violate the California Labor Code. The court, however, held both that the California hours and weights legislation discriminates against women and is therefore unconstitutional and that defendant's refusal to assign plaintiff to Thermal was not a lawful exercise of its discretion as an employer.

Restrictions on the amount of weight a woman can legally lift[28] are under attack in other states. An employer's thirty-five pound limitation[29] was tested in *Bowe v. Colgate-Palmolive Co.*,[30] where the court held it legal and proper for an employer to fix a thirty-five pound maximum weight for carrying or lifting by female employees. In another case, *Weeks v. Southern Bell Telephone & Telegraph Co.*,[31] defendant company took the position that because the job of switchman required lifting weight in excess of thirty pounds, the legal limit in Georgia,[32] a woman could not hold the job. The company conceded that plaintiff had seniority over the male awarded the position and that she was paid $78 per week as opposed to the $135 she would receive if she were a switchman. The sole issue in the case was whether or not sex is a bona fide occupational qualification, entitling defendant to bar a woman, as such, from consideration for the job of switchman, her capacities notwithstanding. The lower court held for defendant, but the Fifth Circuit reversed, finding illegal discrimination based on sex.

Segregated "help wanted" advertisements are another aspect of discrimination against women. Although the Civil Rights Act of 1964 forbids most such ads to be placed in newspapers[33] and forbids discrimination by sex in employment, the Equal Employment Opportunity Commission guidelines[34] nonetheless allowed two columns classified by sex to stand in the newspapers. In July 1968, therefore, the National Organization for Women brought a mandamus suit against the EEOC to compel it to enforce the law as written. The court summarily dismissed the complaint, saying that obviously some jobs were better suited to men and others to women,[35] but the suit did cause the EEOC to change its guidelines to conform with the law.[36] The American Newspaper Publishers Association brought an action to enjoin enforcement of the guidelines;[37] both the district court and the court of appeals found for the EEOC. However, although the *New York Times* and some other New York newspapers have now desegregated their want ads, most newspapers around the country still refuse to abide by the law.

The public accommodations section[38] of the Civil Rights Act of 1964, unlike the employment section, does not forbid discrimination on account of sex. A test case[39] was recently brought in New York against a Syracuse hotel that does not allow women to sit at the bar unescorted, and the action was dismissed. The court emphasized, first, that there was no state action, since the women who sat in at the bar were not arrested; and second, because the public accommodation law does not forbid discrimination on the basis of sex, that the hotel could discriminate if it so wished.[40]

The case was not appealed because the author, whose case it was, thought it would be relatively easy to obtain state action in an arrest. Accordingly, she and another member of the National Organization for Women sat in at several bars, including one in New York City that has not served women for the last one hundred and fourteen years. Although they suffered many indignities, they were not arrested. The author then decided to bring an action in a New York state court under a new section of the state civil rights law[41] that makes it illegal to refuse to serve a customer "without just cause." Summary judgment was granted to defendants and the case was dismissed. The author filed a third case, however, that was heard on August 6, 1969 and that was decided in favor of plaintiff.

III / Private Law

Some colleges have strict rules covering the hours when coeds must be in their dormitories and an inflexible system of signing in and out.[42] Regulation is the product of the idea that a university stands *in loco parentis* to its students, an idea that is hopefully changing. After all, a married woman of eighteen is considered to be "emancipated" from her parents under the law.[43] Why then is a college student living away from home not equally adult? But in any case, the rationale is not consistently applied; male students are not subjected to the same restrictions as women in the use of the dormitories, or even to the requirement that they live on campus. The Oneonta College curfew was challenged, but the case was dismissed on technical grounds without examination of the merits. Possibly because of the suit, however, the college voluntarily rescinded its curfew regulations,[44] so the students were the ultimate winners.

A double standard is also apparent in the law governing married women. Under present law, a married woman loses her name and becomes lost in the anonymity of her husband's name. Her domicile is his no matter where she lives,[45] which means she cannot vote or run for office in her place of residence if her husband lives elsewhere. If she wants an annulment and is over eighteen, in certain cases she cannot get one,[46] but her husband can until he is twenty-one.[47] In practice, if not in theory, she cannot contract for any large amount, borrow money, or get a credit card in her own name. She is, in fact, a non-person with no name.

Women receive little in exchange for this loss of status. Although in theory the husband and wife are one person, the relationship "has worked out in reality to mean . . . the one is the husband."[48] For example, husband and wife do not have equal rights to consortium,[49] the exclusive right to the services of the spouse and to his or her society, companionship, and conjugal affection.[50] Until recently it was everywhere the law that only the husband could recover for loss of consortium, and this is still the law in about two-thirds of the states.[51] The major breakthrough came in 1950 in *Hitaffer v. Argonne Co.*,[52] which reversed the prevailing rule. In a more recent case, *Karczewski v. Baltimore & O.R.R.*,[53] the court concluded, "[m]arriage is no longer viewed as a 'master-servant relationship,'"[54] and in *Owen v. Illinois Baking Corp.*[55] the court held that denying a wife the right to sue for loss of consortium while permitting such suit to a husband violates the equal protection clause.[56]

The unreasonableness of denying an action for loss of consortium to the wife is well expressed by Michigan Supreme Court Justice Smith:

> The gist of the matter is that in today's society the wife's position is analogous to that of a partner, neither kitchen slattern nor upstairs maid. Her duties and responsibilities in respect of the family unit complement those of the husband, extending only to another sphere. In the good times she lights the hearth with her own inimitable glow. But when tragedy strikes it is a part of her unique glory that, forsaking the shelter, the comfort, and warmth of the home, she puts her arm and shoulder to the plow. We are now at the heart of the issue. In such circumstances, when her husband's love is denied her, his strength sapped, and his protection destroyed, in short, when she has been forced by the defendant to exchange a heart for a husk, we are urged to rule that she has suffered no loss compensable at the law. But let some scoundrel dent a dishpan in the family kitchen and the law, in all its majesty, will convene the court, will march with measured tread to the halls of justice, and will there suffer a jury of her peers to assess the damages. Why are we asked, then, in the case before us, to look the other way? Is this what is meant when it is said that justice is blind?[57]

Conclusion

In theory all persons should be equal, but in practice women are less "equal" than men. In all phases of life women are second-class citizens leading legally sanctioned second-rate lives. The law, it seems, has done little but perpetuate the myth of the helpless female best kept on her pedestal. In truth, however, that pedestal is a cage bound by a constricting social system and hemmed in by layers of archaic and anti-feminist laws.

Notes

The author is President, Syracuse Chapter of National Organization for Women. B.A. 1944, J.D. 1954, Syracuse University.

1. See *The Social Evil* (Seligman ed. 1902); George, "Legal, Medical and Psychiatric Considerations in the Control of Prostitution," 60 *Mich. L. Rev.* 717 (1962).

2. No. M-47623 (Circuit Ct., Multnomah County, Ore., Jan. 9, 1967).

3. E.g., Pennsylvania, Connecticut. See statutes upheld in *Ex parte* Gosselin, 141 Me. 412, 44 A.2d 882 (1945); Platt v. Commonwealth, 256 Mass. 539, 152 N.E. 914 (1926).

4. 210 Pa. Super. 156, 232 A.2d 247 (1967).

5. *Pa. Stat.* tit. 61, § 566 (1964), *as amended* (Supp. 1969).

6. 210 Pa. Super. at 164, 232 A.2d at 252. The philosophy of the statute is more cogently, if not convincingly, explained as follows:

   > There is little doubt in the minds of those who have had much experience in dealing with women delinquents, that the fundamental fact is that they belong to a class of women who lead sexually immoral lives. . . .
   >
   > [Such a statute] would remove permanently from the community the feeble-minded delinquents who are now generally recognized as a social menace, and would relieve the state from the ever increasing burden of the support of their illegitimate children.

   Commonwealth v. Daniels, 210 Pa. Super. 156, 171 n.2, 232 A.2d 247, 255 n.2 (1967) (dissenting opinion). Oddly enough, the material quoted from the *Daniels* case was supplied by Philadelphia District Attorney Arlen Specter in a brief urging the *un*constitutionality of the Muncy Act.

7. 430 Pa. 642, 243 A.2d 400 (1968). Shortly thereafter the Pennsylvania legislature enacted a statute that required the court to set a maximum sentence, but prohibited it from setting a minimum term. *Pa. Stat.* tit. 61, § 566 (Supp. 1969).

8. 281 F. Supp. 8 (D. Conn. 1968).

9. *Conn. Gen. Stat. Ann.* § 17—360 (1958).

10. Middletown Press, Aug. 12, 1968, at 1, col. 1 (Middletown, Connecticut).

11. E.g., *Cal. Penal Code* § 274 (West 1955). Prior to its liberalization in 1967, it was similar to statutes in 41 other jurisdictions, Leavy & Kummer, "Criminal Abortion: A Failure of Law," 50 *A.B.A.J.* 52 n.2 (1964).

12. But see Brief for Appellant as Amicus Curiae at 37—38, People v. Belous, 71 Cal. 2d 996, 458 P.2d 194, 80 Cal. Rptr. 354 (1969), reporting that Father Robert Drinan, Dean of Boston College Law School, has come out for

repeal on the grounds that it should be a matter of individual conscience, not law.

13. See, e.g., L. Kanowitz, *Women and the Law: The Unfinished Revolution* 27 (1969):

> Though very few people would urge the legalization of all abortions, the principle of legal equality of the sexes is an additional reason for extending the circumstances under which therapeutic abortions should be legally justified.

14. 71 Cal. 2d 996, 458 P.2d 194, 80 Cal. Rptr. 354 (1969).

15. *Belous* Brief, *supra* note 12, at 10−11 (footnotes omitted).

16. (1969) Assy. Int. No. 3473-A (Mr. Blumenthal).

17. (1969) Assy. Int. No. 1061 (Mrs. Cook).

18. *See* 2 *NOW Acts* 14 (Winter-Spring 1969).

19. New York State Council of Churches Leg. Release No. 8 (Feb. 10, 1969).

20. American Civil Liberties Union Release (March 25, 1968).

21. *Cal. Penal Code* § 274 (West Supp. 1968).

22. Two actions were just filed in New York to have that state's abortion statutes declared unconstitutional. *N.Y. Times*, Oct. 8, 1969, at 53, col. 1; *id.*, Oct. 1, 1969, at 55, col. 3.

23. Oldham, "Sex Discrimination and State Protective Laws," 44 *Denver L. Rev.* 344, 375 (1967) (emphasis added). But see R. Seidenberg, "Our Outraged Remnant," 6 *Psychiatric Opinion*, Oct. 1969, at 18:

> The exaggeration of the difference between the sexes has been used to justify misogyny. Our young people want to make it difficult to distinguish between the sexes to show that everything feminine is not contemptible. One can wear long hair proudly; to be taken for a woman is not something to despair. Make the sexes undifferentiated, and then, perhaps, the mythology of "feminine" and "masculine" will be revealed for what it really is—a ruse to keep women subjugated and to guarantee men an unearned superiority.

24. *Cal. Labor Code* § 1350 (West Supp. 1968):

> No female shall be employed in any manufacturing, mechanical, or mercantile establishment or industry, laundry, . . . cleaning and dyeing establishment, hotel, public lodging house . . . in this state, more than eight hours during any one day of 24 hours or more than 48 hours in one week. . . .

Females covered by the Fair Labor Standards Act, however, are exempt from the prohibitions of § 1350. *Id.* § 1350.5.

25. *Cal. Admin. Code* tit. 8, § 11460 (1968). The division of public welfare is given specific enforcement power of § 1350. *Cal. Labor Code* § 1356 (West Supp. 1968).

26. 284 F. Supp. 950 (C.D. Cal.), *vacated*, 393 U.S. 993 (1968).

27. 293 F. Supp. 1219 (C.D. Cal. 1968).

28. The typical restriction to 30 or 35 pounds is ironic if the goal is to preserve the femininity of women laborers; mothers commonly lift their children until they are 6 or 7 years old, when they weigh at least 70 pounds.

29. Originally instituted because of substantial female employment during World War II, this practice continued even when the men returned to work. Bowe v. Colgate-Palmolive Co., 272 F. Supp. 332, 340 (S.D. Ind. 1967).

30. 272 F. Supp. 332 (S.D. Ind. 1967). The provision was also challenged in Sellers v. Colgate-Palmolive Co., — F.2d — (7th Cir. 1969), which held in favor of the plaintiffs.

     The *Bowe* court did hold, however, that use of a seniority list segregated by sex, which resulted in certain female employees being laid off from employment while males with less plant seniority were retained, resulted in discrimination in violation of the 1964 Civil Rights Act. 272 F. Supp. at 359.

31. 408 F.2d 228 (5th Cir. 1969).

32. Rule 59, promulgated by Georgia Commissioner of Labor, pursuant to *Ga. Code Ann.* § 54–122(d) (1961): "[f]or women and minors, not over 30 pounds." A more flexible rule, setting no specific limitations, replaced Rule 59 in 1968. *See* 408 F.2d at 233.

33. Civil Rights Act of 1964, § 704(b), 78 Stat. 257, 42 U.S.C. § 2000e-3(b) (1964):

     > It shall be an unlawful employment practice for an employer, labor organization, or employment agency to print or publish or cause to be printed or published any notice or advertisement relating to employment by such an employer or membership in or any classification or referral for employment by such a labor organization, or relating to any classification or referral for employment by such an employment agency, indicating any preference, limitation, specification, or discrimination, based on race, color, religion, sex, or national origin, except that such a notice or advertisement may indicate a preference, limitation, specification, or discrimination based on religion, sex, or national origin when religion, sex, or national origin is a bona fide occupational qualification for employment.

34. 31 Fed. Reg. 6414 (1966).

35. The court pointed out that secretaries are obviously female, despite the presence in front of the bench of the male stenographer.

36. 29 C.F.R. § 1604.4 (1969).

37. American Newspaper Pub. Ass'n v. Alexander, 294 F. Supp. 1100 (D.D.C. 1968).

38. 42 U.S.C. § 2000a (1964).

39. DeCrow v. Hotel Syracuse Corp., 288 F. Supp. 530 (N.D.N.Y. 1968).

40. *Id.* at 532. It is interesting to note that the court did not find the hotel's admitted discrimination offensive; this is in accord with public opinion. The *Syracuse Post-Standard* said in a lead editorial:

> The campaign waged for several months by the National Organization for Women (NOW) against Hotel Syracuse for its long-standing policy of refusing to serve drinks to unescorted women at the bar in the Rainbow Lounge has reached another absurd point.
>
> All sororities at Syracuse University have been asked to refuse to patronize Hotel Syracuse "because they discriminate against women at their bar," in a letter from Faith A. Seidenberg, one of three directors of the Central New York Chapter of NOW.
>
> --
>
> Hotel Syracuse has had the no-unescorted-women-at-the-bar rule ever since Prohibition was repealed in an effort "to maintain the dignity of the room" and to discourage undesirables and wouldbe pickups from frequenting the Rainbow Lounge, which is at street level, just off the main entrance to the hotel.
>
> --
>
> Hotel Syracuse should be commended for running a decent place, instead of being subjected to the repeated persecution of sit-ins and boycott efforts. Surely any women's rights group could find a better cause than this!

Syracuse Post-Standard, Nov. 8, 1968, at 12, col. 1.

41. *N.Y. Civ. Rights Law* § 40-e (McKinney Supp. 1969).

42. E.g., Syracuse University at Syracuse, N.Y. Letter sent to parents of freshmen, January 1969 (freshman curfew); State University of New York at Oneonta, Experimental Women's Hours Policy, spring semester 1968 (freshman curfew).

43. E.g., *N.Y. Dom. Rel. Law* § 140(b) (McKinney 1964).

44. State University of New York at Oneonta, Experimental Women's Hours Policy (Rev. Sept. 1968).

45. New York Trust Co. v. Riley, 24 Del. Ch. 354, 16 A.2d 772 (1940). But see *N.Y. Dom. Rel. Law* § 61 (Mckinney 1964).

46. E.g., *Cal. Civ. Code* §§ 56, 82 (West Supp. 1968).

47. E.g., *id.*

48. United States v. Yazell, 382 U.S. 341, 361 (1966) (dissenting opinion).

49. Burk v. Anderson, 232 Ind. 77, 81, 109 N.E.2d 407, 408 (1952) (dictum).

50. Smith v. Nicholas Bldg. Co., 93 Ohio 101, 112 N.E. 204 (1915).

51. See Moran v. Quality Alum. Casting Co., 34 Wis. 2d 542, 549–550 nn. 15 & 16, 150 N.W.2d 137, 140 nn.15 & 16 (1968); Simeone, "The Wife's Action for Loss of Consortium—Progress or No?" 4 *St. Louis U.L.J.* 424 (1957).

52. 183 F.2d 811 (D.C. Cir. 1950).

53.   274 F. Supp. 169 (N.D. Ill. 1967).

54.   *Id.* at 175. The court summarized the rationale of the prevailing rule:

> The early status of women during the sixteenth and seventeenth centuries vitally affected the common law attitude toward relational marital interests. The wife was viewed for many purposes as a chattel of her husband, and he was entitled to her services in the eyes of the law. ... The wife, however, as a "servant" was not entitled to sue for the loss of services of her husband, since in theory he provided none.

> *Id.* at 171.

55.   260 F. Supp. 820 (W.D. Mich. 1966).

56.   "To draw such a distinction between a husband and wife is a classification which is unreasonable and impermissible." *Id.* at 822.

57.   Montgomery v. Stephan, 359 Mich. 33, 48−49, 101 N.W.2d 227, 234 (1960), *quoted with approval,* Millington v. Southeastern Elev. Co., 22 N.Y.2d 498, 503−504, 239 N.E.2d 897, 900, 293 N.Y.S.2d 305, 309 (1968).

Goesaert v. Cleary / The Case of the Female Bartender

Goesaert v. Cleary, 74 F. Supp. 735 (1947)
Goesaert v. Cleary, 335 U.S. 464 (1948)

The institution of law has given credence to the centuries-old argument that there are certain tasks and jobs which women are not qualified to perform simply because they are female. In 1948, the United States Supreme Court upheld the constitutionality of a Michigan statute which made it illegal for a woman to be a bartender unless she was the wife or daughter of a male owner of a licensed liquor establishment. The United States Supreme Court upheld the decision of a three-judge federal court and there appears below both the Supreme Court decision and Judge Picard's lower federal court dissenting opinion. Since the dissent to the Supreme Court's decision is rather brief, the Picard dissent is included to better express the arguments of those who find the Michigan statute discriminatory against women. The three-judge court ruled constitutional the Michigan statute which said, in part, "Each applicant for license [bartending] shall be a male person 21 years of age or over, shall submit a certificate from his local board of health or health officer showing that such person is not affected with any infectious or communicable disease, and shall meet the requirements of the commission: Provided, that the wife or daughter of the male owner of any establishment licensed to sell alcoholic liquor for consumption on the premises may be licensed as a bartender by the commission under such rules and regulations as the commission may establish." Judge Picard disagreed, arguing that the statute was unconstitutional. His opinion is given first, because chronologically it came before the Supreme Court opinion did.

***Goesaert v. Cleary*, 74 F. Supp. 735 (1947)**

Judge Picard dissents:

The only question here is whether the state may disqualify certain women as bartenders while permitting this avenue of employment to other women having less legal right to so act than those prohibited.

Therefore I cannot concur with my respected associates for two reasons:

First, This law in my opinion violates Sec. 1 of the Fourteenth Amendment because it

A. Discriminates between persons similarly situated;

B. Denies plaintiffs equal protection of the laws; and

C. Its proviso that the wife and daughter of a male licensee may act as bartender while denying the same privilege to either the female licensee or her daughter, is palpably arbitrary, capricious and unreasonable, and not based on facts that can reasonably be conceived.

Second, That plaintiffs should be permitted to present evidence before we act on the interlocutory injunction.

First.

It violates Sec. 1 of the Fourteenth Amendment.

The material part of Sec. 1 reads as follows:

"... nor shall any State deprive any person of life, liberty, or property, without due process of law; nor deny to any person within its jurisdiction the equal protection of the laws."

Conceding that the legislature, guarding the health, safety, and morals of the people, under its police power, has a tremendously wide latitude of discretion (Lindsley v. Natural Carbonic Gas Co., 220 U.S. 61, 78, 31 S.Ct. 337, 55 L.Ed. 369, Ann.Cas. 1912C, 160; Carmichael v. Southern Coal & Coke Co., 301 U.S. 495, 510, 57 S.Ct. 868, 81 L.Ed. 1245, 109 A.L.R. 1327);

agreeing that any discriminatory classifications need not be "with mathematical nicety, or because in practice it results in some inequality"
(Lindsley v. Natural Carbonic Gas Co. supra [220 U.S. 61, 31 S.Ct. 340]),
I nevertheless query: What is the purpose of the Fourteenth Amendment
if not to prevent gross, unreasonable discrimination of this kind? Both
the state and federal constitutions provide for checks and balances. Our
legislature has not been given carte blanche to enact any and all kinds of
legislation. As stated in Dobbins v. Los Angeles, 195 U.S. 223, 25 S.Ct. 18,
20, 49 L.Ed. 169:

"The question in each case is whether the legislature has adopted the
statute in exercise of a reasonable discretion, or whether its action be a
mere excuse for an unjust discrimination, or the oppression or spoilation
of a particular class."

No legislature may in effect say "We make this distinction, foolish and
unfair though we know it to be, because we are in the mood." It cannot—
because our courts have vigilantly and consistently closed the entrance
to those fertile fields of unconstitutionality, unfairness and inequality by
reiterating again and again that no law may be capricious, unreasonable
or arbitrary. This law, in my humble opinion, bears the stigma of all three
because:

A. Discriminating Between "Persons Similarly Situated."

Mr. Justice McKenna in Ohio ex rel. Lloyd v. Dollison, 194 U.S. 445,
24 S.Ct. 703, 704, 48 L.Ed. 1062, says:

> "Those contentions are that the Ohio statute denies plaintiff in error
> the equal protection of the law, and deprives him of liberty and property
> without due process of law.
> *"The first contention can only be sustained if the statute treat plaintiff in error
> differently from what it does others who are in the same situation as he,—that is,
> in the same relation to the purpose of the statute."* (Emphasis ours)

Our own Michigan Supreme Court in People v. Case, 153 Mich. 98,
116 N.W. 558, 18 L.R.A., N.S., 657, quoting from a Colorado decision,
(Adams v. Cronin, 29 Colo. 488, 68 P. 590, 63 L.R.A. 61), puts its stamp
of approval on the constitutionality of an ordinance because it "does not
operate as a discrimination between different licensees. It applied equally
to everyone of that class, ..." [153 Mich. 98, 116 N.W. 560] (Note: The
Michigan law cannot pass this test of constitutionality.)

See also State ex rel. Galle v. City of New Orleans, 113 La. 371, 36 So.
999, 67 L.R.A. 76, 2 Ann. Cas. 92, where the court said:

"Ordinances must be general in their character, and operate equally upon all persons within the municipality, of the same class, to whom they relate."

In Watson v. Maryland, 218 U.S. 173, 30 S.Ct. 644, 647, 54 L.Ed. 987, we read:

"The selection of the exempted classes was within the legislative power, subject only to the restriction that it be not arbitrary or oppressive *and apply equally to all persons similarly situated.*" (Emphasis ours)

In the case at bar the Michigan Supreme Court boldly admits that this act discriminates between male and female licensees. In Fitzpatrick v. Liquor Control Commission, 316 Mich. 83, at page 91, 25 N.W.2d 118, at page 121, the court said:

"Plaintiffs claim (and it must be admitted) that in so doing the legislature has discriminated between male and female licensees, as to who may act as bartenders."

Briefly that proviso permits the male owner, his wife and daughter, to act as bartenders in his business, *but* denies the same privilege to both the female owner and her daughter.

If this is not an instance of unjust discrimination against persons similarly situated in the same business, in the same relation to the purpose of the statute and in the same class, it would be difficult to find one.

B. It Denies Plaintiffs Equal Protection of the Laws.

Let us review the admitted facts. According to the bill of complaint this is not a new venture for Mrs. Goesaert. She is not just now going into the liquor business under this new law. She started business, bought property, and incurred obligations under a law that permitted her to do exactly what her license said she could do—own and operate a business.

I accept the well known rule of law that a license to sell liquor is not a property right but a privilege (Glicker v. Michigan Liquor Control Commission, 6 Cir., 160 F. 2d 96), but here the question is not whether this woman will be granted a license. The issue is, having granted her a license, can the legislature arbitrarily and unreasonably change the rules in the middle of the game as against her alone because she happens to be a woman licensee.

In this connection it must be remembered that Michigan's liquor law, Pub.Acts 1933, Ex.Sess., No. 8, § 19, as amended by Pub. Acts 1945, No. 133, section 18.990, subsection 15, Mich.Stat.Ann., provides that one owning a liquor license, even in a community where the number of licensees operating exceeds the legal quota, may have his or her license renewed each succeeding year, and licenses almost automatically continue from year to year. Even quota restrictions do not prevail if such license was held before May 1, 1945. Plaintiff, Goesaert, did have such a license and evidently the legislature recognized in this privilege a property right that should not be restricted or removed. Still, while refusing to change the rules as unfair in one section of the act, in the succeeding section the legislature makes the debated change that has abridged her property rights immeasurably.

Where is the "equal protection" for her?

Under this act a woman whose husband, a male licensee, has just died, finds herself at an added disadvantage. She not only has lost her husband, but neither she nor her daughter may help run the family business as they did when the main breadwinner was alive. Across the street her male competitor may permit his wife and daughter to run his business even if he works in a factory miles away.

Has not this woman by every test of reasoning been deprived of the equal protection of the laws?

One's sense of fair play and justice rebels and it is not strange that in validating the constitutionality of this act in the Fitzpatrick case, supra, the court found it expedient to recall Justice Cooley's admonition in "Constitutional Limitations," viz., that courts cannot "run a race of right, reason, and expediency with the legislative branch of the state government." But to this I feel impelled to add an extract from Liggett Co. v. Baldridge, 278 U.S. 105, 49 S. Ct. 57, 59, 73 L.Ed. 204—

> "A state cannot, *under the guise of protecting the public*, arbitrarily interfere with private business or prohibit lawful occupations or impose unreasonable and unnecessary restrictions upon them.'" (Emphasis ours)

C. The Law is "Palpably Arbitrary, Capricious and Unreasonable."

Lindsley v. National Carbonic Gas Co., supra, cited by my colleagues, and a widely quoted case, holds that the constitutionality of any legislative enactment may be attacked "when it is without any reasonable basis, and therefore is purely arbitrary." And further that, "if any state of facts reasonably can be conceived that would sustain it, the existence of that state of facts at the time the law was enacted must be assumed." This law can be upheld then only if it is not arbitrary and unreasonable under any set of facts that can reasonably be conceived. Well, what facts can those be? The

majority opinion seeks to enumerate by stating that the legislature might
have had in mind, to-wit:

> ". . . that a grave social problem . . . would be mitigated to the vanish-
> ing point in those places where there was a male licensee ultimately
> responsible for the condition and the decorum maintained in his establish-
> ment."

What has been the 14 years' experience of the Liquor Commission on
that point? Have there been more, or less, violations where the licensee
was a woman acting as her own bartender, as compared to licenses held
by males? Has the "decorum" been better or worse?

Another suggested conceivable fact—". . . the self interest of male
licensees in protecting the immediate members of their families would
generally insure a more wholesome atmosphere in such establishments."

What has been the experience here? Would not a widow, for example,
with a valuable license be more determined than a male licensee in
protecting her family and livelihood? Is a father more interested in assuring a "wholesome atmosphere" than a mother?

Further, that the legislature "may also have considered the likelihood
that a male licensee could provide protection for his wife or daughter that
would be beyond the capacity of a woman licensee . . ."

But it must be remembered that no male adult is required to be present
when the wife or daughter is bartender. In fact it is common knowledge
that there are many male licensees who have other jobs, helping out only
in the bar, daytimes, if working nights, or at night when working daytime.
Surely the wife or daughter of a male licensee is just as subject to the
perils of her employment, in the absence of her husband or father, as the
female licensee or her daughter. Has not the female licensee provided
protection to herself and daughter in the past?

We are immediately challenged that this goes to the wisdom of the
legislature and we agree that the wisdom of what the legislature has
done is not the issue. This goes beyond the "wisdom," and we have
searched in vain for the faintest semblance of facts that can be "reasonably
conceived" to bolster this admittedly discriminatory legislation.

Nor can its enactment be logically defended on the theory that the
police power is an inherent right of legislatures in matters of public
health, safety, and morals. It is still necessary that the distinction be
reasonably related to the object of the legislation (New York Rapid Transit
Corp. v New York, 303 U.S. 573, 578, 58 S.Ct. 721, 82 L.Ed. 1024); and in

holding an ordinance which prohibited sale of liquor in dry goods stores unconstitutional (Chicago v. Netcher; 183 Ill. 104, 55 N.E. 707, 709, 48 L.R.A. 261, 75 Am.St.Rep. 93), the court said:

> "The restriction is purely arbitrary, not having any connection with and not tending in any way towards the protection of, the public against the evils arising from the sale of intoxicating liquor."

Can it be contended that it promotes public *safety* to permit only women to act as bartenders who happen to be the wife or daughter of the male owner of the business while neither the woman who owns her own license nor her daughter can so act?

Can it be contended that a woman bartender would promote the *morals* of an establishment if her husband or her father were the licensee more than if she or her mother held the license?

And is it claimed that the male owner is more solicitous of sanitation or *public health* than the female?

On all three points, safety, morals, and health, would not the contrary be more likely to exist?

Something new?

My colleagues cite as "persuasive" but "not controlling" the Michigan decision in Fitzpatrick v. Liquor Control Commission, supra. Let us examine two citations given therein.

On page 124 of 25 N.W.2d it refers to Section 5363 of the Michigan Compiled Laws 1897, to-wit—

> "That this act shall not be so construed as to prevent the wife or other females who are bona fide members of the family of a proprietor of a saloon from tending bar or serving liquors in his saloon."

This may well be the fount from which the present provision in our law drew the breath of life so further analysis is interesting. The words "in *his* saloon" are significant. Seldom if ever fifty years ago were women granted licenses to sell liquor. As a matter of fact women were not frequenters of bars or saloons. There was an ingenious subterfuge labeled "family entrance" but comparatively few women availed themselves of that means of seeking refreshments. Today there is no such prohibition affecting women. They can and are licensees, and can and do frequent places where liquor is sold. The 1897 law has no application.

The second citation refers to the California ordinance, People v.

Jemnez, 49 Cal.App.2d Supp. 739, 121 P.2d 543, 544 claimed by our Michigan Supreme Court to be a "case quite in point with the case at bar." We quote:

> "The provisions of this section shall not apply to the mixing of alcoholic beverages ... *by any on-sale licensee* nor to the mixing of such beverages by the *wife of any licensee* on the premises for which her husband holds an on-sale license." Gen.Laws, Act 3796, § 56.4. (Emphasis ours)

Obviously in California a woman may also be a licensee and it is worthy of note that in California if a woman is the licensee *she may* act as bartender to the same extent as the wife of the male licensee. We agree that the case is in point but for plaintiffs—not defendant.

Not only California but other states having similar legislation have carefully avoided writing in any liquor prohibition that places woman in different categories.

Many of these "similar laws" are cited in defendant's brief but I find upon scrutiny that by inference at least, all favor plaintiffs and not defendant.

In Cronin v. Adams, 192 U.S. 108, 24 S.Ct. 219, 48 L.Ed. 365, a case relating to the constitutionality of a Denver ordinance, we find that women—*all women* including the wife and female children of the owner—were prohibited from entering any saloon.

In People v. Case, supra, the Flint ordinance barred women—*all women*—from being in or about the bar.

In City of Hoboken v. Goodman, 68 N.J. L. 217, 51 A. 1092, the ordinance in question is very significant. It prevented any female from acting as bartender unless she was the wife of the owner *or owned the business herself.*

The California Statutes, Deering's California General Laws, Vol. 2, Act 3796, page 1353, Sec. 56.4, page 1413, also exempted from the class prohibited the wife of the owner *and the owner herself.*

In Nelson, Chief of Police v. State ex rel. Gross, 157 Fla. 412, 26 So.2d 60, the prohibition was against *all women*—no exceptions.

Does it mean nothing that all states passing similar laws have avoided drawing the distinctions between women bartenders that Michigan has?

Can it be that members of the legislatures of those states are less solicitous of their women folks than Michigan? Or has "chivalry" (Fitzpatrick case, supra) returned to the Michigan legislature alone among our forty-eight states?

Conclusion.

For the reasons given and because I firmly believe that if this court endorses this type of discriminating legislation it opens the door for further fine "distinctions" that will eventually be applied to religion, education, politics and even nationalities, I must dissent.

Goesaert v. Cleary, 335 U.S. 464 (1948)

Mr. Justice Frankfurter delivered the opinion of the Court.

As part of the Michigan system for controlling the sale of liquor, bartenders are required to be licensed in all cities having a population of 50,000 or more, but no female may be so licensed unless she be "the wife or daughter of the male owner" of a licensed liquor establishment. Section 19a of Act 133 of the Public Acts of Michigan, 1945, Mich. Stat. Ann. § 18.990 (1) (Cum. Supp. 1947). The case is here on direct appeal from an order of the District Court of three judges, convened under § 266 of the old Judicial Code, now 28 U.S.C. § 2284, denying an injunction to restrain the enforcement of the Michigan law. The claim, denied below, one judge dissenting, 74 F. Supp. 735, and renewed here, is that Michigan cannot forbid females generally from being barmaids and at the same time make an exception in favor of the wives and daughters of the owners of liquor establishments. Beguiling as the subject is, it need not detain us long. To ask whether or not the Equal Protection of the Laws Clause of the Fourteenth Amendment barred Michigan from making the classification the State has made between wives and daughters of owners of liquor places and wives and daughters of non-owners, is one of those rare instances where to state the question is in effect to answer it.

We are, to be sure, dealing with a historic calling. We meet the alewife, sprightly and ribald, in Shakespeare, but centuries before him she played a role in the social life of England. See, *e.g.*, Jusserand, English Wayfaring Life in the Middle Ages, 133, 134, 136–37 (1889). The Fourteenth Amendment did not tear history up by the roots, and the regulation of the liquor traffic is one of the oldest and most untrammeled of legislative powers. Michigan could, beyond question, forbid all women from working behind a bar. This is so despite the vast changes in the social and legal position of women. The fact that women may now have achieved the virtues that men have long claimed as their prerogatives and now indulge in vices that men have long practiced, does not preclude the States from drawing a sharp line between the sexes, certainly in such matters as the regulation of the liquor traffic. See the Twenty-First Amendment and *Carter* v. *Virginia*, 321 U.S. 131. The Constitution does not require legislatures to reflect sociological insight, or shifting social standards, any more than it requires them to keep abreast of the latest scientific standards.

While Michigan may deny to all women opportunities for bartending, Michigan cannot play favorites among women without rhyme or reason. The Constitution in enjoining the equal protection of the laws upon States precludes irrational discrimination as between persons or groups of persons in the incidence of a law. But the Constitution does not require situations "which are different in fact or opinion to be treated in law as though they were the same." *Tigner* v. *Texas*, 310 U.S. 141, 147. Since bartending by women may, in the allowable legislative judgment, give rise to moral and social problems against which it may devise preventive measures, the legislature need not go to the full length of prohibition if it believes that as to a defined group of females other factors are operating which either eliminate or reduce the moral and social problems otherwise calling for prohibition. Michigan evidently believes that the oversight assured through ownership of a bar by a barmaid's husband or father minimizes hazards that may confront a barmaid without such protecting oversight. This Court is certainly not in a position to gainsay such belief by the Michigan legislature. If it is entertainable, as we think it is, Michigan has not violated its duty to afford equal protection of its laws. We cannot cross-examine either actually or argumentatively the mind of Michigan legislators nor question their motives. Since the line they have drawn is not without a basis in reason, we cannot give ear to the suggestion that the real impulse behind this legislation was an unchivalrous desire of male bartenders to try to monopolize the calling.

It would be an idle parade of familiar learning to review the multitudinous cases in which the constitutional assurance of the equal protection of the laws has been applied. The generalities on this subject are not in dispute; their application turns peculiarly on the particular circumstances of a case. Thus, it would be a sterile inquiry to consider whether this case is nearer to the nepotic pilotage law of Louisiana, sustained in *Kotch* v. *Pilot Commissioners*, 330 U.S. 552, than it is to the Oklahoma sterilization law, which fell in *Skinner* v. *Oklahoma*, 316 U.S. 535. Suffice it to say that "A statute is not invalid under the Constitution because it might have gone farther than it did, or because it may not succeed in bringing about the result that it tends to produce." *Roschen* v. *Ward*, 279 U.S. 337, 339.

Nor is it unconstitutional for Michigan to withdraw from women the occupation of bartending because it allows women to serve as waitresses where liquor is dispensed. The District Court has sufficiently indicated the reasons that may have influenced the legislature in allowing women to be waitresses in a liquor establishment over which a man's ownership provides control. Nothing need be added to what was said below as to the other grounds on which the Michigan law was assailed.

Judgment affirmed.

Mr. Justice Rutledge, with whom Mr. Justice Douglas and Mr. Justice Murphy join, dissenting.

While the equal protection clause does not require a legislature to achieve "abstract symmetry" or to classify with "mathematical nicety," that clause does require lawmakers to refrain from invidious distinctions of the sort drawn by the statute challenged in this case.

The statute arbitrarily discriminates between male and female owners of liquor establishments. A male owner, although he himself is always absent from his bar, may employ his wife and daughter as barmaids. A female owner may neither work as a barmaid herself nor employ her daughter in that position, even if a man is always present in the establishment to keep order. This inevitable result of the classification belies the assumption that the statute was motivated by a legislative solicitude for the moral and physical well-being of women who, but for the law, would be employed as barmaids. Since there could be no other conceivable justification for such discrimination against women owners of liquor establishments, the statute should be held invalid as a denial of equal protection.

The Case of the All-Male Jury

Hoyt v. Florida, 368 U.S. 57 (1961)

The law differentiates in many ways the rights and duties of males and females and these differentiations based on sex sometimes appear to discriminate against women. In the area of jury service, state laws vary and even though it is argued that these laws are there "to protect" women, it still remains that the laws are sexually based and at times do discriminate against women. In his book *Women and the Law*, Leo Kanowitz summarizes these state laws:

"As of August 1, 1962, only 21 states permitted women to serve on juries on the same basis as men. Of 14 other states recognizing child care problems as special grounds for exemptions from jury service, only 5 allowed the exemption to both sexes, the remaining 9 making it available to women only. In 15 states, women were allowed an exemption on the basis of their sex alone. In 3 other states women could be exempted for reasons not available to men, such as the nature of the crime in a criminal proceeding or the unavailability of adequate courthouse facilities to accommodate women jurors. In 3 states, women could serve only if they registered with the clerk of the court—an arrangement that is similar to the automatic exemption on the basis of sex alone, but one that obviates the necessity of appearing at the courthouse if a woman chooses not to volunteer her services for jury duty. Finally, in addition to Alabama, two other states, Mississippi and South Carolina, excluded women from jury service entirely, a practice declared unconstitutional in *White v. Crook*."

On February 7, 1966, a three-judge federal district court decided, in *White v. Crook*, that Alabama's statutory exclusion of women from jury duty violated the Fourteenth Amendment's equal protection clause.

In 1961, however, *in Hoyt v. Florida*, the United States Supreme Court upheld the constitutionality of a Florida statute which requires that jurors be taken from "male and female" citizens of the state, "provided, however, that the name of no female shall be taken for jury service unless said person has registered with the clerk of the circuit court her desire to be placed on the jury list." Hoyt argued that the nature of the crime she was charged with, killing her husband by assaulting him with a baseball bat, demanded the inclusion of persons of her own sex on the jury: she argued that the Florida statute had the effect of excluding women from jury duty. The United States Supreme Court found, however, "no substantial evidence whatever in this record that Florida has arbitrarily undertaken to exclude women from jury service, a showing which it was incumbent on appellant [Hoyt] to make. . . ."

Hoyt v. Florida, 368 U.S. 57 (1961)

Mr. Justice Harlan delivered the opinion of the Court.

Appellant, a woman, has been convicted in Hillsborough County, Florida, of second degree murder of her husband. On this appeal under 28 U.S.C. § 1257 (2) from the Florida Supreme Court's affirmance of the judgment of conviction, 119 So. 2d 691, we noted probable jurisdiction,

364 U.S. 930, to consider appellant's claim that her trial before an all-male jury violated rights assured by the Fourteenth Amendment. The claim is that such jury was the product of a state jury statute which works an unconstitutional exclusion of women from jury service.

The jury law primarily in question is Fla. Stat., 1959, § 40.01 (1). This Act, which requires that grand and petit jurors be taken from "male and female" citizens of the State possessed of certain qualifications, contains the following proviso:

> "provided, however, that the name of no female person shall be taken for jury service unless said person has registered with the clerk of the circuit court her desire to be placed on the jury list."

Showing that since the enactment of the statute only a minimal number of women have so registered, appellant challenges the constitutionality of the statute both on its face and as applied in this case. For reasons now to follow we decide that both contentions must be rejected.

At the core of appellant's argument is the claim that the nature of the crime of which she was convicted peculiarly demanded the inclusion of persons of her own sex on the jury. She was charged with killing her husband by assaulting him with a baseball bat. An information was filed against her under Fla. Stat., 1959, §782.04, which punishes as murder in the second degree "any act imminently dangerous to another, and evincing a depraved mind regardless of human life, although without any premeditated design to effect the death of any particular individual. . . ." As described by the Florida Supreme Court, the affair occurred in the context of a marital upheaval involving, among other things, the suspected infidelity of appellant's husband, and culminating in the husband's final rejection of his wife's efforts at reconciliation. It is claimed, in substance, that women jurors would have been more understanding or compassionate than men in assessing the quality of appellant's act and her defense of "temporary insanity." No claim is made that the jury as constituted was otherwise afflicted by any elements of supposed unfairness. Cf. *Irvin* v. *Dowd*, 366 U.S. 717.

Of course, these premises misconceive the scope of the right to an impartially selected jury assured by the Fourteenth Amendment. That right does not entitle one accused of crime to a jury tailored to the circumstances of the particular case, whether relating to the sex or other condition of the defendant, or to the nature of the charges to be tried. It requires only that the jury be indiscriminately drawn from among those eligible in the community for jury service, untrammelled by any arbitrary and systematic exclusions. See *Fay* v. *New York*. 332 U.S. 261, 284–285, and the cases cited therein. The result of this appeal must therefore depend on whether such an exclusion of women from jury service has been shown.

I

We address ourselves first to appellant's challenge to the statute on its face.

Several observations should initially be made. We of course recognize that the Fourteenth Amendment reaches not only arbitrary class exclusions from jury service based on race or color, but also all other exclusions which "single out" any class of persons "for different treatment not based on some reasonable classification." *Hernandez* v. *Texas*, 347 U.S. 475, 478. We need not, however, accept appellant's invitation to canvass in this case the continuing validity of this Court's dictum in *Strauder* v. *West Virginia*, 100 U.S. 303, 310, to the effect that a State may constitutionally "confine" jury duty "to males." This constitutional proposition has gone unquestioned for more than eighty years in the decisions of the Court, see *Fay* v. *New York, supra*, at 289–290, and had been reflected, until 1957, in congressional policy respecting jury service in the federal courts themselves. Even were it to be assumed that this question is still open to debate, the present case tenders narrower issues.

Manifestly, Florida's § 40.01 (1) does not purport to exclude women from state jury service. Rather, the statute "gives to women the privilege to serve but does not impose service as a duty." *Fay* v. *New York, supra*, at 277. It accords women an absolute exemption from jury service unless they expressly waive that privilege. This is not to say, however, that what in form may be only an exemption of a particular class of persons can in no circumstances be regarded as an exclusion of that class. Where, as here, an exemption of a class in the community is asserted to be in substance an exclusionary device, the relevant inquiry is whether the exemption itself is based on some reasonable classification and whether the manner in which it is exercisable rests on some rational foundation.

In the selection of jurors Florida has differentiated between men and women in two respects. It has given women an absolute exemption from jury duty based solely on their sex, no similar exemption obtaining as to men. And it has provided for its effectuation in a manner less onerous than that governing exemptions exercisable by men: women are not to be put on the jury list unless they have voluntarily registered for such service; men, on the other hand, even if entitled to an exemption, are to be included on the list unless they have filed a written claim of exemption as provided by law. Fla. Stat., 1959, § 40.10.

In neither respect can we conclude that Florida's statute is not "based on some reasonable classification," and that it is thus infected with unconstitutionality. Despite the enlightened emancipation of women from the restrictions and protections of bygone years, and their entry into many parts of community life formerly considered to be reserved to men, woman is still regarded as the center of home and family life. We cannot say that it is constitutionally impermissible for a State, acting in pursuit of the general welfare, to conclude that a woman should be relieved from the civic duty of jury service unless she herself determines that such service is consistent with her own special responsibilities.

Florida is not alone in so concluding. Women are now eligible for jury service in all but three States of the Union. Of the forty-seven States where women are eligible, seventeen besides Florida, as well as the District of Columbia, have accorded women an absolute exemption based solely on their sex, exercisable in one form or another. In two of these States, as in Florida, the exemption is automatic, unless a woman volunteers for such service. It is true, of course, that Florida could have limited the exemption, as some other States have done, only to women who have family responsibilities. But we cannot regard it as irrational for a state legislature to consider preferable a broad exemption, whether born of the State's historic public policy or of a determination that it would not be administratively feasible to decide in each individual instance whether the family responsibilities of a prospective female juror were serious enough to warrant an exemption.

Likewise we cannot say that Florida could not reasonably conclude that full effectuation of this exemption made it desirable to relieve women of the necessity of affirmatively claiming it, while at the same time requiring of men an assertion of the exemptions available to them. Moreover, from the standpoint of its own administrative concerns the State might well consider that it was "impractical to compel large numbers of women, who have an absolute exemption, to come to the clerk's office for examination since they so generally assert their exemption." *Fay* v. *New York, supra,* at 277; compare 28 U.S.C. § 1862; H.R. Rep. No. 308, 80th Cong., 1st Sess. A156 (1947).

Appellant argues that whatever may have been the design of this

Florida enactment, the statute in practical operation results in an exclusion of women from jury service, because women, like men, can be expected to be available for jury service only under compulsion. In this connection she points out that by 1957, when this trial took place, only some 220 women out of approximately 46,000 registered female voters in Hillsborough County—constituting about 40 percent of the total voting population of that county—had volunteered for jury duty since the limitation of jury service to males, see *Hall* v. *Florida*, 136 Fla. 644, 662–665, 187 So. 392, 400–401, was removed by § 40.01 (1) in 1949. Fla. Laws 1949, c. 25, 126.

This argument, however, is surely beside the point. Given the reasonableness of the classification involved in § 40.01 (1), the relative paucity of women jurors does not carry the constitutional consequence appellant would have it bear. "Circumstances or chance may well dictate that no persons in a certain class will serve on a particular jury or during some particular period." *Hernandez* v. *Texas, supra*, at 482.

We cannot hold this statute as written offensive to the Fourteenth Amendment.

II

Appellant's attack on the statute as applied in this case fares no better.

In the year here relevant Fla. Stat., 1955, § 40.10 in conjunction with § 40.02 required the jury commissioners, with the aid of the local circuit court judges and clerk, to compile annually a jury list of 10,000 inhabitants qualified to be jurors. In 1957 the existing Hillsborough County list had become exhausted to the extent of some 3,000 jurors. The new list was constructed by taking over from the old list the remaining some 7,000 jurors, including 10 women, and adding some 3,000 new male jurors to build up the list to the requisite 10,000. At the time some 220 women had registered for jury duty in this county, including those taken over from the earlier list.

The representative of the circuit court clerk's office, a woman, who actually made up the list testified as follows as to her reason for not adding others of the 220 "registered" women to the 1957 list: "Well, the reason I placed ten is I went back two or three, four years, and noticed how many women they had put on before and I put on approximately the same number." She further testified: "Mr. Lockhart [one of the jury commissioners] told me at one time to go back approximately two or three years to get the names because they were recent women that had signed up, because in this book [the female juror register], there are no dates at the beginning of it, so we can't—I don't know exactly how far back they do go and so I just went back two or three years to get my names." When read in light of Mr. Lockhart's testimony, printed in the margin, it is apparent that the idea was to avoid listing women who though registered might be disqualified because of advanced age or for other reasons.

Appellant's showing falls far short of giving this procedure a sinister complexion. It is true of course that the proportion of women on the jury list (10) to the total of those registered for such duty (some 220) was less than 5 percent, and not 27 percent as the trial court mistakenly said and the state appellate court may have thought. But when those listed are compared with the 30 or 35 women who had registered since 1952 (note 11, p. 66) the proportion rises to around 33 percent, hardly suggestive of an arbitrary, systematic exclusionary purpose. Equally unimpressive is appellant's suggested "male" proportion which we are asked to contrast with the female percentage. The male proportion is derived by comparing the number of males contained on the jury list with the total number of male electors in the county. But surely the resulting proportion is meaningless when the record does not even reveal how many of such electors were qualified for jury service, how many had been granted exemptions (notes 3 and 4, p. 61), and how many on the list had been excused when first called. (*Id.*)

This case in no way resembles those involving race or color in which the circumstances shown were found by this Court to compel a conclusion of purposeful discriminatory exclusions from jury service. *E.g., Hernandez* v. *Texas, supra; Norris* v. *Alabama,* 294 U.S. 587; *Smith* v. *Texas,* 311 U.S. 128; *Hill* v. *Texas,* 316 U.S. 400; *Eubanks* v. *Louisiana,* 356 U.S. 584. There is present here neither the unfortunate atmosphere of ethnic or racial prejudices which underlay the situations depicted in those cases, nor the long course of discriminatory administrative practice which the statistical showing in each of them evinced.

In the circumstances here depicted, it indeed "taxes our credulity," *Hernandez* v. *Texas, supra,* at 482, to attribute to these administrative officials a deliberate design to exclude the very class whose eligibility for jury service the state legislature, after many years of contrary policy, had declared only a few years before. (See p. 64, *supra.*) It is sufficiently evident from the record that the presence on the jury list of no more than ten or twelve women in the earlier years, and the failure to add in 1957 more women to those already on the list, are attributable not to any discriminatory motive, but to a purpose to put on the list only those women who might be expected to be qualified for service if actually called. Nor is there the slightest suggestion that the list was the product of any plan to place on it only women of a particular economic or other community or organizational group. Cf. *Thiel* v. *Southern Pacific Co.,* 328 U.S. 217; *Glasser* v. *United States,* 315 U.S. 60, 83—87. And see also *Fay* v. *New York, supra,* at 287.

Finally, the disproportion of women to men on the list independently carries no constitutional significance. In the administration of the jury laws proportional class representation is not a constitutionally required factor. See *Akins* v. *Texas,* 325 U.S. 398, 403; *Cassell* v. *Texas,* 339 U.S. 282, 286—287; *Fay* v. *New York, supra,* at 290—291.

Finding no substantial evidence whatever in this record that Florida has arbitrarily undertaken to exclude women from jury service, a showing which it was incumbent on appellant to make, *Hernandez* v. *Texas, supra,* at 479—480; *Fay* v. *New York, supra,* at 285, we must sustain the judgment of the Supreme Court of Florida. Cf. *Akins* v. *Texas, supra.*

Affirmed.

The Chief justice, Mr. Justice Black and Mr. Justice Douglas, concurring.

We cannot say from this record that Florida is not making a good faith effort to have women perform jury duty without discrimination on the ground of sex. Hence we concur in the result, for the reasons set forth in Part II of the Court's opinion.

The Senate Holds Hearings,
The House Debates, and the
Presidents Receive Recommendations

The Senate Holds Hearings on the
Equal Rights Amendment

On May 5, 6, and 7, 1970, the Subcommittee on Constitutional Amendments of the Committee on the Judiciary of the United States Senate conducted hearings on Senate Joint Resolution 61, the "Equal Rights" amendment. The Joint Resolution read:

Resolved by the Senate and House of Representatives of the United States of America in Congress assembled (two-thirds of each House concurring therein), That the following article is proposed as an amendment to the Constitution of the United States, which shall be valid to all intents and purposes as part of the Constitution when ratified by the legislatures of three-fourths of the several states:

Article —

Section 1. Equality of rights under the law shall not be denied or abridged by the United States or by any State on account of sex. Congress and the several States shall have power, within their respective jurisdictions, to enforce this article by appropriate legislation.

Section 2. This article shall be inoperative unless it shall have been ratified as an amendment to the Constitution by the legislatures of three-fourths of the several States.

Section 3. This amendment shall take effect one year after the date of ratification.

Senator Birch Bayh presided and opened the hearings with some remarks about the status of women in the United States and discrimination practiced against them.

Many individuals and groups presented testimony before the committee. The statement of Jean Witter, Chairman of the Equal Rights Amendment Committee of the National Organization for Women (NOW), appears below. She presents arguments for the passage of the Equal Rights Amendment and counters some of the arguments against the amendment. She discusses, among other things, the amendment's ramifications and implications in relation to the draft and the international scene; also, she reviews the three routes open to women to achieve constitutional equality.

Miss Witter's statement is followed below by the testimony of three women from the Washington Women's Liberation Movement. The three women, who use the names of Emma Goldman, Sarah Grimke, and Angelina Grimke (all historical figures who worked for women's rights), charge that the amendment "cannot guarantee real equality"; that Congress is merely trying to "co-opt a growing women's liberation revolution." After a short statement to the committee, the women turned to the spectators in the Senate hearing room and Angelina Grimke argued that what was needed was not the amendment under consideration, but a total transformation in our society. After a short address to the audience, ending with "Free our sisters, free ourselves, all power to the people," the three women left the room.

Their testimony is followed below by the statement of Mortimer Furay, Metropolitan Detroit AFL-CIO Council. Mr. Furay argues that the amendment is not only unnecessary, but will have the effect of repealing "the thousands of laws, rules, regulations, directives, opinions, which now protect women from insidious and destructive working conditions visited upon them largely because of their biological composition and background." He argues that the biological difference between women and men means there has always existed a division of labor based on sex. The differentiations in the work and social roles of men and women, he states, are "destined to last as long as society will endure. . . ." Mr. Furay contends that the equality guaranteed by the Fourteenth Amendment is sufficient and indeed, "if the 14th amendment has not brought equality under the law, to our women, how can anyone postulate that an equal rights amendment will do it, an amendment that removes from the statute books the very laws which help raise women a part way up to the position of male, if only in the marketplace of their hire?"

In the end, the 91st Senate did not enact the Equal Rights Amendment.

Statement of Jean Witter

Introduction

The U.S. Congress finds itself increasingly in the position of having to answer the question, "Why are you still beating your wife?" Further delay in the passage of the Equal Rights Amendment is indefensible. To deny Constitutional Equality to over half the U.S. population in 1970, in an era when people are becoming increasingly aware of human rights and human dignity, is incomprehensible, inexcusable, and will in fact become tantamount to political suicide before long.

Only the fact that the Equal Rights Amendment has been "the best kept secret of the 20th century" has allowed Congressmen to return to their seats session after session, while they have denied our women Constitutional Equality and the full recognition as first class citizens. The fact that Senate hearings are being held in May, when six months ago there were more than enough sponsors to pass the amendment insults every woman voter in the country. Since 1970 is an election year Congress will probably adjourn in early August and little action will occur after mid-July. Effectively, there are only two short months for the passage of the Equal Rights Amendment. One cannot help but to surmise that the members of Congress expect the Amendment to die a quiet death and to be quietly resurrected to start from scratch again in the new Congress in 1971. American women have better things to do with their time, even if Congress appears not to.

The Equal Rights Amendment will not die a quiet death in 1970! If the Equal Rights Amendment is not passed in 1970, its ghost will stalk the voting polls in November! If the Amendment is not passed in 1970, American women must de-seat the present Congress and replace them with legislators who are responsive to the electorate.

Status of women council favors the amendment

I do not intend to repeat the arguments so ably presented in the March 1970 Memorandum, "The Proposed Equal Rights Amendment to the U.S. Constitution" prepared by the study group on equal legal rights for the Citizen's Advisory Council on the Status of Women.[1] The Council as you know in Feb. 1970 declared in favor of the Equal Rights Amendment. [A copy of this later memorandum appears in the hearing record in connection with the testimony of Mrs. Cutwillig.]

Rather than to repeat the material presented by the Council, I intend to build onto the material and arguments presented in the Council's thorough study.

Discriminatory laws

It is well-known that many laws discriminate on the basis of sex. It has not been emphasized, however, that nearly every form of discriminatory law has been either repealed or never existed in some states.

Some states do have:

Separate legal domicile for either spouse.

Inheritance laws that are identical for both men and women.

The same lower limit to the marriage age for both sexes.

The same jury duty obligations for both men and women.

Child support laws applying equally to both parents.

Property laws that apply equally for men and women.

Joint guardianship of children.

Labor standards that apply equally to men and women.

. . . and so on, in nearly every area of discriminatory law.

The fact that a condition of non-discrimination on account of sex does exist in some states in nearly every area of disputable legislation, does prove that the system of sex discrimination under the law is not essential and that people living under the equal situation find that situation not a problem and not a hardship. The argument that the Equal Rights Amendment should not be passed because of the many changes that would be required in state laws is a poor one; on the contrary, the Equal Rights Amendment may be of great benefit to the states in helping them to update their laws, and encouraging more uniformity in family law from state to state.

Protective legislation

The Equal Rights Amendment was once opposed by some groups because it was a threat to protective legislation, or protective labor laws for women. In recent years protective legislation has proven to be restrictive legislation. In the past five years 17 states have repealed all or part of their protective laws. Delaware, for example, repealed its protective labor laws in 1965 with no ill effects.

Ohio has announced recently that it will no longer enforce the protective labor laws since they are in conflict with Title VII of the Civil Rights Act of 1964.

In Pennsylvania the new Sex Amendment to the Pa. Human Relations Act has, by the statement of Pennsylvania's Attorney General, impliedly repealed that Pa. Protective Labor Laws.[2] The staff and machinery for the enforcement of these laws no longer exists. There have been no complaints.

Protective labor laws can no longer stand in the way of the passage of the Equal Rights Amendment; they are on the way out of existence even without the Amendment. The strict enforcement of Title VII of the Civil Rights Act of 1964 would eventually supersede the protective labor laws.

Similarly, the strict enforcement of Title VII would supersede many other state laws that may discriminate in employment situations.

Stop discriminatory laws

When the Equal Rights Amendment is a part of the U.S. Constitution, laws that discriminate on the basis of sex will not be passed since they would be unconstitutional. The Amendment will thus protect both men and women from injustice on account of their sex.

The old English common law v. modern common law

When our U.S. Constitution was written in 1787, the Old English Common Law was then in use in the English speaking world, including our thirteen colonies. Under the Old English common law, women were not regarded as persons under the law; women were regarded as chattel, as property. Consequently, when a legal document or constitution contained words such as people or person, these words did not mean women and men, but men only.

Bearing in mind that words like people and person did not orginally mean women in a legal document, such as a constitution, if we read again our Constitution looking particularly for changes which were made to give our women coverage under the Constitution, we find only one such change; namely, our 19th Amendment gave our women the right to vote. Women are covered by our U.S. Constitution for three minutes twice a year in the voting booth. Other than this our women are covered by our State laws and by a few specific Federal laws, but not by the U.S. Constitution. Only our men have the full protection of the U.S. Constitution. The Equal Rights Amendment is needed to rectify this situation—and the sooner, the better!

With the advent of woman suffrage, state constitutions have gradually come to be interpreted that words such as person and people do mean both men and women. In other words, under the present common law, state constitutions are gradually being interpreted as protecting both sexes equally. Why then, hasn't the U.S. Constitution gradually come to include both sexes under the common law? If it were not for the 10th Amendment, this probably would happen. The 10th Amendment states: "The powers not delegated to the U.S. by the Constitution" . . . "the reserves to the States" . . . "or to the people."

Therefore, when women are admitted into a state legislature, it is because words like citizen or person in the state constitution are being interpreted by the common law to include women. The common law is allowing the legal meaning of such words to change to mean both men and women in state law.

However, when women were admitted into Congress, it was not because the word person in the U.S. Constitution was being interpreted by the common law to include women. It was because the method of selecting state representatives to Congress is determined by the states and is a matter of States' Rights as protected by the 10th Amendment, a power reserved to the States. Not to admit Jeannette Rankin, the first woman Representative, in 1917 as the Representative from Montana, would have been an abridgement of States' Rights as protected by the 10th Amendment.

Since all laws regarding women were originally regarded as being in the realm of "powers reserved to the States," a constitutional amendment is needed in order to clearly give to U.S. women the equal protection of the U.S. Constitution. The Equal Rights Amendment is needed because the 10th Amendment cannot allow this change in interpretation of the U.S. Constitution to come about by common law interpretation. Neither can it be denied that such a basic right as equality under the law between the sexes, should be clearly spelled out in the words of a Constitutional Amendment.

Some women did not want suffrage

"Equality of rights under the law" for both men and women in the form of the Equal Rights Amendment is an essential step, but full enforcement may take up to a century. Certainly, not every eligible woman registered to vote after the passage of the 19th Amendment, and some of our older women have never considered voting. In recent elections, however, the number of women who voted exceeded the number of men who voted; and the percentage of college educated female voters exceeded the percentage of college educated male voters.[3] The fact that some women were not ready to accept suffrage at the time of the passage of the 19th Amendment was fortunately not permitted to stand in the way of giving suffrage to their daughters.

Similarly, let us now not be blinded from taking this essential step in the full emancipation of U.S. women by the fact that some women are not yet ready or anxious for full equality. We must not continue to deny our daughters equal opportunity. Our daughters must have Constitutional Equality even if many older women and men are not able to accept immediately all of the implications and manifestations of Constitutional Equality for women.

Three routes to constitutional equality

U.S. women could possibly achieve Constitutional Equality by two routes in addition to the route of the Equal Rights Amendment. Neither of the other two methods would assure the immutable protection to both men and women that will be assured by the Equal Rights Amendment.

The Supreme Court route

Women could eventually achieve Constitutional Equality by Supreme Court decision. If the Supreme Court ruled that several sex discrimination laws were unconstitutional according to the 14th Amendment, women would then have the "equal protection of the law."[4] However, there is no assurance that the next Supreme Court decision would not reverse the previous decisions, thereby again denying Constitutional Equality to our women again. The Supreme Court in one case, Adkins v. Children's Hospital, 261 U.S. 525 (1923), held an act of Congress fixing minimum wage standards for women to be unconstitutional.[5] The doctrine expressed in the Adkins case was soon reversed by subsequent Supreme Court rulings.[6] All other Supreme Court rulings before and after the Adkins case have held that differences in the law based on sex are not unreasonable and therefore, constitutional.

It may be a long, arduous and expensive route for women to achieve Constitutional equality by Supreme Court interpretation of the 14th Amendment. Since it was not the original intent of Congress that women should have the "equal protection of the laws" when the 14th Amendment was passed in 1868, the Supreme Court could justify excluding women from coverage under the 14th Amendment indefinitely. It is after all the function of the Supreme Court to interpret the Constitution and its amendments according to the original intent of Congress and not to change the Constitution or its intent. The Constitution states in Article I: "ALL legislative Powers herein granted shall be vested in a Congress of the U.S." It is therefore the function of the Congress, and not of the Supreme Court, to change the law of the land. The U.S. Congress should not abdicate its legislative power to the Supreme Court by taking the stand the Supreme Court should change the original meaning of the 14th Amendment to include women. It is clearly the responsibility of the Congress under the Constitution to pass the Equal Rights Amendment; men and women must have the equal protection of the Constitution, and it is the duty of the Congress to bring this about by exercise of its Constitutionally ensured legislative powers.

Further, the Constitution in Article V states: "The Congress, whenever two-thirds of both Houses shall deem it necessary, shall propose Amendments to this Constitution." Since 75 Senators are sponsors for the Equal Rights Amendment, far more than two-thirds of the Senate, there would appear to be a clear mandate from the Constitution for the immediate passage of the Equal Rights Amendment, without change, by the U.S. Senate.

The U.S. Constitution as a Model for the World.—The Constitution of the U.S. has long been considered a model document; it has been read and studied by political science students throughout the world. To not include within the Constitution or its Amendments the provision for equality of rights under the law regardless of sex, would be a serious omission of a right which is basic to every citizen. Such a basic right should not be left to the Supreme Court to take away as the times change. The U.S. Constitution is incomplete as a model document without the Equal Rights Amendment.

"Appropriate Legislation" Route.—Constitutional Equality for women could also be accomplished by "appropriate legislation" under the 14th Amendment, Section 5.[7] Recently such "appropriate legislation" was passed to reduce the voting age to 18 (See H. R. 4249).[8] But the best age at which citizens should start voting may change over the centuries, and is not the subject for a constitutional amendment, although an amendment was thought by some to be necessary. The rights guaranteed in the Equal Rights Amendment are basic human rights and should be clearly and unequivocally stated as part of the U.S. Constitution.

I have considered having a bill introduced in Congress to clearly extend "the equal protection of the law" in the 14th Amendment to cover both men and women, specifically stating that sex shall not be considered a reasonable ground for discrimination under the law. Such a bill is provided for in the 14th Amendment, Section 5: "this amendment may be enforced by appropriate legislation."

Such a bill could pass with only a majority vote in each House. It would certainly be quicker than a constitutional amendment and could possibly accomplish the purpose. However, a similar bill could repeal or qualify the bill at a later date. And of course, the Supreme Court may eventually declare the law unconstitutional in that it was not the original intent of the 14th Amendment to give women "the equal protection of the laws." While I believe such a bill should be considered as a temporary measure to extend the 14th Amendment to women immediately, the Equal Rights Amendment must become a part of our Constitution to protect both men and women for all time.

The draft for women

Does the Equal Rights Amendment imply that women should be subject to the draft or compulsory military service as well as men? Many older and middle aged people in the U.S. seem much against the draft for women, mostly I believe, because it was something they never considered for themselves when they were draft age. It is interesting that the young people who are draft age are very open to the idea of drafting women. They realize that women in some countries are already subject to military service and do serve in the armed forces on the same basis as men.

Many of those working for women's rights, myself included, very much oppose war as a way of solving international problems. As an individual, I favor a well-funded Dept. of Peace and a national peace program equivalent in scope and intensity to our present defense and space programs. But in spite of such aspirations, we must recognize that equality of responsibility does imply that as long as men are being drafted, women should be drafted as well.

However, a valid question can be raised as to whether women do indeed have any obligation to serve in the armed forces. Since women in practice have been denied access to policy-making position, they have not been involved in the decisions leading to military involvement. One can argue that women, as a group, have no responsibility to risk their lives to carry out policy decisions from which they as a group are barred. This is a valid point.

However, the same argument can be made on the basis of age; that is, the young should not be asked to implement the decisions of the old.

Perhaps it is equally unfair, and even uncivilized, to draft the young men to carry out the military decisions of the old men. The fact remains that we have always done this, and we are still doing it today. The case can be made that the draft is just as unfair to young men as it would be to young women. Therefore, we must consider drafting women as long as we draft anyone.

While certainly the disadvantages of being subject to the draft out-weigh the advantages, it should be noted that there are certain advantages. Women who are not drafted do not share the following benefits:

Valuable in-service training (even for high school drop-outs).

Correction of physical problems.

Opportunity to travel.

Learning to live and cooperate with others.

Opportunity to learn leadership.

Additional benefits after discharge from service:

Educational opportunities, scholarships.

Veterans bonuses.

Veterans loans.

Continuation of G.I. Insurance.

Medical treatment in V.A. hospitals.

Veterans preference in federal and state employment:

Civil Service lists.

Extra points on Civil Service tests.

Much less likely to lose government job during Reduction-In-Force.

Life-long respect due to those who have served the nation.

Women who are not drafted share neither the disadvantages or the benefits.

Congress has the power to draft women now

It should be emphasized that not passing the Equal Rights Amendment will not ensure that women will not be drafted in the future. Congress already has the power to include women in any conscription and the Equal Rights Amendment would not affect the power of Congress.[11] The Equal Rights Amendment, however, would imply that women would be required to register for military service and would be called for induction on the same basis as men.

The effect of drafting women

A number of countries already do draft women.[12] Women are drafted and serve in the armed forces on the same basis as men in Israel, Cuba, Red China. In countries where women do serve in the armed forces on the same basis as men, the status of women is very high. The young women in Israel are not aware of a "women problem"—they are completely equal with men.[12]

Of course, just as men are exempt from the draft for reasons of health or responsibility, many women would also be exempt for like reasons.

On the whole the advantages to American women because of being subject to the draft are greater than the disadvantages. If American women are to step into their rightful place in the nation, they must accept full responsibility as well as rights. At this point in history, a part of full responsibility includes the draft.[9,10]

If some do object to people, male or female, being drafted, then it is up to those of us who object to the draft to change the world so that the draft can become a part of our primitive history. Until that time, women and men must share equal responsibility in being subjected to the draft.

Women cannot be denied constitutional equality
because they bear the burden of reproduction

In the year 1900 to speak of "equality of rights under the law" for women would have been a purely academic, if not meaningless, consideration because women were in no position to demand equality of rights, and no group has ever received rights without first demanding them. Most women were involved almost continuously in the reproductive processes throughout their adult years, until shortly before their death—on the average at the age of 48 years.

In 1970 only 40 percent of U.S. women have one or more children under age eighteen, and of these mothers nearly 10 percent are also the head of a house hold.[13] Who is to say that these women and U.S. women of past generations should not share the "equal protection of the laws" under our Constitution? Who is to say that the bearing of rifles in the past by our men was more important to the nation than bearing of children? And who is to say that the men of our nation deserved full Constitutional protection for carrying their share of the burdens, but the women did not? It is a grave miscarriage of justice that has denied U.S. women Constitutional Equality until 1970! Certainly women are human beings and deserve to be accorded equal treatment under the law. Women cannot be denied Constitutional Equality because they bear the burden of reproduction!

In 1970 60 percent of the U.S. women do not have a child under age eighteen.[13] To deny equal opportunity to 60 percent of the U.S. women who do not have a child under 18 years of age, because of biological sex differences is senseless, as well as unconscionable. Indeed, we must recognize motherhood as a temporary condition and encourage our young mothers to realize that they can expect to do other things in addition to being a parent, just as men do.

International implications

Women in Pakistan have Constitutional Equality.[16] Many nations of the world have Constitutional Equality for their women. It is internationally embarrassing that U.S. purports to be a leader among nations and yet continues to deny Constitutional Equality to over half of its citizens.

Senator Eugene McCarthy, recent presidential canditate and chief sponsor of the Equal Rights Amendment, found it necessary to vote against the U.N. Convention on the Political Rights of Women in 1967.[14,15] Senator McCarthy, in so voting, recognized that it would be inconsistent for the U.S. to ratify the U.N. Convention on the Political Rights for Women because U.S. women have only the right to vote under the U.S. Constitution (the right to vote is covered in Article I of the U.N. Convention).

While the ratification by the Senate of the U.N. Convention would not give full Constitutional Equality to U.S. women, it would extend Federal coverage into areas now covered only by State law, and for this reason may even be unconstitutional. Quoting from the U.N. Convention on the Political Rights for Women:

"Article II. Women shall be eligible for election to all publicly elected bodies, established by national law, on equal terms with men, and without discrimination.

"Article III. Women shall be entitled to hold public office and to exercise all public functions, established by national law, on equal terms with men, without discrimination."

Ratification of a U.N. Convention has the force of an international treaty and under the Constitution would become the law of the land. Ratification of the U.N. Convention on the Political Rights for Women would not be just a statement that U.S. favors rights for women in other countries, but since our own women have only the right to vote under the U.S. Constitution, it would extend the rights of U.S. women under Federal law into the two areas covered by Article II and Article III, which are now covered for women only by State law.

Until the Equal Rights Amendment is passed, the U.N. Convention on the Political Rights for Women cannot be passed; to do so would be to infringe on States rights as guaranteed by the 10th Amendment; namely, that "the powers not delegated to the U.S. by the Constitution" ... "are reserved to the States" ... "or to the people."

If the U.S. is to retain its place of leadership among the nations, the Equal Rights Amendment must be passed. The Equal Rights Amendment as part of the U.S. Constitution would then delegate certain powers to the U.S. (that were formerly reserved to the States), and subsequently the ratification of the U.N. Convention of the Political Rights for Women would then be possible under this new constitutional amendment.

World crisis

The problems of the world today that must be solved *soon* are of such a magnitude that we cannot continue to waste our human talent. If we do not encourage our women to fully utilize their talents to help to solve the critical problems of the world today, none of us may survive to criticize our present poor judgment or prejudice. The clear statement of Constitutional Equality for U.S. women in an amendment to the U.S. Constitution can serve as a mandate and a challenge to our women. The Equal Rights Amendment is needed NOW! Please act with all due haste.

The Amendment must pass both Houses in the next two months or it will die again. The U.S. Congress cannot afford to take upon themselves the responsibility of further penalizing the nation by continuing to discourage our women at this time; a time when the population explosion is already a reality. At a time when over 10 million people in the world die yearly from starvation, our women must be encouraged to participate in the mainstream; they must have reason to believe that there are other rewarding endeavours for women besides producing a large family.[17]

For the U.S. Congress to kill the Equal Rights Amendment for the 24th time would be a crime not only against the 51 percent of the population who are women, but against the survival and well-being of the nation as a whole.

Notes

1. Citizen's Advisory Council on the Status of Women, "The Proposed Equal Rights Amendment to the U.S. Constitution, A. Memorandum," March 1970.

2. Pa. Manufacturers Assn., Legislative Bulletin, No. 31, Harrisburg, Pa., Nov. 28, 1969.

3. U.S. Dept. of Commerce, "Voter Participation in the National Election Nov. 1964," Series P—20, No. 143, Oct. 25, 1965
   1966 Supplement, Series P—20, No. 160, Feb. 2, 1967

4. President's Commission on the Status of Women, American Women, 1963

5. Encyclopedia Britanica, "Women, Legal Position of," 1945

6. President's Commission on the Status of Women, Report of the Committee on Civil and Political Rights, GPO, 1963

7. N. Y. Times, "Lowering Voting Age Is an Idea Whose Time Has Come," p. 12, March 29, 1970

8. 91st Congress, 2nd Sess., H. R. 4249, "Voting Rights Act Amendments of 1970," Title III, passed by the House, Dec. 11, 1969, passed by the Senate, April 2, 1970

9. Hughes, Judge Sarah T., "Should Women Be Left Behind?" National Business Woman, Oct. 1969

10. Mead, Margaret, "The Case for Drafting All Boys—and Girls," Redbook Magazine, Sept. 1966

11. National Federation of Business and Professional Women, "Some Questions and Answers on Equal Rights Amendment," Nov. 1968

12. Borgese, Elisabeth Mann, Ascent of Woman, Braziller, N.Y., 1963

13. U.S. Dept. of Commerce, Statistical Abstract of the U.S., 1968

14. 90th Cong., 1st Sess., Senate Foreign Relations Committee, "Hearings on Human Rights Conventions," 1967

15. Swayzee, Elizabeth N., "Action Needed in Human Rights Year," The Bridge, Jan. 1968 (?)

16. Senate Reports, most recent, 87th Cong., 2nd Sess., Rept. No. 2192, 1962

17. Ehrlich, Paul R., The Population Bomb, Ballantine Books, N.Y., 1968.

Our next witnesses represent the Washington Women's Liberation Movement.

I would be grateful if you ladies would identify yourselves for our record, please.

Statement of Emma Goldman, Women's Liberation, Washington, D.C., Accompanied by Sarah Grimké, Angelina Grimké

Miss Sarah Grimké: We are here representing the Washington D.C. Women's Liberation. We do not use our own names because we are speaking for the group and any three of us could be speaking here today.

We have come here today to support our sisters who have been working since 1923 for the passage of this amendment to guarantee equal constitutional rights.

At the same time we recognize the fears of working women that an equal rights amendment may be used exploitatively against us rather than to guarantee rights. Equal rights under the law will give women the confidence to struggle further for liberation.

The nature of the male supremacist system which viciously discriminates against women in all levels of our society will be exposed. No woman could be against equality under the law, but we know that the amendment cannot guarantee real equality.

For example, the 13th, 14th, and 15th Amendments promised, constitutional equality to black men, but now, after 100 years of legalistic doubledealing in the legislatures and the courts, black people have learned that they must struggle in the streets and seize what is rightfully theirs. For women, as for blacks, equal rights are a beginning.

We know, moreover, that the Constitution was written to protect the privilege and status of white men. We do not come here to ask for our freedom. We are going to take it. It is rightfully ours.

As was said more than 100 years ago, I ask no favors for my sex. I surrender not our claim to equality. All I ask our brethren is that they will take their feet from off our necks and permit us to stand upright on the ground on which God has designed us to occupy.

Miss Goldman: These hearings are being held at a time when it is obvious that women are standing up for their rights. We know that this amendment will be passed by Congress in a vain attempt to absorb the growing pressure exerted by women in their own behalf.

The liberation of women has become the issue of the 1970's. The mass media—television, comic strips, magazines from the Atlantic Monthly to Family Circle—has distorted, manipulated and exploited the women's movement. Add now the U.S. Congress, close on the heels of Playboy Magazine, manifests its blatant hypocrisy by frantically searching for a way to co-opt a growing women's revolution.

We are aware the system will try to appease us with their paper offerings. We will not be appeased! Our demands can only be met by a total transformation of society which you cannot legislate, you cannot co-opt, you cannot control. The struggle belongs to the people.

Miss Angelina Grimké: That concludes our testimony to the Senate, such as it is represented here, but we still have a few things we would like to say to the people and particularly the women who are here.

So we talk to the people who are here. [Standing and facing the audience.]

At best, they offer women equal jobs with equal pay under this amendment. But we know that this is only an equal right to be exploited in a market economy based on profit and not on human needs; that even then women who work in a home will not be paid for the work that they do. And they still have the responsibility for the home whether they have outside employment or not.

They offer us equal access to higher education, but we know and especially today, that this is an equal opportunity to be shot and slaughtered on the campus.

The amendment will place equal responsibility on men and women for alimony, divorce, and child custody. But it does not deal with the reasons for failed marriages: the nuclear family which cannot meet human emotional needs. The nuclear family which is an isolated unit of the husband, wife and children, in this society takes no responsibility for children. We must, all of us, men and women, take up this responsibility. We are experimenting in new forms of cooperative and communal living. We are working to provide free 24-hour a day child care, community controlled.

The amendment will give us equal social security benefits, but what use are equal social security benefits in a country where all the necessities of life—food, clothes, housing—cost money and inflation is wildly out of control. The health industry makes over 2\frac{1}{2}$ billion profit each year after taxes. At the same time most of our people just simply cannot afford to be sick or old. We are working for free health care, for safe contraception and for abortion on demand.

They offer us an equal chance to kill and to die for the U.S. imperialism. We oppose the draft for both men and women. But like our sisters in Vietnam and Cambodia, we will fight for the liberation of oppressed peoples wherever we are.

Finally, they offer us equal representation on juries and equal criminal penalties within a totally corrupt and repressive judicial system. So-called justice for the Panther women in New Haven means being without bail in solitary confinement, being pregnant with no medical care, giving birth under armed guard, having the baby taken away by the State without the mother's consent, and later being used as a bribe for false testimony.

Constitutional amendments will not make any difference to these things, only revolutionary change can meet the demands that women are making today.

Free our sisters, free ourselves, all power to the people. [Leaving the room.]

Senator Bayh: Will you ladies care to stay for any questions or do you prefer not to?

Would someone like to question these ladies if they would stay for questions?

Senator Cook: Mr. Chairman

Senator Bayh: I don't think that is indispensable, but I have a question that I think would be appropriate.

I would like them to clarify some of the concerns they have. Senator Cook?

Senator Cook: Mr. Chairman, I would like to move that the last lady's remarks, be excluded from the record. I so move because of her statement that her testimony had been concluded and because I feel her remarks were intended for the audience rather than for the committee.

I also want to say, as an enthusiastic cosponsor of this amendment, that if I were to make a speech to a comparable group, which was unwilling to be questioned, I may not have extended the courtesy to such a group as you extended to them on this occasion.

I only say this because I think these hearings should be put in true perspective without the use of intimidation by either the witnesses or the committee.

Senator Bayh: I think the Senator from Kentucky, in his own inimical fashion, has put the previous remarks in proper perspective.

If the Senator has no serious objections, and in deference to our previous witnesses, I would like to consult them. If they desire to have their remarks listed in the record, then I see no reason why they should not be in the record. We don't need to agree with all the assumptions and conclusions. If they desire that they be part of the record, whether their position before the committee was just symbolic rather than substantive, I have no objection to these remarks being in the record.

Senator Cook: Obviously I want my remarks to state how I feel about the actions of the previous witness. I think that when witnesses are invited to testify it is because the committee wants to do the best job that it can. If it is the desire of the Chairman to keep those remarks in the record obviously it will be done.

However, I want my remarks to follow her remarks, because I think the record should show that after the first two witnesses concluded their remarks they got up from the witness table, faced the audience, and said that they wished to speak to the audience, not to the committee, for the purpose of the record.

Senator Bayh: We will take the appropriate steps to see that the posture, as well as the postulation of the witnesses, is included in the record.

I, of course, suppose that some committee chairmen and subcommittee chairmen might be concerned about manifestations of support or dissent exhibited in the hearing room. I do not care to follow this policy myself, realizing the extent to which strong feelings are involved in a matter such as this. The reason I was hopeful that the witnesses would permit us to explore their thoughts more fully is that the Chairman has recognized the strong show of support on the part of those who are presently in the hearing room, yet there seems to be significant support for some of the statements of the last witnesses and for the conclusion that the Chair was drawing, that they were opposed to the efforts to amend the Constitution in this fashion.

I am not sure that is a reasonable conclusion, and that is why I wanted these witnesses to clarify whether they were or were not in favor of this; indeed, one following their reasoning would have to conclude they saw no reason for the 13th, 14th, and 15th amendments.

Heaven only knows our history reflects the length of time it took to implement those amendments, but without those amendments it seems we would have been even harder pressed to do the job that was long overdue.

We ask the indulgence of the next witnesses, the three groups remaining, if they would permit us to recess and return at 2:15.

(Thereupon, at 1:15 p.m., the subcommittee took a recess, to reconvene at 2:15 p.m., the same day.)

Afternoon session

Senator Bayh: Our next witness is Mr. Mortimer Furay, Metropolitan Detroit AFL-CIO Council.

Mr. Furay.

**Statement of Mortimer Furay,
Metropolitan Detroit AFL-CIO Council**

Mr. Furay: I am here today representing the Detroit Metropolitan AFL—CIO Council, the organized labor group of my community.

I have been employed in the labor movement since 1937, most of that time representing women who worked—and worked, I might say, with their hands, not in a professional category, but women who worked with their hands.

I feel it an honor to be the first to speak against adoption of the so-called "Equal Rights Amendment," Senate Joint Resolution 61.

I might call on the indulgence of the committee to say that I cannot help but remember what happened to Andy Warhol who was shot by a feminist.

First of all, I feel the passage of this legislation is unnecessary since women are covered by the provisions of the 14th amendment guaranteeing all persons equal treatment under law. As if, indeed, any legal act of and by itself can guarantee anything. But more to the point, unless this proposal includes the Hayden retention proviso, it will repeal the thousands of laws, rules, regulations, directives, opinions, which now protect women from insidious and destructive working conditions visited upon them largely because of their biological composition and background.

[Voice from the audience.]

Senator Bayh: If the witness will yield, just as we permitted great flexibility this morning and tried to provide the maximum courtesy to all our witnesses, I trust that everyone will proceed accordingly this afternoon.

Please continue.

Mr. Furay: These laws are the result of years of research, debate, social action of momentous proportion for adoption and years of court testing. They have had subsequent reappraisals and amendments. While many are obsolete and inadequate, they constitute a protective force absolutely mandatory for women's protection.

The proponents of this legislation know not of the havoc they will wreak upon our women workers, their marriages, and familiar obligations. The irony is that this is being done in the name of women's liberation. I want to concentrate my testimony to rebut those who claim the difference between the sexes is minimal and we therefore no longer need protective legislation.

The proponents of pseudo-equality charge that modern industrial and technological methods of production has reduced the need for women's protective legislation. But the opposite is the case. Experts in the field of biomechanics have pointed out that the Second Industrial Revolution of mechanization and automation has created great changes in our workforce. And I would like to cite three of them:

1. Women are far more numerous in the workforce and therefore their safety and well-being constitutes a far greater concern than ever before. We are now talking about more than one-third of our national workforce.

2. Women are more intimately connected with mechanical schedules than they were a decade ago. They spend five to six times as much time of the day, touching, moving, or manipulating something mechanical.

3. For the first time in our history, more than 50 percent of the women in the workforce are married.

Researchers in the field of industrial medicine are beginning to explore the problems of female employment and as a result have uncovered a mass of information that points out the need for special concern, special protective legislation. Certainly, it rebuts those who are recommending the vacating of protective legislation.

Dr. Anna Baetjer in her book "Women in Industry" warns "women should not be required to work more than 55 to 60 hours a week even under very pressing circumstances. Most authorities recommend a maximum of 48 hours." That's why we in Michigan are fighting to retain our present, albeit obsolete, 54-hours maximum workweek law for women.

That's why the AFL—CIO Council of Detroit supported the fight of Stephanie Prociuk, of the United Auto Workers Union, in her suit against the Occupational Safety Standards Commission of the State of Michigan when they attempted to repeal the hours limitation law under the guise of the mistaken notion that the days of female exploitation are over.

It was during that legal battle that the Ad Hoc Committee Against the Repeal of Protective Legislation rallied the women of Michigan to support litigation that would enjoin the State from repealing protective laws.

They induced Dr. Erwin Tichauer, the worldwide authority on biomechanic medical engineering of the New York University Medical Center Institute of Rehabilitation Medicine, to testify as to his studies on the functional anatomy of the body. His testimony covered the locomotor performance, efficiency, sources of trauma, injury, fatigue, accident proneness, and the effects of work places on the physical health and safety of female workers, all subject matters of protective legislation.

What he had to say, unchallenged by the attorney-general of the State of Michigan, led Circuit Court Judge George T. Martin, to permanently restrain the Occupational Safety Standards Commission from repealing the Michigan maximum hour law. Dr. Tichauer's testimony induced the following paraphrasing for presentation here.

He pointed out that while industrial mechanization has improved conditions for the workers of America, it has created a whole new set of problems.

While the workload has been consistently lower in industry, a by-product of that change had been an increase in work stress on relatively small parts of the anatomy. Previously, people worked with their arms, back, hands—now they only push buttons and therefore, the work stress is concentrated, say, on the tip of the finger.

It is the women who are largely engaged in manipulative work, in requiring intensive application of effort for the entire working day. While operations have been simplified, the entire body is no longer used but certain muscle groups, repetitive movement patterns and certain parts of the anatomy of women are being stressed intensively for the entire day, while other parts are at rest.

This has led to an imbalance in work stress in respect to individual body segments in many female occupations. As a result, this concentrated work stress has created fatigue factors over long periods of time for women who, because of their structure, are unable to cope with it from both a medical, as well as from a plain physical discomfort point of view. This excessive concentrated work strain appearing after intervals of time is the overriding factor in the increased hazard to the health and safety of women so involved.

Because of these factors, women now need the protection of State protective legislation more than ever before—not less. To wipe out such legislation by enacting the proposed pseudo-equal rights amendment, as I have said before, without benefit of the Hayden proviso retaining all such current protection, would be a real blow to women resulting in further enslavement rather than their liberation.

Those who think equality will be gained by legislation are either ignorant or naive. My introductory course in sociology at Wayne University, long ago, dispelled any such belief in that panacea route. I was cited the passage in Tacitus "Quid leges sine moribus?" "What are laws without mores?"

I remember the postulation "When the mores are adequate, laws are unnecessary; and when the mores are inadequate, laws are useless." The mores on the status of women are inadequate and unreflective of sex equality. All our norms on this subject are designed by the evil power of male chauvinism. The statutes, the rules and regulations, the customs and folkways, the taboos and fashions, the rites and rituals, the ceremonies and conventions, and finally even etiquette of our society are blocks to accomplishing the objectives of true sex equality.

Our entire culture is captivated by chauvinism. You can forget the inscription on the pediment of Langdell Hall at Harvard's famous law school "Non sub homine, sed sub Deo et Lege"—"Not under man but under God and Law"—for the corruption on this subject is all pervasive.

Simone de Beauvoir, the French sociologist, correctly reminds us that in all societies:

> It is a woman who has been subject and slave, man who has been ruler and master. Woman is vassal, receptacle utensil, the nearest tool of man. She is conquered, subdued, vanquished in sexual encounter as in life. Man takes, woman gives. Man acts, woman waits. Man is always the one, woman the other. Always destined to wander in the world of man and never in the world of her own.

There is no genuine equality in the two sexes. Woman is always the other, never the one. Condemned to an eternal alterity and religious platitudes. "Blessed be God that he did not make me a woman," so runs the Hebrew prayer. Among the blessings for which Plato thanked God was first that he had "been born free and not a slave" and second, "that he was a man and not a woman." Herein lies the philosophical basis for male chauvinism supported by Aristotle who also maintained that "a female is a female by virtue of a certain lack of qualities." Do you wonder where the religious basis for our chauvinism comes from? St. Paul said:

The man is not of the woman, but the woman of the man. Neither was the man created for the woman but the woman for the man. For the husband is the head of the wife, as Christ is the head of the church. Let the wives be to their own husband in everything.

And we wonder where our double standard comes from.

John Chrysostom ascertained that "among all savage beasts, none is found so harmful as woman." St. Thomas Aquinas said she "was an imperfect man and an incidental being." The Genesis says that it was Eve who made the man eat the apple and it is she in consequence who is the author of his misfortune. This obvious male chauvinism must be counteracted because it is one of the roots of the evil.

It is man that has made the mores, they are the ones that created religions and philosophies, they occupy the center of the world stage. There has never been equality between the sexes, there is no equality now. The double standards of conduct assuredly still exist even though there has been a constantly narrowing gap between the privileges of the sexes.

Are women the marginal people destined forever to remain on the fringes of history? That condition must be rectified. If there is a woman problem and the intensity of the denials confirms the fact, it exists because biology places certain limitations upon cultural aspirations. To reconcile two careers, one based on physiological fulfillment and the other upon cultural creativity, this was the problem for which our society has found no satisfactory solution, but find one we must.

Women and men alike occupy many different statuses, but for women, the norms attached to these statuses pull them more frequently in two different directions and leave them in conflict caught between contradictory events. A woman can never forget her sex. On the role of sex to women, Margaret Mead has so aptly written:

A woman's life is punctuated by a series of specific events. The beginning of physical maturity at the menarche, end of virginity, pregnancy and birth, finally the menopause, the reproductive period as a woman is definitely over, however zestful she may be as an individual.

Each of these events because once past, can never be retraced, is momentous for a woman, whereas a man's ability to command an army or to discover a new drug is less tied to the way his body functions sexually. Sex in its whole meaning, from courtship through parenthood, means more to a woman than it does to a man although sexual acts may have more urgency for men than for women.

Senator Bayh: Would you yield just a moment?

Mr. Furay: Yes.

Senator Bayh: Have you had the good fortune to get to know Dr. Mead?

Mr. Furay: I have met her, I do not know her.

Senator Bayh: How old a lady would you say she is?

Mr. Furay: I would think she is in her seventies.

Senator Bayh: I suppose from all of these things that she describes for women she is probably beyond that point. Do you suggest that she is not making a significant contribution in many, many ways to this country right now?

Mr. Furay: I think Margaret Mead has made a greater contribution to the cause of women than any other woman in America, as a sociologist and as an anthropologist. I feel that the remarks she has made relative to this subject bear more listening to than those of any other person in the country.

Senator Bayh: It seems to me that if you take Margaret Mead's contribution and put that in proper perspective, it totally refutes what you are saying. [Applause.]

Please, let us permit our witness to respond.

She testified before our committee when we were discussing the 18-year-old vote. She did not relate the sexual attributes or the physical characteristics of a man or woman's sexual ability to their ability to comprehend, to their ability to contribute.

We are talking about apples and oranges; we are talking about different things.

Mr. Furay: I think her study, Senator, of the sex behavior and the sex patterns of people both from the primitive and from a modern point of view is unmatched by any other anthropologist in the world.

Senator Bayh: Yes. But with all due respect, I do not see how what she says here pertains to the problem of whether we should pass this amendment or not. She is saying that there are sexual differences between man and women. Can anybody deny that? What we are talking about is her ability to produce and to be treated as an equal in other areas.

Mr. Furay: That is exactly what I propose in my argument.

Senatory Bayh: You may continue. I just wanted to make a point. Senator Cook?

Senator Cook: Mr. Chairman, I will ask questions at the conclusion of this testimony.

Mr. Furay: To continue:

It was Mira Komarovsky who had to blast the President of a woman's college for claiming that a knowledge of cooking is more important than a knowledge of Kantian philosophy.

Since the days of Adam and Eve, there has been a sexual division of labor though not determined in any particular way. There is such a division in all societies, and it is fairly uniform because women bear the children in all societies. When we begin to talk about sex this is the one thing that we cannot forget. This is the one thing that Margaret Mead keeps reminding us of. The sexual division of labor is done on a biological base. The differences in the sex status can vary only within the limit of sexual capacities. Among these are the most important—the reproductive functions of the female, the physical strength of the male. The exceptions upon complete examination confirm the rule. These are facts with which we must reckon. These are conditions which we must understand in order to correct.

George Murdock, one of society's most famous anthropologists and sociologists, in a study of 220 nonliterate societies discovered regularities in the sexual division of labor. In those societies, warfare, metal working, hunting and fishing were predominantly male activities. Cooking, the manufacture and repair of clothing, pottery, and firemaking are predominantly female activities. Agriculture, on the contrary, was shared by both sexes.

In civilized society, we similarly find a sexual division of labor, which remains to this day. In view of the slowly growing equality between the sexes, it is somewhat surprising to note the number of voluntary associations still limited to one sex. The Cubs, the Brownies, the Boy Scouts, the Girl Scouts, YMCA, and the YWCA, are but a few examples where men and women do approximately the same things but do them in separate associations.

In spite of the decreasing emphasis on the sexual criteria in many occupations, it still persists. The separation of sexes is both a cultural and social phenomenon. It is deeply ingrained. Culturally speaking, men and women have a different status and conform to different norms, not only in our society but in all societies. This has been a stubborn deterrent to solve the sex equality problem.

Amran Scheinfeld, author of "Women and Men" made this observation:

> There is an important difference between the group principle as applied to any two races, two nations or two economic or social classes, and as applied to the two sexes as groups. Given time, individuals of any given race, national or social group can cross over, blend with, or be completely absorbed into another race, nation or society. Biological barriers need not be in the way. But the situation with sexes as a group is entirely different. No other such distinction and unalterable division of mankind exists, where it can never be possible for the two groups to merge and where, with each generation, men and women start off with the same biological dividing line between them and the same general tendencies toward differentiations in their work and social roles.

This kind of differentiation then is destined to last as long as human society will endure, few of us would not have it that way. In no society do male and females do the same thing, occupy the same status, share identical interests, conform to the same norms, or aspire to the same kinds of achievement. All societies channel the conduct of sexes in different directions just as they signalize the difference by a distinction in dress. But this does not mean that we cannot nor should not provide equality of treatment.

It need not be the same, but it should be equal. If the 14th amendment that removes from the statute books the very laws which help raise anyone postulate that an equal rights amendment will do it, an amendment that removes from the statute books the very laws which help raise women a part way up to the position of male, if only in the marketplace of their hire?

It is going to take the executive, legislative, and judicial branches of our Federal Government, our State, city and county governments combined with all the civic, religious, fraternal, political community, labor organizations to just start the job of bringing equality to women.

All the public media will have to join all of our educational institutions, from nursery school to college, to disseminate our intentions. Our economy must be marshalled, our power structures mandamused and our entire familial structures must be completely reoriented, if the desire for sex equality is to become a reality. It will take, not brassiereless Fridays, nor broom-riding frolics, but the complete mobilization of our social institutions to do that job.

Women must learn John Donne's lesson "no woman is an island" and men must learn the Jeffersonian maxim "freedom is indivisible" if we are to win this fight.

Will the passage of an equal rights amendment prevent the employers of this Nation from subtly discriminating against women by designing their buildings, factories, laundries, furniture, machines, tools, and fixtures for men, as they now do? Of course not. We live in a society so male-oriented that the forms of discrimination assault women every second of their lives. They are discriminated against covertly and overtly, grossly and in the most subtle fashions!

Take the matter of simple tool design. The charts and hard data for body measurements used in determining dimension of tools and hardware which come in contact with workers have been designed in an industrial environment largely geared to men. As research for design progresses and data for measurement was sought, it came from available statistics.

There is a great amount of data available on men but much less available on women, surprisingly less. Generally speaking, it is a common occurrence that a woman has to adapt herself to a tool or a machine designed for the body contours and body measurement of men. Though the situation is being corrected, it will take from 10 to 15 years for new information to filter through the design process. Most of the information supplied industry for tool, furniture, and machine design comes from the "Measurement of Man," charts published by the Whitney Library of Design or the "Human Factor in Design" published by the Mitre Corp.

What data there is compiled for women deals largely with type-writers. Research now going on is 7 years behind the change in the work force. It takes at least 5 years to get the results of research into production. It will, therefore, be a long time before machines will be properly designed for women. This is a matter of concern about the health and safety of working women.

When Dr. Tichauer was asked the question by the Circuit Court "What is the effect of the extension of the workday beyond 10 hours a day and beyond 54 hours a week for women?" This is a law that would be repealed if the amendment were passed, he answered.

"Considering the normal state of affairs among women, that most have another job to do by looking after household and domestic chores, it would definitely be detrimental to occupational safety and it would certainly not enhance their health and well-being. I would also say that even if they have no domestic work, the length of the work day beyond 10 hours would, in my opinion, increase her accident proneness and would, worst of all, render her more liable to off-the-job accidents such as are caused by erratic movements which would end by her burning herself on the kitchen stove, using an iron, or being involved in traffic accidents."

[Voices from the audience.]

Senator Cook: Mr. Chairman, as a result of having visited some college campuses where I did not have the right to speak I hope that all here today would understand that everyone has a right to speak. I would also hope that every lady in this room would give those of differing opinion an opportunity to be heard.

I am not sure that all of Mr. Furay's statements are relevant to the amendment to the Constitution. I find his point concerning existing equal rights legislation especially irrelevant.

Senator Bayh: The point is well taken.

Mr. Furray, please continue.

Mr. Furay: When asked "Are women more susceptible to injury, to accidents than men because of differences between men and women." he answered:

> In certain fields of manufacturing activity or domestic activity, yes. In other fields, no. This cannot be answered categorically. Women are structurally different from men. They have a different anatomy, not only in the quality of their organs, but also by dimensions which affect the mechanical advantage or disadvantage of the muscles employed. The ability to perform mechanically, the ability to produce work output, is related to the lean muscle mass of the body. This is undoubtedly less in the case of women. Women have certain different respiratory characteristics, the vital capacity of respiration in the case of women is lower, so if you compare the physique of women and men, her work tolerance, her endurance, are definitely lower.
>
> When you have a group of people who engage in a task which is heterogeneous, men and women, old and young, all workers of equal efficiency and at equal levels of physiological health and well-being at the beginning, only as the length of the task lengthens, will individual differences become more apparent. In many occupations, there are numerous situations where the efficiency of woman is not impaired for 6, 7 8, 9, 10

hours, and then all of a sudden, the limit of activity of work tolerance has been reached and efficiency drops, and personal levels of comfort drop and accident risks increase. The first aspect as to the difference between men and women, are many having home duties. The second factor, is the anatomical differences between men and women, the muscle structure, the number, and extent of the muscle structure, also the body measurements with respect to muscle.

When asked if any known statistic indicates a comparison between male and female muscle power, he answered:

The National Safety Council states in its manual that the endurance of women to perform is one-third less than that of men.

He responded to this question, "Do you have any figure indicating the extent to which women have a difference in their respiratory quality?" by testifying:

Most researchers, including myself, have found this vital capacity to be 20 percent less. The operating characteristics of the respiratory system relate to oxygen transport to the tissues, to the muscles, and determines the combustion efficiency. If a woman has less muscle mass, the amount of oxygen she needs to perform will also be less. Like in a motor car, the size of the engine being smaller, her fuel intake and the oxygen intake to burn this fuel will be less. This ability to inhale less of oxygen affects the ability in much the same way as with a motor car. A small engine has difficulties on a long climb that might be performing very well in the city. In the same way, a trained athlete develops large muscle capacity that he must have, and therefore, develops great endurance and greater peak performance levels. It might not always affect their ability to produce average performances, but many examples show that the ability to perform at peaks is impaired in women. Scholars and students of the subject, including myself, ascribe this to the combined effect of less muscle mass and less respiratory capacity.

We learned from Dr. Tichauer's testimony, the real impact of male chauvinist antiquated concepts, deeply rooted superstitutions upon the life of our women. We learned the disastrous effects upon them as wage earners. We were shocked to learn of our ignorance-induced complicity in this matter.

We finally learned to value what protective laws we have and the need to improve them, expand their scope and broaden their coverage. We learned enough to oppose, with determination and resolution, the repeal of any law designed to protect women, whether it be to satisfy the selfish needs of some employer, or the misdirected action of some of our citizenry infatuated with the concept of power unaware of power's awesomeness and responsibility. Under both categories, we place the supporters of the equal rights amendment.

Please do not pass this legislation because you will have contributed to the darkness on the matter and added to the plight of the working women of America. . . .

The House Debates the Equal Rights Amendment

While the 91st Senate did not pass the Equal Rights Amendment, the 91st House of Representatives did. On August 10, 1970, the House of Representatives debated House Joint Resolution 264 (same as S.J. 61). First, the motion to discharge the Committee on the Judiciary from consideration of the amendment was debated. After the vote for discharge was passed by a vote of 332 to 22, the Equal Rights Amendment itself was debated. Below are portions of that debate. First, Mrs. Griffiths speaks for the discharge motion and Mr. Celler speaks against it. This is followed by Mr. Celler's remarks in opposition to the Equal Rights Amendment. Speeches by Congresswomen Green and Chisholm supporting the amendment follow Mr. Celler's remarks.

On August 10, 1970, the United States House of Representatives passed the Equal Rights Amendment by a 350 to 15 vote.

Representative Martha W. Griffiths
Speaks in Support of the Discharge Motion

Mrs. Griffiths: Mr. Speaker, for 47 consecutive years this amendment has been introduced into the Congress of the United States. For 26 years both parties in their political conventions have endorsed it; the Republican Party has endorsed it for 30 years. Yet it has been 22 years since the Judiciary Committee of the House has even held a hearing on it. On the eve of the 50th birthday of women suffrage, it appears reasonable to me that the proponents of this legislation, who are more than a majority of this House, have a right to have this legislation discussed. We ask only 1 hour to convince you that the amendment is fair and reasonable; and I will yield 15 minutes of that hour at the request of the gentleman from New

York (Mr. Celler) to Judiciary members for debate who may oppose it.

Give us a chance to show you that those so-called protective laws to aid women—however well-intentioned originally—have become in fact restraints, which keep wife, abandoned wife, and widow alike from supporting her family. . . .

**Representative Emanuel Celler Speaks
against the Discharge Motion**

Mr. Celler: Mr. Speaker, I oppose the motion to discharge the Committee on the Judiciary from consideration of House Joint Resolution 264, proposing an amendment to the Constitution of the United States relative to equal rights for men and women. What we are being asked to do is to vote on a constitutional amendment, the consequences of which are unexamined, its meaning nondefined, and its risks uncalculated.

On July 16, 1970, I placed in the *Congressional Record* the notice that the Judiciary Committee would hold hearings on September 16. Certainly, if the House is asked to vote on a constitutional amendment of this magnitude, it must have before it a record of expert testimony upon which to base its collective judgment. You should know that the Judiciary Committee has not been idle in preliminary staff study consideration of the possible affects of the amendment. The American Law Division of the Library of Congress has been requested to and has delivered to the committee samplings of the laws of 11 States and the District of Columbia relating to support, custody, divorce, separation and alimony which could be abrogated, for good or evil, by the adoption of this constitutional amendment—Alabama, Alaska, California, Colorado, District of Columbia, Hawaii, Illinois, Massachusetts, Nevada, New York, Pennsylvania and Texas.

I quote some portions thereof:

> So far as we can ascertain, no definitive legal analysis has ever been undertaken which purports to examine in detail any of the ramification of these problems; and since no State has adopted a constitutional amendment of similar purpose, no court decision precedents exist that might provide some basis for prediction. This report, therefore, can do more than express our views in the form of what we believe is at best only reasonable speculation, as to some of the more significant aspects of domestic relations law, statutory and case law, which might be subject to reevaluation in the light of a possible "Equal Rights" Amendment."

Subsequent to the receipt of the American Law Division of the Library of Congress report, I wrote to the attorneys general of each State asking for information for committee use as to what laws, if any, could be affected by the proposal. The replies are now coming in. The attorney general of Texas has sent this committee a list of State laws which as he states may or may not be affected. He cannot make a definitive reply any more than could the Library of Congress. Can we? Do we know? We cannot even begin to speculate until a body of information is before us, derived from considered testimony, analysis and exact information such as we have sought from the 50 States.

According to Prof. Paul Freund of the Harvard Law School, concurred in by numerous other legal scholars, every provision of law concerning woman would raise a constitutional issue which would have to be resolved in the courts. Others argue that women presently have the same constitutional protection under the fifth and 14th amendments that they would have upon adoption of the equal rights amendment. Maybe they are right; maybe they are wrong. Can we afford to grope in the dark without any concrete evidence.

Each of us is in a sense blindfolded. How can we discharge our responsibilities without even the knowledge of which laws of the very States which sent us here could be abrogated, voided, or changed. Some should be, others not. But at the very least, we should know. Only hearings can produce that body of knowledge. The committee has already begun its work; we ask only for the opportunity to complete it.

Further, on June 30, July 7 and 13, and August 4, our colleagues Mikva, Griffiths, Ryan, and William D. Ford introduced a proposal to carry out the recommendations of the Presidential Task Force on Women's Rights and Responsibilities. The proposal is specific, its direction clear, its provisions immediately operative upon enactment. The two proposals, the equal rights amendment and the Women's Equality Act of 1970, as it is termed, should be considered together in committee hearings. The concrete versus the abstract should be joined in issue so that again, the Members of this body can judge and vote with chapter and verse before them.

Let us not leap into the thicket until we can at the very least know a bit about the terrain on which we will land, and where it will lead.

After just 1 hour of debate should this motion prevail, we shall be asked to vote on a constitutional amendment.

Feminists clamor for equal rights. Nobody can deny that women should have equality under the law. But ever since Adam gave up his rib to make a woman, throughout the ages we have learned that physical, emotional, psychological and social differences exist and dare not be disregarded.

Neither the National Women's Party nor the delightful, delectable and dedicated gentlelady from Michigan (Mrs. Griffiths) can change nature. They cannot do it.

Beyond that, let me say that there is as much difference between a male and a female as between a horse chestnut and a chestnut horse—and as the French say, Vivé la difference.

Any attempt to pass an amendment that promises to wipe out the effects of these differences is about as abortive as trying to fish in a desert—and you cannot do that.

There is no really genuine equality and I defy anyone to tell me what "equality" in this amendment means. Even your five fingers—one is not equal to the other—they are different.

You know, as a matter of fact, there is only one place where there is equality—and that is in the cemetery.

Women have thrown off many shakles with the help of men. I admit some shackles remain. Our duty is to abolish distinctions based on sex except such as are reasonably justified by differences in physical structure or biological or social function. The equal rights amendment would eliminate all distinctions in legal treatment of men and women even when the fundamental reasonableness and common sense of such differences is apparent.

For example, under the Federal Jury Selection Act of 1968, women with children today may seek and obtain an excuse from Federal Jury duty on the grounds of undue hardship or extreme inconvenience.

Will women hereafter be prohibited from requesting such excuse from jury service—because a man cannot have such an excuse? Where is the equality then? Man has the right to say that if women have the right, then men should have the right.

The adoption of a blunderbuss amendment would erase existing protective female legislation with the most disastrous consequences.

You would have scores of thousands of working women without the proper protection from oppressive and fatal practices.

Some feminists casually say—We do not want protection, we want liberation.

Will you tell that to the female factory worker and to the female farmworker and get their reply? It would require very buoyant prescience to predict the effects of this amendment. Scores and scores of laws— State, municipal, and Federal Government—make distinctions in their applications, and, therefore, it would be impossible to determine exactly what the consequences would be. I say let us at least have hearings before we pass upon an amendment as important as this one. . . .

Representative Emanuel Celler Speaks against the Equal Rights Amendment

Mr. Celler: I rise in opposition to House Joint Resolution 264.

Mr. Speaker, remember that the joint resolution would create equal rights for men as well as equal rights for women. If a right is accorded to a woman and not to a male, that male has a right to object to that woman's right as not accorded to him.

Where would that apply? It would apply to the State laws of alimony. Strangely, it may relate to State laws concerning rape, to military service, support of the family, domicile, age of consent, the bastardy laws, and a whole slew of other laws that time does not permit me to mention.

We have assiduously in the Congress avoided giving jurisdiction to the Federal Government in domestic relations, marital, and divorce matters. But we would be plunged into that cockpit by the adoption of this amendment, because one of the provisions of the amendment states that the Federal Government has the right to enforce the provisions of the amendment. The intrusion of the hand of the Federal Legislature and the Federal courts into the very delicate personal relationships of husband and wife and their relationship to their children, including custody and bastardy laws, as I said before, age of consent, and so forth, would bring grief untold.

Remember also that there is no time limit specified for ratification of the amendment. Examine House Joint Resolution 264 and you will see how loosely it has been drawn, how incompletely it has been conceived. This amendment could roam around State legislatures for 50 years. Customarily we provide that ratification must occur within 7 years of its submission to the States. But there is no provision of that sort in this resolution. There is unlimited time for the States to ratify it. Ultimately, the Congress will be confronted with the responsibility of determining the validity of State legislature approval.

Do you want to approve an amendment of that sort with such a loose end? Think carefully about that, ladies and gentlemen.

It has been said by the distinguished Speaker—and I have the highest regard for his opinion, but even a cat can look at a king—he says it is a historic step forward. I say it is a historic step backward. Labor spent years and years to get protective legislation for factoryworkers and farmworkers.

At one fell swoop this amendment would wipe out all those protective laws that we, after arduous toil, sought to put on the statute books. And the feminists cavalierly, as I said before, would say, "we do not want protection, we want liberation." I say "Tell that to the Marines." Tell that to the female farmworkers. Tell that to the female factoryworkers. Then get your reply. They want these protections: protection against arduous labor; protection against manual and heavy weight-lifting requirements; protection against night work; protection in reference to certain rest periods. These all would go by the board, because they are not accorded to men. Think about that before you vote for this amendment.

As I said, we would just dump the Congress into the cockpit of domestic and marital relations concerning alimony, divorce, domicile, and community property as well as child custody, support and maintenance. We have addressed ourselves over many years against specific wrongs leveled against women. We have arrested many kinds of discriminations against women. That has been done with the help of men. I have been in the forefront of that kind of battle. I struggled long and arduously for passage of title VII of the Civil Rights Act of 1967, giving equality to women in employment. We passed the equal pay law for equal work for women. We passed hundreds of statutes. Hundreds have been passed in the States and in the Federal Government.

That is the way to proceed in these matters and not by using this blunderbuss proposal that will wipe out all the good as well as the bad. I do not want to wipe out the good. This unfortunately would wipe out the good.

There are over 20 million married women who are nonworking full-time homemakers. What about those homemakers? I am not speaking of the professional women who are in the forefront of this demand for this amendment. What about the homemakers? We do not hear from them, but they are vitally interested. Close to 60 percent of the women in the labor force are married and must depend upon their husbands for the majority of the family income. Thus, there are approximately 44 million who depend upon their husbands to provide the primary support for the family, and eminent authorities maintain that the equal rights amendment would abolish the common rule whereby a husband has the primary right to support his family.

Thus, I hope that the amendment will be voted down.

Mr. Speaker, I do not oppose this proposed amendment lightly; I have devoted many years of my life pursuing the goal of equality of opportunity for all people. Nor do I oppose the so-called equal rights amendment with the patronizing smugness of the male. Discriminations against women do exist as has been time and time again conclusively shown. The inequality in pay scales, the inequality to access to higher education, to high posts in business and Government, to cite but a few, cannot be justified or defended and the understandable passion to break these barriers to equality cannot be dismissed.

If the equal rights amendment supplied the remedy I would be among the first to rise in its support. It does not. It is, I am sorry to state, a deft, vague ear- and eye-catching slogan, deceiving in its simplicity and dangerous because of its very simplicity. It is an abstraction, the words of which are not susceptible to definition or to clarity of meaning. Even the proponents of the legislation disagree on intent. There are those supporting the amendment who believe that that which differentiates necessarily discriminates, that only identity of treatment can destroy discrimination. Other proponents declare that it will in no wise affect operation of law based on functional differences.

It interests me greatly that the Citizens' Advisory Council on the Status of Women, in a statement issued in March of 1970 in defense of the equal rights amendment, talks about the "probable meaning and effect" of that amendment. We are asked to throw a rock into a churning sea with only guesswork as to what the waves will bring to the shores. It states unequivocally:

> The amendment would restrict only governmental action and would not apply to purely private action.

Yet we know that the courts more and more have extended right of suits to private action. Quo vadis? Possibly into the private quarrels, private wishes, private adjustments of two joined in matrimony? . . .

**Representative Edith Green Speaks
in Support of the Equal Rights Amendment**

Mrs. Green of Oregon: Mr. Speaker, first of all, may I pay my respects to the gentlewoman from Michigan for her courage and for her determination in bringing this amendment to the floor today, after years and years of neglect in the Judiciary Committee. I cannot express too strongly my admiration and my respect for her. She has already outlined to us the failure of the Supreme Court to act to bring full constitutional rights to women. May I suggest that her logic, her legal competence, her articulateness recommend her for a position on the highest court. There is nothing that would have pleased me more than had the previous administration appointed her as the first woman Justice to the U.S. Supreme Court.

Mr. Speaker, after listening to some of the debate, may I say it actually seems incredible to me that in the last quarter of the 20th century, we are still debating whether or not the majority of the American people have equal rights under the Constitution.

It has been said that if this amendment is passed it will create profound social changes. May I say to you, it is high time some profound social changes were made in our society. A bit later, I intend to suggest where some of these changes should occur. I hope that the debate today will not be based on "vive la difference" arguments, but rather with the words of Walt Whitman in mind: "That whatever degrades another degrades me, and whatever is said or done returns at last to me."

If we have the power and we do not act to remove the barriers that result in waste and injustice and frustration, then society is the loser, and any kind of discrimination is degrading to the individual and harmful to society as a whole.

Women know that there is no such thing as equality per se but only equal opportunity to——and this is what women want: equal rights and equal opportunity to make the best one can of one's life within one's capability and without fear of injustice or oppression or denial of those opportunities.

That is really what we are asking today.

Now what are the facts? Several years ago the Congress under the leadership of the gentleman from New York (Mr. Celler) passed the civil rights bill including title VII which said that there should be no discrimination in employment based on race, color, creed, national origin, or sex.

Congress, in passing that, did not state a preference of ending one kind of discrimination over the other. Any preference that has been made has been an administrative preference. The Equal Employment Opportunity Commission has referred many complaints to the Justice Department—Complaints about discrimination based on race and complaints about discrimination based on sex. The Justice Department has taken up many where discrimination because of race has occurred. But until last month the Justice Department had not instituted a single case where a complaint was sent over from the Equal Employment Opportunity Commission a complaint of discrimination because of sex.

How prevalent is discrimination based on sex? What impact does it have on our Nation socially and economically. The disproportion in employment has become the criterion by which discrimination against members of ethnic minorities stands confirmed.

It seems no less applicable as to discrimination against women. Let us look at Civil Service. In the Civil Service grades of 3, 4, 5, and 6 where the salaries are low there are many women employed. But what about the policy positions: grade levels 16, 17, and 18. In each one of these grade levels where the salaries are from $25,000 to $35,000, less than 1 percent of the positions are filled by women. Ninety-nine percent of the positions in each of these grade levels are filled by men.

Let us go to the other end of the financial spectrum, let us take the apprenticeship program which is under the jurisdiction of the Congress, I am advised that there are now 278,000 positions in the apprenticeship program nationwide. Only 1 percent of these are held by girls and 99 percent are held by boys.

Let us look at the Job Corps which was voted by this Congress. Some of us tried to get 50 percent of those positions made available to girls. On my own committee there was strong opposition to this and we could never get, by legislation or by administrative act, a program which would provide equal opportunities for girls and boys. This year girls have the highest percentage of positions that they have ever had in the history of the program. This year 29 percent of the Job Corps positions are filled by girls, 71 percent are held by boys. Members of the Education and Labor Committee of this Congress argued against making any more positions available for girls.

When we look at the need, when we look at the unemployment rate among 16- to 21-year-old youth, the highest unemployment rate in the Nation is among nonwhite girls between 16 and 21. In recent weeks we have heard about the economic impact in our society when there is 5 or 6 percent unemployment, but among nonwhite girls, looking for jobs, the unemployment rate is 37.7 percent. Boys not only have 99 percent of the apprenticeship program slots and 71 percent of the Job Corps positions but also this year and each of the preceding years the military has taken about 100,000 boys who are below standard for special training. The military will not take any girl who is not a high school graduate—or a high school equivalency—and also one who scores higher on the test than is required for the boys.

What kind of impact does this form of legal discrimination have? When we bar girls from the kind of training which will enable them to have employable skills such as apprenticeship and meaningful Job Corps programs or something similar, the result is disastrous. Studies by the Women's Bureau show that girls must literally go into prostitution or have a baby so they can get on welfare in order to physically survive and then society places the sordid stigma on these girls who have "gone wrong" when actually society has refused to give them the opportunity to receive training. When this condition exists I suggest it is not the girl so much who is sick but I suggest that it is society which is sick.

And what a sad commentary on our society today when various studies of fourth and fifth grade classes have been made, 99 percent of the boys are glad that they are boys, but 30 to 40 percent of the girls wish that they were boys because boys have greater opportunities. What does this say to a society that leaves that kind of an imprint on a girl so young? The search for identity and dignity is shared by each individual whichever his or her sex, whatever his or her race, whatever his or her national origin.

All of us, men and women, black and white, share not only a spiritual and moral involvement with mankind but an economically, socially, and politically dependent involvement which should make the action and fate of the least of us—of great consequence to the rest of us.

Discrimination is as corrosive and brutalizing to those who discriminate as it is to those who are its objects. In short we are all its victims—those who perpetuate it, those who tolerate it, those who bear its brunt.

My concern today and in past years is based not only on the documented need for brainpower of women, but, also, because I see in it a surrender on the part of young women to myths about themselves which have no relation to reality.

What about education? The latest statistics which I have show that

53.1 percent of the female high school graduates get into college; 70.3 percent of the male high school graduates get into college. I am advised that last year in Virginia 21,000 girl applicants for college were rejected. Not one single boy applicant was rejected. In many colleges we still find that a higher grade point average is required for a girl than for a young man. In one department of a prestigious school in the District of Columbia girls of the second level, academically, are admitted while boys are accepted on the basis of highest scores first. Why? A limited number of girls is admitted and they do not take the girls who have the highest scores.

The 1970 census shows that in full time year around employment, if you are an eighth grade graduate and male the average salary is $7,140. If you are an eighth grade graduate and female the average salary $3,970. If you are a high school graduate and male the average salary is $9,100. If you are a high school graduate and female the average salary is $5,280. If you are a college graduate and male—according to the 1970 census— the average salary is $13,320; if you are a college graduate and female the average salary is $7,930. Starting salaries are lower; promotions are fewer for women.

At the graduate level discrimination intensifies. According to the latest figures I have—which are 1966—two thirds of the master's degrees have gone to men and 88 percent of the Ph. D.s have gone to men. Arbitrary age limits have been placed on women for admission to graduate work. And in some cases for women this age limit is 35. This works a particular hardship on women who have left the labor market to rear children and want to reenter at the age of 35 or 40 with 25 or 30 years of productive service from which society would benefit.

In the halls of academe, women are more welcome in lower paid jobs than at the higher paid jobs. The median salary for women full professors is $11,649 and the medial salary for a male full professor is $12,768— a differential of over $1100. In order to get the equal pay for equal work bill passed in this Congress in 1963, we were forced to accept an exemption for equal pay for equal work for women who were in executive, administrative, or professional jobs. It is my hope that this year we will remove that exemption.

The proportion of women in the professions is lower in this country than in most industrialized countries throughout the world. Professionally, women in the United States constitute only 9 percent of all professions; 8 percent of all scientists; 3.5 percent of all lawyers, and 1 percent of all engineers. Women constitute only 6.7 percent of all physicians—an especially interesting percentage when one observes that over 60 percent of the doctors in the Soviet Union are women.

Several years ago a Rockefeller report stated:

> Ultimately—the source of the greatness of any nation is in the individuals who constitute the living substance of the nation—an undiscovered talent, a wasted skill, a misapplied ability is a threat to the capacity of a free people to survive.

Let me discuss briefly the economic conditions faced by the working women of this country. At issue is not whether women should work; at issue is not labor but economic reward and opportunities. The facts are that as of 1970, 31,293,000 women are working. I noticed that the labor unions are opposing this amendment today. For years union negotiators negotiated contracts where identical work was performed by men and by women and written into the contract was a provision paying women less than the men. Even today there are various kinds of polite subterfuges to get around the Equal Pay Act of 1963. Promotions have been far more difficult for women. In talking about full-time year around employees, a decade ago women's median salary was 64 percent of that of men. In 1968 women's median salary is 58 percent of that of men. While other parts of our society have improved their economic status—for women there has been a 6 percent decrease in comparison in this decade.

The evidence shows that 41 percent of the poor children in the United States are completely dependent on the earnings of women and even more than 41 percent would be if women were not willing to take these low-paying jobs. Numerically, discrimination based on sex affects far more individuals than does discrimination based on race. There are more white women in the United States in the lowest income brackets than all of the Negro men and Negro women combined in lowest income brackets. This has tremendous implications for a society that talks about poverty and disadvantaged children. Equal efforts ought to be made to correct injustice whether it is discrimination because of sex or discrimination because of race.

The facts are that women—like men—work for compelling economic reasons. May I suggest that the female rebellion of these years has sound economic causes.

To fail to provide equal educational opportunities, to fail to apply equal economic rewards, and to fail to apply the creative, intellectual, and physical talents of women to the menagerie of ills of a great society can only bring profound regret when we mark the balance sheet for the American experiment at the turn of the century.

If we do succeed in beating our swords into plowshares—no hand dare lay idle at that plowshare if we are to seek a better tomorrow for our children.

Playwright Bernard Shaw wrote:

> The great secret, Eliza, is not having bad manners or good manners or any other particular sort of manners, but having the same manner for all human souls; in short, behaving as if you were in Heaven, where there are no third class carriages and where one soul is as good as another.

The secret in our democracy is not having certain rights for those whose color is white or those whose color is black, not having certain rights for males and others for females; not having certain rights for certain ones who are in power, but having equal rights and equal opportunities for all.

It has already been said that women have been working for the equal rights amendment for almost half a century.

Jane Addams wrote:

> It requires an unfaltering courage to act year after year in the belief that the hoary abominations of society can only be done away with through the steady impinging of fact on fact—of interest on interest—of will on will.

To my colleagues may I say that women's courage, women's hopes are beginning to falter when they realize that the "daily impinging of fact upon fact" has done little to persuade the men in the National legislative body and in the State legislatures to correct an injustice that has existed since our country was born. I suggest that the time is long since past when women should be required to be treated as second-class citizens and not entitled to the same equal rights under the Constitution as are the male members of our society.

The search for human identity and dignity is not uniquely any one person's. Every man and every woman pursues the search for his and her place in the sun where each may stand with a sense of self-respect and self-worth equal to that of all other human beings. No sex, no nationality, no race of people has a monopoly on this desire for full human fulfill-ment. . . .

Representative Shirley Chisholm Speaks
in Support of the Equal Rights Amendment

Mrs. Chisholm: Mr. Speaker, House Joint Resolution 264, before us to-day, which provides for equality under the law for both men and women, represents one of the most clear-cut opportunities we are likely to have to declare our faith in the principles that shaped our Constitution. It provides a legal basis for attack on the most subtle, most pervasive and most institutionalized form of prejudice that exists. Discrimination against women, solely on the basis of their sex, is so widespread that it seems to many persons normal, natural and right. Legal expression of prejudice on the grounds of religious or political belief has become a minor problem in our society. Prejudice on the basis of race is, at least, under systematic attack. There is reason for optimism that it will start to die with the present older generation. It is time we act to assure full equality of opportunity to those citizens who, although in a majority, suffer the restrictions that are more commonly imposed on minorities, to women.

The argument that this amendment will not solve the problem of sex discrimination is not relevant. If the argument were used against a civil rights bill—as it has been used in the past—the prejudice that lies behind it would be embarrassing. Of course laws will not eliminate prejudice from the hearts of human beings. But that is no reason to allow prejudice to continue to be enshrined in our laws—to perpetuate injustice through inaction.

The amendment is necessary to clarify countless ambiguities and inconsistencies in our legal system. For instance, the Constitution guarantees due process of law, in the fifth and 14th amendments. But the applicability of due process to sex distinctions is not clear: Women are excluded from some State colleges and universities. In some States, restrictions are placed on a married woman who engages in an independent business. Women may not be chosen for some juries. Women even receive heavier criminal penalties than men who commit the same crime.

What would the legal effects of the equal rights amendment really be? The equal rights amendment would govern only the relationship between the State and its citizens—not relationships between private citizens.

The amendment would be largely self-executing, that is, any Federal or State laws in conflict would be ineffective 1 year after date of ratification without further action by the Congress or State legislatures.

Opponents of the amendment claim its ratification would throw the law into a state of confusion and would result in much litigation to establish its meaning. This objection overlooks the influence of legislative history in determining intent and the recent activities of many groups preparing for legislative changes in this direction.

State labor laws applying only to women, such as those limiting hours of work and weights to be lifted, would become inoperative unless the legislature amended them to apply to men. As of early 1970 most States would have some laws that would be affected. However, changes are being made so rapidly as a result of the title VII of the Civil Rights Act of 1964, it is likely that by the time the equal rights amendment would become effective, no conflicting State laws would remain.

In any event, there has for years been great controversy as to the usefulness to women of these State labor laws. There has never been any doubt that they worked a hardship on women who need or want to work overtime and on women who need or want better paying jobs, and there has been no persuasive evidence as to how many women benefit from the archaic policy of the laws. After the Delaware hours law was repealed in 1966, there were no complaints from women to any of the State agencies that might have been approached.

Jury service laws not making women equally liable for jury service would have to be revised.

The selective service law would have to include women, but women would not be required to serve in the Armed Forces where they are not fitted any more than men are required to serve. Military service, while a great responsibility, is not without benefits, particularly for young men with limited education or training. Since October 1966, 246,000 young men who did not meet the normal mental or physical requirements have been given opportunities for training and correcting physical problems. This opportunity is not open to their sisters. Only girls who have completed high school and meet high standards on the educational test can volunteer. Ratification of the amendment would not permit application of higher standards to women.

Survivorship benefits would be available to husbands of female workers on the same basis as to wives of male workers. The Social Security Act and the civil service and military service retirement acts are in conflict.

Public schools and universities could not be limited to one sex and could not apply different admission standards to men and women. Laws requiring longer prison sentences for women than men would be invalid, and equal opportunities for rehabilitation and vocational training would have to be provided in public correctional institutions.

Different ages of majority based on sex would have to be harmonized.

Federal, State, and other governmental bodies would be obligated to follow nondiscriminatory practices in all aspects of employment, including public school teachers and State university and college faculties.

What would be the economic effects of the equal rights amendment? Direct economic effects would be minor. If any labor laws applying only to women still remained, their amendment or repeal would provide opportunity for women in better-paying jobs in manufacturing. More opportunities in public vocational and graduate schools for women would also tend to open up opportunities in better jobs for women.

Indirect effects could be much greater. The focusing of public attention on the gross legal, economic, and social discrimination against women by hearings and debates in the Federal and State legislatures would result in changes in attitude of parents, educators, and employers that would bring about substantial economic changes in the long run.

Sex prejudice cuts both ways. Men are oppressed by the requirements of the Selective Service Act, by enforced legal guardianship of minors, and by alimony laws. Each sex, I believe, should be liable when necessary to serve and defend this country.

Each has a responsibility for the support of children.

There are objections raised to wiping out laws protecting women workers. No one would condone exploitation. But what does sex have to do with it? Working conditions and hours that are harmful to women are harmful to men; wages that are unfair for women are unfair for men. Laws setting employment limitations on the basis of sex are irrational, and the proof of this is their inconsistency from State to State. The physical characteristics of men and women are not fixed, but cover two wide spans that have a great deal of overlap. It is obvious, I think, that a robust woman could be more fit for physical labor than a weak man. The choice of occupation would be determined by individual capabilities, and the rewards for equal work should be equal.

This is what it comes down to: artificial distinctions between persons must be wiped out of the law. Legal discrimination between the sexes is, in almost every instance, founded on outmoded views of society and the prescientific beliefs about psychology and physiology. It is time to sweep away these relics of .he past and set future generations free of them.

Federal agencies and institutions responsible for the enforcement of equal opportunity laws need the authority of a Constitutional amendment. The 1964 Civil Rights Act and the 1963 Equal Pay Act are not enough; they are limited in their coverage—for instance, one excludes teachers, and the other leaves out administrative and professional women. The Equal Employment Opportunity Commission has not proven to be an adequate device, with its powers limited to investigation, conciliation and recommendation to the Justice Department. In its cases involving sexual discrimination, it has failed in more than one-half. The Justice Department has been even less effective. It has intervened in only one case involving discrimination on the basis of sex, and this was on a procedural point. In a second case, in which both sexual and racial discrimination were alleged, the racial bias charge was given far greater weight.

Evidence of discrimination on the basis of sex should hardly have to be cited here. It is in the Labor Department's employment and salary figures for anyone who is still in doubt. Its elimination will involve so many changes in our State and Federal laws that, without the authority and impetus of this proposed amendment, it will perhaps take another 194 years. We cannot be parties to continuing a delay. The time is clearly now to put this House on record for the fullest expression of that equality of opportunity which our founding fathers professed.

They professed it, but they did not assure it to their daughters, as they tried to do for their sons.

The Constitution they wrote was designed to protect the rights of white, male citizens. As there were no black Founding Fathers, there were no founding mothers—a great pity, on both counts. It is not too late to complete the work they left undone. Today, here, we should start to do so.

In closing I would like to make one point. Social and psychological effects will be initially more important than legal or economic results. As Leo Kanowitz has pointed out:

> Rules of law that treat of the sexes per se inevitably produce far-reaching effects upon social, psychological and economic aspects of male-female relations beyond the limited confines of legislative chambers and court-rooms. As long as organized legal systems, at once the most respected and most feared of social institutions, continue to differentiate sharply, in treatment or in words, between men and women on the basis of irrelevant and artificially created distinctions, the likelihood of men and women coming to regard one another primarily as fellow human beings and only secondarily as representatives of another sex will continue to be remote. When men and

women are prevented from recognizing one another's essential humanity by sexual prejudices, nourished by legal as well as social institutions, society as a whole remains less than it could otherwise become.

The Presidents Receive Recommendations

The role of presidents in bringing about equality and justice for the women of America has mostly been in the form of establishing task forces and commissions to study the status of women and their rights and responsibilities. Studies are undertaken and recommendations are presented, but for the most part the efforts of presidents have ended there. In 1961, President Kennedy established by Executive Order 10980 the President's Commission on the Status of Women, which presented its recommendations to Mr. Kennedy in 1963; those recommendations appear below. In 1969, President Nixon's Presidential Task Force on Women's Rights and Responsibilities presented its recommendations with a somewhat greater sense of urgency than the Kennedy Commission did. That urgency, however, has not been reflected in Mr. Nixon's implementation of the recommendations. What is striking about the two sets of recommendations, one in 1963 and the other in 1969, is the similarity between them. The problems of 1963 remain the problems of 1969: job discrimination, unequal educational opportunities, inadequate childcare centers, unfair taxation policies, inequality under the law, and so on. The reader is invited to compare the recommendations of these two documents with the demands of contemporary women's liberation spokeswomen and organizations; for instance, compare the recommendations with the Statement of Purpose of the National Organization for Women (see p. 259).

**Recommendations of President Kennedy's Commission
on the Status of Women, 1963**

Education and counseling

Means of acquiring or continuing education must be available to every adult at whatever point he or she broke off traditional formal schooling. The structure of adult education must be drastically revised. It must provide practicable and accessible opportunities, developed with regard for the needs of women, to complete elementary and secondary school and to continue education beyond high school. Vocational training, adapted to the nation's growing requirement for skilled and highly educated manpower, should be included at all of these educational levels. Where needed and appropriate, financial support should be provided by local, state, and federal governments and by private groups and foundations.

In a democracy offering broad and everchanging choices, where ultimate decisions are made by individuals, skilled counseling is an essential part of education. Public and private agencies should join in strengthening counseling resources. States and school districts should raise their standards for state employment service counselors and school guidance counselors. Institutions offering counseling education should provide both course content and ample supervised experience in the counseling of females as well as males, adults as well as adolescents.

The education of girls and women for their responsibilities in home and community should be thoroughly re-examined with a view to discovering more effective approaches, with experimentation in content and timing, and under auspices including school systems, private organizations, and the mass media.

Home and community

For the benefit of children, mothers, and society, child-care services should be available for children of families at all economic levels. Proper standards of child care must be maintained, whether services are in homes or in centers. Costs should be met by fees scaled to parents' ability to pay, contributions from voluntary agencies, and public appropriations.

Tax deductions for child-care expenses of working mothers should be kept commensurate with the median income of couples when both husband and wife are engaged in substantial employment. The present limitation on their joint income, above which deductions are not allowable, should be raised. Additional deductions, of lesser amounts, should be allowed for children beyond the first. The 11-year age limit for child-care deductions should be raised.

Family services under public and private auspices to help families avoid or overcome breakdown or dependency and establish a soundly based homelife, and professionally supervised homemaker services to meet emergency or other special needs should be strengthened, extended, or established where lacking.

Community programs under public and private auspices should

make comprehensive provisions for health and rehabilitation services, including easily accessible maternal and child health services, accompanied by education to encourage their use.

Volunteers' services should be made more effective through coordinated and imaginative planning among agencies and organizations for recruitment, training, placement, and supervision, and their numbers augmented through tapping the large reservoir of additional potential among youth, retired people, members of minority groups, and women not now in volunteer activities.

Women in employment

Equal opportunity for women in hiring, training, and promotion should be the governing principle in private employment. An Executive order should state this principle and advance its application to work done under federal contracts.

At present, federal systems of manpower utilization discourage part-time employment. Many able women, including highly trained professionals, who are not free for full-time employment, can work part time. The Civil Service Commission and the Bureau of the Budget should facilitate the imaginative and prudent use of such personnel throughout the government service.

Labor standards

The federal Fair Labor Standards Act, including premium pay for overtime, should be extended to employment subject to federal jurisdiction but now uncovered, such as work in hotels, motels, restaurants, and laundries, in additional retail establishments, in agriculture, and in nonprofit organizations.

State legislation, applicable to both men and women, should be enacted, or strengthened and extended to all types of employment, to provide minimum-wage levels approximating the minimum under federal law and to require premium pay at the rate of at least time and a half for overtime.

The normal workday and workweek at this moment of history should be not more than 8 hours a day and 40 hours a week. The best way to discourage excessive hours for all workers is by broad and effective minimum-wage coverage, both federal and state, providing overtime of at least time and a half the regular rate for all hours in excess of 8 a day or 40 a week.

Until such time as this goal is attained, state legislation limiting maximum hours of work for women should be maintained, strengthened, and expanded. Provisions for flexibility under proper safeguards should allow additional hours of work when there is a demonstrated need. During this interim period, efforts should continuously and simultaneously be made to require premium rates of pay for all hours in excess of 8 a day or 40 a week.

State laws should establish the principle of equal pay for comparable work.

State laws should protect the right of all workers to join unions of their own choosing and to bargain collectively.

Security of basic income

A widow's benefit under the federal old-age insurance system should be equal to the amount that her husband would have received at the same age had he lived. This objective should be approached as rapidly as may be financially feasible.

The coverage of the unemployment-insurance system should be extended. Small establishments and nonprofit organizations should be covered now through federal action, and state and local government employees through state action. Practicable means of covering at least some household workers and agricultural workers should be actively explored.

Paid maternity leave or comparable insurance benefits should be provided for women workers; employers, unions, and governments should explore the best means of accomplishing this purpose.

Women under the law

Early and definitive court pronouncement, particularly by the United States Supreme Court, is urgently needed with regard to the validity under the Fifth and Fourteenth Amendments of laws and official practices discriminating against women, to the end that the principle of equality become firmly established in constitutional doctrine.

Accordingly, interested groups should give high priority to bringing under court review cases involving laws and practices which discriminate against women.

The United States should assert leadership, particularly in the United Nations, in securing equality of rights for women as part of the effort to define and assure human rights; should participate actively in the formulation of international declarations, principles, and conventions to improve the status of women throughout the world; and should demonstrate its sincere concern for women's equal rights by becoming a party to appropriate conventions.

Appropriate action, including enactment of legislation where necessary, should be taken to achieve equal jury service in the states.

State legislatures, and other groups concerned with the improvement of state statutes affecting family law and personal and property rights of married women, including the National Conference of Commissioners on Uniform State Laws, the Council of State Governments, the American Law Institute, and state Commissions on the Status of Women, should move to eliminate laws which impose legal disabilities on women.

Women as citizens

Women should be encouraged to seek elective and appointive posts at local, state, and national levels and in all three branches of government.

Public office should be held according to ability, experience, and effort, without special preferences or discriminations based on sex. Increasing consideration should continually be given to the appointment of women of demonstrated ability and political sensitivity to policy-making positions.

Continuing leadership

To further the objectives proposed in this report, an Executive order should:

1. Designate a Cabinet officer to be responsible for assuring that the resources and activities of the federal government bearing upon the Commission's recommendations are directed to carrying them out, and for making periodic progress reports to the President.

2. Designate the head of other agencies involved in those activities to serve, under the chairmanship of the designated Cabinet officer, as an interdepartmental committee to assure proper coordination and action.

3. Establish a citizens committee, advisory to the interdepartmental committee and with its secretariat from the designated Cabinet officer, to meet periodically to evaluate progress made, provide counsel, and serve as a means for suggesting and stimulating action.

Recommendations of President Nixon's Presidential Task Force on Women's Rights and Responsibilities, 1969

December 15, 1969.

The President,
The White House, Washington, D.C.

Dear Mr. President: As President of the United States, committed to the principle of equal rights for all, your leadership can be crucial to the more than half our citizens who are women and who are now denied their full constitutional and legal rights.

The quality of life to which we aspire and the questioning at home and abroad of our commitment to the democratic ideal make it imperative that our nation utilize to the fullest the potential of all citizens.

Yet the research and deliberations of this Task Force reveal that the United States, as it approaches its 200th anniversary, lags behind other enlightened, and indeed some newly emerging, countries in the role ascribed to women.

Social attitudes are slow to change. So widespread and pervasive are discriminatory practices against women they have come to be regarded, more often than not, as normal. Unless there is clear indication of Administration concern at the highest level, it is unlikely that significant progress can be made in correcting ancient, entrenched injustices.

American women are increasingly aware and restive over the denial of equal opportunity, equal responsibility, even equal protection of the law. An abiding concern for home and children should not, in their view, cut them off from the freedom to choose the role in society to which their interest, education, and training entitle them.

Women do not seek special privileges. They do seek equal rights. They do wish to assume their full responsibilities.

Equality for women is unalterably linked to many broader questions of social justice. Inequities within our society serve to restrict the contribution of both sexes. We have witnessed a decade of rebellion during which black Americans fought for true equality. The battle still rages. Nothing could demonstrate more dramatically the explosive potential of denying fulfillment as human beings to any segment of our society.

What this Task Force recommends is a national commitment to basic changes that will bring women into the mainstream of American life. Such a commitment, we believe, is necessary to healthy psychological, social, and economic growth of our society.

The leader who makes possible a fairer and fuller contribution by women to the nation's destiny will reap dividends of productivity measurable in billions of dollars. He will command respect and loyalty beyond measure from those freed from second-class citizenship. He will reaffirm, at a time of renewed worldwide emphasis on human rights, America's fitness for leadership in the community of nations.

His task will not be easy, for he must inspire and persuade government and the private sector to abandon outmoded attitudes based on false premises.

Without such leadership there is danger of accelerating militancy or the kind of deadening apathy that stills progress and inhibits creativity.

Therefore, this Task Force recommends that the President:

1. Establish an Office of Women's Rights and Responsibilities, whose director would serve as a special assistant reporting directly to the President.

2. Call a White House conference on women's rights and responsibilities in 1970, the fiftieth anniversary of the ratification of the suffrage amendment and establishment of the Women's Bureau.

3. Send a message to the Congress citing the widespread discriminations against women, proposing legislation to remedy these inequities, asserting Federal leadership, recommending prompt State action as a corollary, and calling upon the private sector to follow suit.

The message should recommend the following legislation necessary to ensure full legal equality for women:

a. Passage of a joint resolution proposing the equal rights amendment to the Constitution.

b. Amendment of Title VII of the Civil Rights Act of 1964 to (1) remove the burden of enforcement from the aggrieved individual by empowering the Equal Employment Opportunity Commission to enforce the law, and (2) extend coverage to State and local governments and to teachers.

c. Amendment of Titles IV and IX of the Civil Rights Act of 1964 to authorize the Attorney General to aid women and parents of minor girls in suits seeking equal access to public education, and to require the Office of Education to make a survey concerning the lack of equal educational opportunities for individuals by reason of sex.

d. Amendment of Title II of the Civil Rights Act of 1964 to prohibit discrimination because of sex in public accommodations.

e. Amendment of the Civil Rights Act of 1957 to extend the jurisdiction of the Civil Rights Commission to include denial of civil rights because of sex.

f. Amendment of the Fair Labor Standards Act to extend coverage of its equal pay provisions to executive, administrative, and professional employees.

g. Amendment of the Social Security Act to (1) provide benefits to husbands and widowers of disabled and deceased women workers under the same conditions as they are provided to wives and widows of men workers, and (2) provide more equitable retirement benefits for families with working wives.

h. Adoption of the liberalized provisions for child care in the family assistance plan and authorization of Federal aid for child care for families not covered by the family assistance plan.

i. Enactment of legislation to guarantee husbands and children of women employees of the Federal government the same fringe benefits provided for wives and children of male employees in those few areas where inequities still remain.

j. Amendment of the Internal Revenue Code to permit families in which both spouses are employed, families in which one spouse is disabled and the other employed, and families headed by single persons, to deduct from gross income as a business expense some reasonable amount paid to a housekeeper, nurse, or institution for care of childern or disabled dependents.

k. Enactment of legislation authorizing Federal grants on a matching basis for financing State commissions on the status of women.

4. The executive branch of the federal government should be as seriously concerned with sex discrimination as with race discrimination, and with women in poverty as with men in poverty.

Implementation of such a policy will require the following Cabinet-level actions:

a. Immediate issuance by the Secretary of Labor of guidelines to carry out the prohibition against sex discrimination by government contractors, which was added to Executive Order 11246 in October 1967, became effective October 1968, but remains un-implemented.

b. Establishment by the Secretary of Labor of priorities, as sensitive to sex discrimination as to race discrimination, for manpower training programs and in referral to training and employment.

c. Initiation by the Attorney General of legal actions in cases of sex discrimination under section 706(e) and 707 of the Civil Rights Act of 1964, and intervention or filing of amicus curiae briefs by the Attorney General in pending cases challenging the validity under the 5th and 14th amendments of laws involving disparities based on sex.

d. Establishment of a women's unit in the Office of Education to lead efforts to end discrimination in education because of sex.

e. Collection, tabulation, and publication of all economic and social data collected by the Federal government by sex as well as race.

f. Establishment of a high priority for training for household employment by the Secretary of Labor and the Secretary of Health, Education, and Welfare.

5. The President should appoint more women to positions of top responsibility in all branches of the Federal government, to achieve a more equitable ratio of men and women. Cabinet and agency heads should be directed to issue firm instructions that qualified women receive equal consideration in hiring and promotions.

Women's Liberation: Contemporary Challenges, Problems, and Goals

National Organization for Women/ Statement of Purpose (1966)

The following statement was adopted at the organizing conference of NOW in Washington, D.C., October 29, 1966.

Statement of Purpose

We, men and women who hereby constitute ourselves as the National Organization for Women, believe that the time has come for a new movement toward true equality for all women in America, and toward a fully equal partnership of the sexes, as part of the world-wide revolution of human rights now taking place within and beyond our national borders.

The purpose of NOW is the take action to bring women into full participation in the mainstream of American society now, exercising all the privileges and responsibilities thereof in truly equal partnership with men.

We believe the time has come to move beyond the abstract argument, discussion and symposia over the status and special nature of women which has raged in America in recent years; the time has come to confront, with concrete action, the conditions that now prevent women from enjoying the equality of opportunity and freedom of choice which is their right, as individual Americans, and as human beings.

NOW is dedicated to the proposition that women, first and foremost, are human beings, who, like all other people in our society, must have the chance to develop their fullest human potential. We believe that women can achieve such equality only by accepting to the full the challenges and responsibilities they share with all other people in our society, as part of the decision-making mainstream of American political, economic and social life.

We organize to initiate or support action, nationally, or in any part of this nation, by individuals or organizations, to break through the silken curtain of prejudice and discrimination against women in government, industry, the professions, the churches, the political parties, the judiciary, the labor unions, in education, science, medicine, law, religion and every other field of importance in American society.

Enormous changes taking place in our society make it both possible and urgently necessary to advance the unfinished revolution of women toward true equality, now. With a life span lengthened to nearly 75 years it is no longer either necessary or possible for women to devote the greater part of their lives to child-rearing; yet childbearing and rearing which continues to be a most important part of most women's lives—still is used to justify barring women from equal professional and economic participation and advance.

Today's technology has reduced most of the productive chores which women once performed in the home and in mass-production industries based upon routine unskilled labor. This same technology has virtually eliminated the quality of muscular strength as a criterion for filling most jobs, while intensifying American industry's need for creative intelligence. In view of this new industrial revolution created by automation in the mid-twentieth century, women can and must participate in old and new fields of society in full equality—or become permanent outsiders.

Despite all the talk about the status of American women in recent years, the actual position of women in the United States has declined, and is declining, to an alarming degree throughout the 1950's and '60's. Although 46.4 percent of all American women between the ages of 18 and 65 now work outside the home, the overwhelming majority—75 percent—are in routine clerical, sales or factory jobs, or they are household workers, cleaning women, hospital attendants. About two-thirds of Negro women workers are in the lowest paid service occupations. Working women are becoming increasingly—not less—concentrated on the bottom of the job ladder. As a consequence full-time women workers today earn on the average only 60 percent of what men earn, and that wage gap has been increasing over the past twenty-five years in every major industry group. In 1964, of all women with a yearly income, 89 percent earned under $5,000 a year; half of all full-time year round women workers earned less than $3,690; only 1.4 percent of full-time year round women workers had an annual income of $10,000 or more.

Further, with higher education increasingly essential in today's society, too few women are entering and finishing college or going on to graduate or professional school. Today, women earn only one in three of the B.A.'s and M.A.'s granted, and one in ten of the Ph.D.'s.

In all the professions considered of importance to society, and in the executive ranks of industry and government, women are losing ground. Where they are present it is only a token handful. Women comprise less than 1 percent of federal judges; less than 4 percent of all lawyers; 7 per-cent of doctors. Yet women represent 51 percent of the U.S. population. And, increasingly, men are replacing women in the top positions in secondary and elementary schools, in social work, and in libraries—once thought to be women's fields.

Official pronouncements of the advance in the status of women hide not only the reality of this dangerous decline, but the fact that nothing is being done to stop it. The excellent reports of the President's Commission on the Status of Women and of the State Commissions have not been fully implemented. Such Commissions have power only to advise. They have no power to enforce their recommendations; nor have they the free-dom to organize American women and men to press for action on them. The reports of these Commissions have, however, created a basis upon which it is now possible to build.

Discrimination in employment on the basis of sex is now prohibited by federal law, in Title VII of the Civil Rights Act of 1964. But although nearly one-third of the cases brought before the Equal Employment Opportunity Commission during the first year dealt with sex discrimina-tion and the proportion is increasing dramatically, the Commission has not made clear its intention to enforce the law with the same seriousness on behalf of women as of other victims of discrimination. Many of these cases were Negro women, who are the victims of the double discrimina-tion of race and sex. Until now, too few women's organizations and official spokesmen have been willing to speak out against these dangers facing women. Too many women have been restrained by the fear of being called "feminist."

There is no civil rights movement to speak for women, as there has been for Negroes and other victims of discrimination. The National Organization for Women must therefore begin to speak.

We believe that the power of American law, and the protection guaranteed by the U.S. Constitution to the civil rights of all individuals, must be effectively applied and enforced to isolate and remove patterns of sex discrimination, to ensure equality of opportunity in employment and education, and equality of civil and political rights and responsibilities on behalf of women, as well as for Negroes and other deprived groups.

We realize that women's problems are linked to many broader questions of social justice; their solution will require concerted action by many groups. Therefore, convinced that human rights for all are indivisible, we expect to give active support to the common cause of equal rights for all those who suffer discrimination and deprivation, and we call upon other organizations committed to such goals to support our efforts toward equality for women.

We do not accept the token appointment of a few women to high-level positions in government and industry as a substitute for a serious continuing effort to recruit and advance women according to their individual abilities. To this end, we urge American government and industry to mobilize the same resources of ingenuity and command with which they have solved problems of far greater difficulty than those now impeding the progress of women.

We believe that this nation has a capacity at least as great as other nations, to innovate new social institutions which will enable women to enjoy true equality of opportunity and responsibility and society, without conflict with their responsibilities as mothers and homemakers. In such innovations, America does not lead the Western world, but lags by decades behind many European countries. We do not accept the traditional assumption that a woman has to choose between marriage and motherhood, on the one hand, and serious participation in industry or the professions on the other. We question the present expectation that all normal women will retire from job or profession for 10 or 15 years, to devote their full time to raising children, only to reenter the job market at a relatively minor level. This, in itself, is a deterrent to the aspirations of women, to their acceptance into management or professional training courses, and to the very possibility of equality of opportunity or real choice, for all but a few women. Above all, we reject the assumption that these problems are the unique responsibility of each individual woman, rather than a basic social dilemma which society must solve. True equality of opportunity and freedom of choice for women requires such practical, and possible innovations as a nationwide network of childcare centers, which will make it unnecessary for women to retire completely from society until their children are grown, and national programs to provide retraining for women who have chosen to care for their own children full-time.

We believe that it is as essential for every girl to be educated to her full potential of human ability as it is for every boy—with the knowledge that such education is the key to effective participation in today's economy and that, for a girl as for a boy, education can only be serious where there is expectation that it will be used in society. We believe that American educators are capable of devising means of imparting such expectations to girl students. Moreover, we consider the decline in the proportion of women receiving higher and professional education to be evidence of discrimination. This discrimination may take the form of quotas against the admission of women to colleges, and professional schools; lack of encouragement by parents, counsellors and educators; denial of loans or fellowships; or the traditional or arbitrary procedures in graduate and professional training geared in terms of men, which inadvertently discriminate against women. We believe that the same serious attention must be given to high school dropouts who are girls as to boys.

We reject the current assumptions that a man must carry the sole burden of supporting himself, his wife, and family, and that a woman is automatically entitled to lifelong support by a man upon her marriage, or that marriage, home and family are primarily woman's world and responsibility—hers, to dominate—his to support. We believe that a true partnership between the sexes demands a different concept of marriage, an equitable sharing of the responsibilities of home and children and of the economic burdens of their support. We believe that proper recognition should be given to the economic and social value of home-making and child-care. To these ends, we will seek to open a reexamination of laws and mores governing marriage and divorce, for we believe that the current state of "half-equality" between the sexes discriminates against both men and women, and is the cause of much unnecessary hostility between the sexes.

We believe that women must now exercise their political rights and responsibilities as American citizens. They must refuse to be segregated on the basis of sex into separate-and-not-equal ladies' auxiliaries in the political parties, and they must demand representation according to their numbers in the regularly constituted party committees—at local, state, and national levels—and in the informal power structure, participating fully in the selection of candidates and political decision-making, and running for office themselves.

In the interests of the human dignity of women, we will protest, and endeavor to change, the false image of women now prevalent in the mass media, and in the texts, ceremonies, laws, and practices of our major social institutions. Such images perpetuate contempt for women by society and by women for themselves. We are similarly opposed to all policies and practices—in church, state, college, factory, or office—which, in the guise of protectiveness, not only deny opportunities but also foster in women self-denigration, dependence, and evasion of responsibility, undermine their confidence in their own abilities and foster contempt for women.

NOW will hold itself independent of any political party in order to mobilize the political power of all women and men intent on our goals. We will strive to ensure that no party, candidate, president, senator, governor, congressman, or any public official who betrays or ignores the principle of full equality between the sexes is elected or appointed to office. If it is necessary to mobilize the votes of men and women who believe in our cause, in order to win for women the final right to be fully free and equal human beings, we so commit ourselves.

We believe that women will do most to create a new image of women by *acting* now, and by speaking out in behalf of their own equality, freedom, and human dignity—not in pleas for special privilege, nor in enmity toward men, who are also victims of the current, half-equality between the sexes—but in an active, self-respecting partnership with men. By so doing, women will develop confidence in their own ability to determine actively, in partnership with men, the conditions of their life, their choices, their future and their society.

Joan Brown, Peggy Way, and Helen Fannings/ Liberation Struggle Generates Tension on Race, Sex Issues

The three women participating in the following conversation attempt to answer such questions as: Will the liberation of the black woman come from the women's liberation or from the liberation of all black people? What are some of the difficult relationships between black and white women? Why are there so few black women participating in women's liberation organizations and activities? Is the identity problem of the white woman different from the identity problem of the black woman? What has been and is the church's role in women's liberation? What influence does the economic system of this country have on the status of women? During the course of the conversation there evolve statements about the similarities and dissimilarities between the struggles of blacks and women in their efforts to achieve "liberation."

(Three Chicago area women involved in various struggles for liberation recently were asked to share their thoughts with each other. The women were Joan Brown, consultant for human relations, YWCA of Metropolitan Chicago; Peggy Way, coordinator of Metropolitan Ministry and assistant professor at the University of Chicago divinity school; and Helen Fannings, housing consultant, Leadership Council for Metropolitan Open Communities. As an opening gambit they were asked: "Efforts for liberation are often presented in such a way that the themes are defined by men. As women, black and white, how do you define your own struggles for liberation?" Following are some excerpts from the conversation, as recorded and condensed by Haselden fellow Michael Stone.)

Joan Brown: To begin with, I don't subscribe to the idea of a women's liberation movement as such, principally because I think that black women have to be concerned with the liberation of all black people, and that a black woman will really find her role in relationship to that struggle. That is a little different, I think, from the women's liberation movement, as it is usually defined.

Peggy Way: I sometimes understand my participation with women's liberation as growing partly out of jealously for what you have as blacks. That may sound strange, but so many of the women in women's liberation

---

came out of the civil rights movement, and saw how blackness became the source of identity and health, became the positive thrust, the joy and the hope and the spirit. And I think probably more of us than would admit it were working *for* blacks rather than *with* blacks, though we didn't realize that until things became blacker and blacker, and what were we left with? We didn't want to become whiter and whiter, because that wasn't our identity. So I think that maybe some of us in women's liberation are seeking a reification of who we are out of loss of the identity we thought we were developing in the movement.

J. B.:   I think we see that in the reactions to SNCC's putting white people out of the movement because it had become clear that they were only going to confuse things. At the same time, I hope that white women are really trying to understand their own oppression, because if this country could ever unlock the riddle of why women, particularly white women, are treated the way they are—as sexual objects, etc.—that understanding might lead to other possibilities.

P. W.:   It would seem to me that a black woman can take part in freeing men much more freely than a white woman can. In a sense, the white man is the enemy of black *people* and is also the enemy of the white *woman*. You are a black man's woman and you are working for your man's freedom in a way I can't. The black man doesn't need to be your enemy, whereas in my situation, the white man really is my enemy. In relation to what Joan said, my liberation must be in terms of the oppression I experience.

Helen Fannings: That makes the relationship entirely different. Black women have to see their struggle first as the struggle for black people. And then, perhaps very privately in our own way, we are going to have to redefine what the black woman's role as a woman may be. Certainly we can no longer be out in front of our men where the white man has put us.

J. B.:   Also, I think there is a very serious question between white women and black women. Look at the experiences young black women are having on college campuses as they see young black men falling prey—that is the only way I can define it—to young white girls who have a great many material things to offer and who are experimenting with their own sexuality—something completely contrary (despite what white people say) to black mores and black folkways. To be a "sister" to a white woman, in all the ways that word can be defined, is to be friends with an enemy. I don't mean we can't be "friends," or that we can't have a relationship we both understand, or that we can't work together on common tasks, but we certainly cannot be *sisters*. That is a hangover from the old, liberal kind of posture.

I

P. W.:   Frequently at women's liberation meetings the question is raised, why aren't there any black sisters?

J. B.:   They know why.

P. W.:   That's right. I think more people are now realizing that the black woman has a thing she has to do. It's not our thing. We have to define what *we* need to do, and I guess this is where I sometimes fall into a certain amount of despair. I think it is much *harder* to define what the white woman should be doing now than what the black woman should be doing.

J. B.:   Everybody is going to be forced to confront herself. There is no longer any escape. We have a little syllogism in which we conclude that old rich white men are the enemy. Now, everybody has got to understand why they are the enemy. It may be not because they are intrinsically bad but because they have the most to protect, in terms of material investment, so that the choice to be made ultimately is whether they are going to hold onto what they have. The other dynamic is that because the white woman is beginning to understand that the white man is the enemy, she is after the black man. But that is not going to work either.

H. F.:   That is an extremely poor plan.

P. W.:   What all this does is to leave the white woman without a man. The freer a white woman becomes, the less chance she has of having a man. You look around, and white men are uptight, they're not free, they run things badly, and you get caught up with hostility. Speaking as a white woman—as someone in the church—I work every day with frightened white men. I keep looking around with great hopefulness that somewhere I'll find a man who is liberated. In women's liberation we try to say that men shouldn't have to be stronger than women, that we can work together as persons and figure out our relationships together. I think we still have an ethos, however, in which women like to have men who are whole and strong, and our culture isn't producing white men like that. I think that the more active women become in women's liberation—especially younger women—the further they separate themselves off from men who are their peers and their age, and that is very painful. It is very hard to formulate an exciting identity out of those you are against. Women's liberation has to figure out that it isn't merely against white men. It still has to retain that emphasis, though, because the white man is the enemy. At the same time we really are concerned about the liberation of the white man—and all people—because we don't want to be liberators who merely oppress another group.

J. B.: If you are for something, you don't have to worry about the enemy. Once we had the slogan of Black Power, it called into question all kinds of other power. You didn't have to say you were against some other kind of power. All you said was you were for Black Power. You didn't have to be against white people. You said that because of what you had as a black in the black community, you didn't want to move into their community. I used to give talks in the suburbs, and I'd tell the people that it was absolutely ludicrous for them to fear that I was going to move out there, because there was nothing out there for me. Then the whole discussion would turn around, because it was inconceivable to them that a black person would not want what they had.

H. F.: They felt you *had* to be desirous of what they had.

II

P. W.: I am unclear as to how to develop a value system related to women's liberation. I think there is a real danger of doing the kind of thing we did with integration, of having a value system that becomes rhetoric rather than reality, and I'm interested in a value system that is very specific.

J. B.: It has to do with contradictions and inconsistencies. Let me give you an example. One of my students a young white girl, is very clear about herself. One day in a meeting I saw her smoking Virginia Slims. I said, "Do you realize what you're doing when you smoke that brand?" "It's such a little thing," she said. Yes, it is a little thing, yet everything we've been talking about is caught up in it. If you talk about the need for a woman to be her own person and be recognized as such and you still smoke Virginia Slims, which say "You've come a long way," to me that is a basic contradiction. Once you recognize that contradiction and make up your mind that you're not going to deal that way, you get so you can recognize it right off, and you begin to minimize or terminate your participation in a great number of things. I simply cannot go to movies and see Barbra Streisand or look at Wayne Cochran, because I *know* that's James Brown's style. And I can't look at old fast black Jimmy Brown on the screen when he's hugging white women, either.

P. W.:   Do black women have any heroines, black image women? I don't see those images existing for a large number of white women, and that creates a great difficulty. I do a sort of cultural analysis of white women in three generations. First, there are what I call the "grandmothers," the Jane Addamses, the women's suffragette women, basically a healthy generation of women who were out in the streets establishing settlement houses, working on legislative matters and the like. Then there are the "mothers," the average white women in the suburbs who developed this fear that you blacks want to move out there too. Essentially this is a very fearful generation of women, who took most of their identity from the white man—who himself didn't have any identity to speak of—and who took the rest of their identity from producing kids who had to look like their mothers thought they ought to look. A very unfortunate generation. Finally, I look at the present women's liberation generation, whom I call the "daughters." They don't have any identity images among the "mothers." I think that the black woman may not need this kind of femininity image, because she has the black image to identify with. I think you blacks have a richer history to repossess than do white women, and you are farther along in the process. I think that if the women's liberation movement is going to be a freeing thing for white women—and then, hopefully, for white men—somebody has to be thinking about how we can say, as Operation Breadbasket does, "I am somebody." Not, "I am somebody because I'm your master," or "I am somebody because *he* tells me I am." How do we get rid of that? In that sense, we have a negative task also—that of ceasing to be the wrong somebody.

J. B.:   That's no different, actually, from what blacks had to do in getting rid of feelings of being nobody, feelings of inferiority and all that. I left the ghetto for the first time to go to the University of Illinois, and it almost killed me, because I could not understand what those people were talking about, why all of a sudden I was so unique. All of those years in the black community I had been It, Miss It, and suddenly I was in a different environment where people were constantly telling me and showing me that I was nobody. Going through that, you have to turn around this denial and reinforce what you really know, that you are somebody. Either you believe there is an intrinsic worth in being human, or you don't believe it. If you do, then you have to give up all that has kept you from being human—just give it up. That's the first step, I would think.

H. F.:   It demands becoming a different kind of person; that is, deciding for yourself that what you are you can't continue to be. And I don't know if white women are really ready to do that yet, to realize that "what I have been" is really very destructive.

III

P. W.:   Do you see any age differences? Most of the women in the liberation movement are relatively young. By and large, there aren't any of what I call the "mothers" among them. There are a few "grandmothers," and they and I get along just fine, but the mothers and I have a great deal of difficulty.

H. F.:   I wonder why.

P. W.:   To follow through what you were saying, the "mothers" may be at the threshold of realizing what it would mean to be free but still aren't really willing to go through with it. They have their home, their kids. So many of the "mothers" generation seem to have adopted their identities producing good white kids, but those good white kids now have long hair and like blacks, and they just don't give the mothers identity any more. These women were taught by the whole culture that their identity as a woman is to produce socially acceptable kids. I think about how many women have been ruined by this attitude, how it has wasted the resources of our culture, so I am committed to women's liberation, but I have very few illusions. I don't think there are going to be millions of white women suddenly freed up. But I think that through women's liberation we may have more freedom than we have now, especially as we have more options, and I think of it as producing the kinds of people who are going to create the new culture. I think I've got to the point where I feel that maybe as a white person the best I can do right now is try to free up a few people to engage in that creative process. I see very few places where people are trying to free up white women. The church ought to be one of those places. Women constitute, at least in the white church, about 60 percent of the membership, and their participation is even higher.

H. F.:   That's true of all churches. The strongest groups in most churches are the women's groups—not only women's societies, but women's aux-iliaries, and this kind of thing. Here are all these little ladies getting together very frequently and being very busy—very dedicated—really feeling that they are involved in something. But they don't relate to the liberation thing, and somehow you have to reach them with what the contradiction is all about.

P. W.:   I've had to decide whether or not to stay in the church. Every time I change jobs I have to decide whether I really want to stay, and I have just about decided I will, because here is this place with all these women with whom nobody is working at all.

H. F.:   I've become pretty involved in the church, too, though I had completely dropped out. I'm not back now because I think this is where it's at, but because from a black point of view I see that there are some resources here that can be used by the black community, and that right now they are just going down the drain.

IV

J. B.:   I think that anybody who wants to be and stay liberated simply cannot participate in the structures as they currently exist because after you make one little step, if you get into a nonsupportive system it pulls you back. Do you know what I mean?

H. F.:   You say, "as they currently exist." Does that mean that you don't have any hope that you can do anything about changing the situation?

J. B.:   Oh, no, none whatever. I begin with the assumption that the churches don't have any commitment to solving anything but the symptoms of the problem—though if the commitment were there, then the churches certainly have the resources. If you believe that the No. 1 problem with poor people in a capitalistic society is lack of money, and then you realize that the three major religious faiths have more money than the five major corporations in America, you know that that's a real resource. But the churches are fooling around, playing these games on people, and praying, and what have you, but I don't know of any in-stances in which there have been direct grants to people who need the money. So we're not even dealing with the solution, which we all know: in a capitalistic society, people need money.

P. W.:   I guess one of the things that interests me in women's liberation, Joan, is that, as far as the woman's role goes, it doesn't matter what economic order we function under. I suspect that as a woman I would find myself in a lowly state whether I was with the most militant people or the most conservative people. There is an order of sexual discrimination that functions regardless of the political system. Another set of structures might conceivably find blacks in a different position, but I'm not at all sure that another set of structures would remove the negative images about the competency of women.

V

J. B.:   Of course, a lot of women like the position they're in, isn't that so? I think white women really dig the dependency thing.

P. W.:   When you have the kind of identity structure going that you have now, that's precisely what happens. You just do *accept*, and you don't raise questions, and to me the problem about white women right now is, how do you get them to raise the questions? And that means, I think, that we are farther back than you, at least in the sense of a basic identity. And that probably means we are going to have to come together as a women's liberation movement so that we can dare to raise those questions.

J. B.:   As a black woman I don't even feel that that is my problem or my responsibility. Under the circumstances, I wouldn't be part of a *women's* lib movement for anything in the world.

H. F.:   That is your problem, Peggy. We just don't have time for it. The thing that's missing in the women's liberation movement is the whole question of survival. And that is the essential question. What you are talking about is a female-male type of problem that you are trying to solve. We're talking about a whole culture whose people have really, really, been fouled up.

Shirley Chisholm / Racism and Anti-Feminism

In the following selection, New York Congresswoman Shirley Chisholm discusses the reasons why more women have not become involved in the women's liberation movement and the forces which are responsible for the hesitancy of women to become involved in their own liberation. Women, says Mrs. Chisholm, must "refuse to accept the old—the traditional—roles and stereotypes." These must be replaced with positive thoughts about femininity. "We must move outside the walls of our stereotypes but we must retain the values on which they were built," Mrs. Chisholm advises. She asks that women become "revolutionaries" in the fashion of Christ, Gandhi, and King, in a society which she sees as "both racist and anti-feminist."

Women take an active part in society and in particular do they take a part in the present social revolution. And I find the question, do women dare to liberate themselves, as much of an insult as I would the question, "Are you, as a black person, willing to fight for your rights?"

America has been sufficiently sensitized as to whether or not black people are willing to both fight and die for their rights to make the question itself asinine and superfluous. America is not yet sufficiently aware that such a question applied to women is equally asinine and superfluous.

I am both black and a woman. That is a good vantage point from which to view at least two elements of what is becoming a social revolution; the American Black Revolution and the Women's Liberation Movement. But it is also a horrible disadvantage. It is a disadvantage because America, as a nation, is both racist and anti-feminist. Racism and anti-feminism are two of the prime traditions of this country.

For any individual, challenging social traditions is a giant step, a giant step because there are no social traditions which do not have corresponding social sanctions, the sole purpose of which is to protect the sanctity of the traditions.

Thus when we ask the question "Do women dare?" we are not asking if women are capable of a break with tradition so much as we are asking,

Chisholm, "Racism and Anti-Feminism," *The Black Scholar*, January—February 1970, pp. 40—45. Reprinted by permission of the author and publisher.

"Are they capable of bearing with the sanctions that will be placed upon them?"

Coupling this with the hypothesis presented by some social thinkers and philosophers that in any given society the most active groups are those that are nearest to the particular freedom that they desire, it does not surprise me that those women most active and vocal on the issue of freedom for women are those who are young, white, and middle-class; nor is it too surprising that there are not more from that group involved in the Women's Liberation Movement.

There certainly are reasons why more women are not involved. This country as I said is both racist and anti-feminist. Few, if any, Americans are free of the psychological wounds imposed by racism and anti-feminism.

A few weeks ago while testifying before the Office of Federal Contract Compliance, I noted that anti-feminism, like every form of discrimination, is destructive both to those who perpetrate it and to their victims, that males with their anti-feminism, maim both themselves and their women.

In *Soul On Ice* Eldridge Cleaver pointed out how America's racial and sexual stereotypes were supposed to work. Whether his insight is correct or not, it bears close examination.

Cleaver, in the passage "The Primeval Mitosis," describes in detail the four major roles. There is the white female who he considers to be "Ultra-feminine" because ". . . she is required to possess and project an image that is in sharp contrast to . . ." the white male's image as the "Omnipotent Administrator . . . all brain and no body."

He goes on to identify the black female as "Subfeminine" or "Amazon" by virtue of her assignment to the lowly household chores and those corresponding jobs of tedious nature. He sums up the role of the black male as the "Supermasculine Menial, all body and no brain," because he was expected to supply society with its source of brute power.

What the roles and strange interplay between them have meant to America, Cleaver goes on to point out quite well.

What he does not say and what I think must be said is that because of the bizarre aspects of their roles and the influence that non-traditional contact among them has on the general society, blacks and whites, males and females, must operate almost independently of each other in order to escape from the quicksands of psychological slavery. Each—black male and black female, white female and white male—must escape first from their own historical trap before they can be truly effective in helping others to free themselves.

Therein lies one of the major reasons that there are not more women involved in the Women's Liberation Movement. Women cannot, for the most part, operate independently of males because they often do not have sufficient economic freedom.

In 1966 the median earnings of women who worked full-time for the whole year was less than the median income of males who worked full-time for the whole year. In fact, white women workers made less than black male workers, and of course, black women workers made the least of all.

Whether it is intentional or not women are paid less than men for the same work, no matter what their chosen field. Whether it is intentional or not, employment for women is regulated still more in terms of the jobs that are available to them. This is almost as true for white women as it is for black women.

Whether it is intentional or not, when it becomes time for a young high-school girl to think about preparing for her career, her counselors, whether they be male or female, will think first of her so-called "natural" career—housewife and mother—and begin to program her for a field with which marriage and children will not unduly interfere.

That is exactly the same as the situation of the young blacks or Puerto Ricans whom the racist counselor advises to prepare for service-oriented occupations because he does not even consider the possibility of their entering the professions.

The response of the average young lady is precisely the same as the response of the average young black or Puerto Rican—tacit agreement—because the odds do seem to be stacked against them.

This is not happening as much as it once did to young minority-group people. It is not happening because they have been radicalized and the country is becoming sensitized to its racist attitudes and the damage that it does.

Young women must learn a lesson from that experience!

They must rebel—they must react to the traditional stereotyped education mapped out for them by the society. Their education and training is programmed and planned for them from the moment the doctor says, "Mr. Jones, it's a beautiful baby girl!", and Mr. Jones begins deleting mentally the things that she might have been and adds the things that society says that she *must* be.

That young woman (for society begins to see her as a stereotype the moment that her sex is determined) will be wrapped in a pink blanket (pink because that is the color of her caste) and the unequal segregation of the sexes will have begun.

Small wonder that the young girl sitting across the desk from her counselor will not be able to say "No" to educational, economic, and social slavery. Small wonder, because she has been a psychological slave and programmed as such since the moment of her birth!

On May 20th of last year I introduced legislation concerning the equal employment opportunities of women. At that time I pointed out that there were three and one-half million more women than men in America but that women held only two percent of the managerial positions; that no women sit on the AFL-CIO Council or the Supreme Court; that only two women had ever held Cabinet rank and that there were at that time only two women of Ambassadorial rank in the Diplomatic Corps. I stated then as I do now that this situation is outrageous.

In my speech on the Floor that day I said:

It is true that part of the problem has been that women have not been aggressive in demanding their rights. This was also true of the black population for many years. They submitted to oppression and even co-operated with it. Women have done the same thing. But now there is an awareness of this situation, particularly among the younger segment of the population.

As in the field of equal rights for blacks, Spanish-Americans, the Indians and other groups, *laws* will not change such deep-seated problems overnight. But they can be used to provide protection for those who are most abused, and begin the process of evolutionary change by compelling the insensitive majority to re-examine its unconscious attitudes.

The law cannot do it for us, we must do it ourselves. Women in this country must become revolutionaries. We must refuse to accept the old—the traditional—roles and stereotypes.

We must reject the Greek philosopher's thought, "It is thy place, woman, to hold thy place and keep within doors." We must reject the thought of St. Paul who said "Let the woman learn in silence." And we must reject the Nietzschean thought "When a woman inclines to learning there is something wrong with her sex apparatus."

But more than merely rejecting we must replace those thoughts and the concepts that they symbolize with positive values based on female experience.

A few short years ago if you called most Negroes black it was tantamount to calling them niggers. But now black is beautiful and black is proud. There are relatively few people, white or black, who do not recognize what has happened.

Black people have freed themselves from the dead weight of the albatross of blackness that once hung around their neck. They have done it by picking it up in their arms and holding it out with pride for all the world to see. They have done it by embracing it—not in the dark of the moon but in the searing light of the white sun. They have said "Yes" to it and found that the skin that was once seen as symbolizing their shame is in reality their badge of honor.

Women must come to realize that the superficial symbolisms that surround us are negative only when we ourselves perceive and accept them as negative. We must begin to replace the old negative thoughts about our femininity with positive thoughts and positive actions affirming it and more.

But we must also remember that that will be breaking with tradition and we must prepare ourselves—educationally, economically and psychologically—in order that we will be able to accept and bear with the sanctions that society will immediately impose upon us.

I am a politician. I detest the word because of the connotations that cling like slime to it but for want of a better term I must use it.

I have been in politics for twenty years and in that time I have learned a few things about the role of women in politics.

The major thing that I have learned is that women are the backbone of America's political organizations. They are the letter-writers and envelope-stuffers, the telephone-answerers; they are the campaign-workers and organizers. They are the speech writers and the largest number of potential voters.

Yet they are but rarely the standard-bearers of elected officials. Perhaps it is in America, more than any other country, that the inherent truth of the old bromide "The power behind the throne is a woman" is most readily apparent.

Let me remind you once again of the relatively few women standard-bearers on the American political scene. There are only ten United States Representatives. There is only one Senator and there are no Cabinet members who are women. There are no women on the Supreme Court and only a small percentage of lady judges at the Federal Court level who might be candidates.

It is true that at the state level the picture is somewhat brighter just as it is true that the North presents a surface that is somewhat more appealing to the black American when compared with the South. But even though in 1967 there were 318 women in various state legislatures, the percentage is not good when compared with the fact that in almost all fifty states there are more women of voting age than there are men; and that in each state the number of women of voting age is increasing at a greater rate than the number of men. Nor is it an encouraging figure when compared with the fact that in 1966 there were not 318 but 328 women in the state legislatures.

Secondly I have learned that the attitude held by the high school counselors that I mentioned earlier is a general attitude held by political bosses. A few years ago a politician remarked to me about a potential young female candidate, "Why invest all the time and effort to build up the gal into a household name when she's pretty sure to drop out of the game to have a couple of kids at just about the time we're ready to run her for mayor?"

I have pointed out time and time again that the harshest discrimination that I have encountered in the political arena is anti-feminism—both from males and brainwashed "Uncle Tom" females.

When I first announced that I was running for the United States Congress last year, both males and females advised me, as they had when I ran for the New York State Assembly, to go back to teaching, a woman's vocation, and leave the politics to the men.

One of the major reasons that I will not leave the American political scene—voluntarily, that is—is because the number of women in politics is declining.

There are at least two million more women than men of voting age but the fact is that while we get out the vote we often do not get out *to vote*. In 1964, for example, 72 percent of registered males voted while only 67 percent of registered females voted. We seem to be a political minority by choice.

I believe that women have a special contribution to make to help bring order out of chaos because they have special qualities of leadership which are greatly needed today. These qualities are the patience, tolerance and perseverance which have developed in many women because of their suppression. If we can add to these qualities a reservoir of information about techniques of community action we can indeed become effective harbingers of change. Women must participate more in the legislative process because, even with the contributions that I have just mentioned, the single greatest contribution that women could bring to American politics would be a spirit of moral purpose.

But unfortunately women's participation in politics is declining, as I have noted. Politics is not the only place that we are losing past gains, though. Columnist Clayton Fritchey in a column *Woman in Office*, noted that "although more women are working, their salaries keep falling behind men's. Some occupations are (still) closed by law to women. Key property laws favor men. In 1940 women held 45 percent of all professional and technical positions as against 37 percent today."

The decline is a general one. But it is because it is a decline that I believe that the true question is not whether or not women dare to move. Women have always dared! The question which now faces us is "Will women dare move in numbers sufficient to have an effect on their own attitudes toward themselves and thus change the basic attitudes of males and the general society?"

Women will have to brave the social sanctions in great numbers in order to free themselves from the sexual, psychological, and emotional stereotyping that plagues us. Like black people we will have to raise our albatross with pride.

It is not feminine egoism to say that the future of mankind may very well be ours to determine. It is simply a plain fact. The softness, warmth, and gentleness that are often used to stereotype us are positive human values; values that are becoming more and more important as the general values of the whole of mankind slip more and more out of kilter.

The strength that marked Christ, Gandhi, and Martin Luther King was a strength born not of violence but of gentleness, understanding and genuine human compassion.

We must move outside the walls of our stereotypes but we must retain the values on which they were built.

No, I am not saying that we are inherently those things that the stereotypes impute that we are; but I am saying that because of the long-enforced roles we have had to play we should know by now that the values are good ones to hold and I am saying that by now we should have developed the capacity to not only hold them but to also dispense them to those around us.

This is the reason that we must free ourselves. This is the reason that we must become revolutionaries in the fashion of Christ, Gandhi, King and the hundreds of other men and women who held those as the highest of human values.

There is another reason. In working toward our own freedom we can also allow our men to work toward their freedom from the traps of their stereotypes.

We are challenged now as we never were before. The past twenty years, with its decline for women in employment and government, with its status quo attitude toward the preparation of young women for certain professions, make it clear that evolution is not necessarily always a process of positive forward motion. Susan B. Anthony, Carrie Nation and Sojourner Truth were not evolutionaries. They were revolutionaries, as are many of the young women of today. More women and more men must join their ranks.

New goals and new priorities, not only for this country, but for all mankind, must be set. Formal education will not help us do that. We must therefore depend on informal learning.

We can do that by confronting people with their own humanity and their own inhumanity. Confronting them wherever we meet them—in the church, in the classroom, on the floors of Congress and the state legislatures, in bars and on the streets. We must reject not only the stereotypes that others hold of us but also the stereotypes that we hold of ourselves and others.

In a speech made a few weeks ago to an audience that was predominantly white and all female I suggested the following if they wanted to create change:

> You must start in your own homes, your own schools and your own churches . . . I don't want you to go home and talk about integrated schools, churches or marriages when the kind of integration you are talking about is black with white.
>
> I want you to go home and work for—fight for—the integration of male and female—human and human. Franz Fanon pointed out in *Black Skins, White Masks* that the Anti-Semitic was eventually the Anti-Negro. I want to say that both are eventually the Anti-Feminist. And even further, I want to indicate that all discrimination is eventually the same thing— Anti-Humanism.

That is my challenge for us today, whether we are male or female.

Myrna Wood and Kathy McAfee / Bread and Roses

The women's liberation movement has raised many questions regarding organization and tactics which will help bring about the "liberation" women seek. One of those questions is whether it is wiser for the women to establish their own organizations (dominated by women) or to work with and through already established "revolutionary" groups and organizations which have other goals besides women's liberation. Myrna Wood and Kathy McAfee argue that the advantages to women are greater if they work through their own organizations which specifically have as their goal women's liberation than to work through such organizations as the Students for a Democratic Society. Of SDS, the authors say: ". . . the question of women's liberation is raised only as an incidental, subordinate aspect of programs around 'the primary struggle,' antiracism. (Although most people in SDS now understand the extent of black people's oppression, they are not aware of the fact that the median wage of working women (black and white) is lower than that of black males.) The male domination of the organization has not been affected by occasional rhetorical attacks on male chauvinism and, most important, very little organizing of women is being done." The authors argue that exploitation of women cuts across economic, racial, and social lines: working class women, bourgois women, and upper-class women are all exploited. In the end, the authors see the hope of success for women's liberation coming from the working-class women; further, ". . . the struggle must be instigated by militant women; liberation is not handed down from above."

Through reprints and pamphlets, the women's liberation movement has given this selection by Myrna Wood and Kathy McAfee wide circulation across the country.

A great deal of confusion exists today about the role of women's liberation in a revolutionary movement. Hundreds of women's groups have sprung up within the past year or two, but among them, a number of very different and often conflicting ideologies have developed. The growth of these movements has demonstrated the desperate need that many women feel to escape their own oppression, but it has also shown that organization

Wood and McAfee, "Bread and Roses," *Leviathan*, June 1969. Reprinted by permission of the publisher.

around women's issues need not lead to revolutionary consciousness, or even to an identification with the left. (Some groups mobilize middle class women to fight for equal privileges as businesswomen and academics; others maintain that the overthrow of capitalism is irrelevant for women.)

Many movement women have experienced the initial exhilaration of discovering women's liberation as an issue, of realizing that the frustration, anger, and fear we feel are not a result of individual failure but are shared by all our sisters, and of sensing—if not fully understanding—that these feelings stem from the same oppressive conditions that give rise to racism, chauvinism and the barbarity of American culture. But many movement women, too, have become disillusioned after a time by their experiences with women's liberation groups. More often than not these groups never get beyond the level of therapy sessions; rather than aiding the political development of women and building a revolutionary women's movement, they often encourage escape from political struggle.

The existence of this tendency among women's liberation groups is one reason why many movement activists (including some women) have come out against a women's liberation movement that distinguishes itself from the general movement, even if it considers itself part of the left. A movement organized by women around the oppression of women, they say, is bound to emphasize the bourgeois and personal aspects of oppression and to obscure the material oppression of working class women *and men*. At best, such a movement "lacks revolutionary potential" (Bernadine Dohrn, N.L.N., V.4, No.9). In SDS, where this attitude is very strong, questions about the oppression and liberation of women are raised only within the context of current SDS ideology and strategy; the question of women's liberation is raised only as an incidental, subordinate aspect of programs around "*the* primary struggle," anti-racism. (Although most people in SDS now understand the extent of black people's oppression, they are not aware of the fact that the median wage of working women, (black and white) is lower than that of black males.) The male domination of the organization has not been affected by occasional rhetorical attacks on male chauvinism and most important, very little organizing of women is being done.

Although the reason behind it can be understood, this attitude toward women's liberation is mistaken and dangerous. By discouraging the development of a revolutionary women's liberation movement, it avoids a serious challenge to what, along with racism, is the deepest source of division and false consciousness among workers. By setting up (in the name of Marxist class analysis) a dichotomy between the "bourgeois," personal and psychological forms of oppression on the one hand, and the "real" material forms on the other, it substitutes a mechanistic model of class relations for a more profound understanding of how these two aspects of oppression depend upon and reinforce each other. Finally, this anti-women's liberationist attitude makes it easier for us to bypass a confrontation of male chauvinism and the closely related values of elitism and authoritarianism which are weakening our movement.

I

Before we can discuss the potential of a women's liberation movement, we need a more precise description of the way the oppression of women functions in a capitalist society. This will also help us understand the relation of psychological to material oppression.

(1) *Male Chauvinism—the attitude that women are the passive and inferior servants of society and of men—sets women apart from the rest of the working class.* Even when they do the same work as men, women are not considered workers in the same sense, with the need and right to work to provide for their families or to support themselves independently. They are expected to accept work at lower wages and without job security. Thus they can be used as a marginal or reserve labor force when profits depend on extra low costs or when men are needed for war.

Women are not supposed to be independent, so they are not supposed to have any "right to work." This means, in effect, that although they do work, they are denied the right to organize and fight for better wages and conditions. Thus the role of women in the labor force undermines the struggles of male workers as well. The boss can break a union drive by threatening to hire lower paid women or blacks. In many cases, where women are organized, the union contract reinforces their inferior position, making women the least loyal and militant union members. (Standard Oil workers in San Francisco recently paid the price of male supremacy. Women at Standard Oil have the least chance for advancement and decent pay, and the union has done little to fight this. Not surprisingly, women formed the core of the back to work move that eventually broke the strike.)[1]

In general, because women are defined as docile, helpless, and in-ferior, they are forced into the most demeaning and mindrotting jobs—

from scrubbing floors to filing cards—under the most oppressive conditions where they are treated like children or slaves. Their very position reinforces the idea, even among the women themselves, that they are fit for and should be satisfied with this kind of work.

(2) *Apart from the direct, material exploitation of women, male supremacy acts in more subtle ways to undermine class consciousness.* The tendency of male workers to think of themselves primarily as men (i.e., powerful) rather than as workers (i.e., members of an oppressed group) promotes a false sense of privilege and power, and an identification with the world of men, including the boss. The petty dictatorship which most men exercise over their wives and families enables them to vent their anger and frustration in a way which poses no challenge to the system. The role of the man in the family reinforces aggressive individualism, authoritarianism, and a hierarchical view of social relations—values which are fundamental to the perpetuation of capitalism. In this system we are taught to relieve our fears and frustrations by brutalizing those weaker than we are: a man in uniform turns into a pig; the foreman intimidates the man on the line; the husband beats his wife, child, and dog.

(3) *Women are further exploited in their roles as housewives and mothers, through which they reduce the costs (social and economic) of maintaining the labor force.* All of us will admit that inadequate as it may be American workers have a relatively decent standard of living, in a strictly material sense, when compared to workers of other countries or periods of history. But American workers are exploited and harassed in other ways than through the size of the weekly paycheck. They are made into robots on the job; they are denied security; they are forced to pay for expensive insurance and can rarely save enough to protect them from sudden loss of job or emergency. They are denied decent medical care and a livable environment. They are cheated by inflation. They are "given" a regimented education that prepares them for a narrow slot or for nothing. And they are taxed heavily to pay for these "benefits."

In all these areas, it is a woman's responsibility to make up for the failures of the system. In countless working class families, it is mother's job that bridges the gap between week to week subsistence and relative security. It is her wages that enable the family to eat better food, to escape their oppressive surroundings through a trip, an occasional movie, or new clothes. It is her responsibility to keep her family healthy despite the cost of decent medical care; to make a comfortable home in an unsafe and unlivable neighborhood; to provide a refuge from the alienation of work and to keep the male ego in good repair. It is she who must struggle daily to make ends meet despite inflation. She must make up for the fact that her children do not receive a decent education and she must salvage their damaged personalities.

A woman is judged as a wife and mother—the only role she is allowed—according to her ability to maintain stability in her family and to help her family "adjust" to harsh realities. She therefore transmits the values of hard work and conformity to each generation of workers. It is she who forces her children to stay in school and "behave" or who urges her husband not to risk his job by standing up to the boss or going on strike.

Thus the role of wife and mother is one of social mediator and pacifier. She shields her family from the direct impact of class oppression. She is the true opiate of the masses.

(4) *Working class women and other women as well are exploited as consumers.* They are forced to buy products which are necessities, but which have waste built into them, like the soap powder the price of which includes fancy packaging and advertising. They also buy products which are wasteful in themselves because they are told that a new car or TV will add to their families' status and satisfaction, or that cosmetics will increase their desirability as sex objects. Among "middle class" women, of course, the second type of wasteful consumption is more important than it is among working class women, but all women are victims of both types to a greater or lesser extent, and the values which support wasteful consumption are part of our general culture.

(5) *All women, too, are oppressed and exploited sexually.* For working class women this oppression is more direct and brutal. They are denied control of their own bodies, when as girls they are refused information about sex and birth control, and when as women they are denied any right to decide whether and when to have children. Their confinement to the role of sex partner and mother, and their passive submission to a single man are often maintained by physical force. The relative sexual freedom of "middle class" or college educated women, however, does not bring *them* real independence. Their sexual role is still primarily a passive one; their value as individuals still determined by their ability to attract, please, and hold onto a man. The definition of women as docile and dependent, inferior in intellect and weak in character cuts across class lines.

A woman of any class is expected to sell herself—not just body but her entire life, her talents, interests, and dreams—to a man. She is expected to give up friendships, ambitions, pleasures, and moments of time to herself in order to serve his career or his family. In return, she receives not only her livelihood but her identity, her very right to existence, for unless she is the wife of someone or the mother of someone, a woman is nothing.

In this summary of the forms of oppression of women in this society, the rigid dichotomy between material oppression and psychological oppression fails to hold, for it can be seen that these two aspects of oppression reinforce each other at every level. A woman may seek a job out of absolute necessity, or in order to escape repression and dependence at home. In either case, on the job she will be persuaded or forced to accept low pay, indignity and a prison-like atmosphere because a woman isn't supposed to need money or respect. Then, after working all week turning tiny wires, or typing endless forms, she finds that cooking and cleaning, dressing up and making up, becoming submissive and childlike in order to please a man is her only relief, so she gladly falls back into her "proper" role.

All women, even including those of the ruling class, are oppressed as women in the sense that their real fulfillment is linked to their role as girlfriend, wife or mother. This definition of women is part of bourgeois culture—the whole superstructure of ideas that serves to explain and reinforce the social relations of capitalism. It is applied to all women, but it has very different consequences for women of different classes. For a ruling class woman, it means she is denied real independence, dignity, and sexual freedom. For a working class woman it means this too, but it also justifies her material super-exploitation and physical coercion. Her oppression is a total one.[2]

II

It is true, as the movement critics assert, that the present women's liberation groups are almost entirely based among "middle class" women, that is, college and career women; and the issues of psychological and sexual exploitation and, to a lesser extent, exploitation through consumption, have been the most prominent ones.

It is not surprising that the women's liberation movement should begin among bourgeois women, and should be dominated in the beginning by their consciousness and their particular concerns. Radical women are generally the post war middle class generation that grew up with the right to vote, the chance at higher education and training for supportive roles in the professions and business. Most of them are young and sophisticated enough to have not yet had children and do not have to marry to support themselves. In comparison with most women, they are capable of a certain amount of control over their lives.

The higher development of bourgeois democratic society allows the women who benefit from education and relative equality to see the contradictions between its rhetoric (every boy can become president) and their actual place in that society. The working class woman might believe that education could have made her financially independent but the educated career woman finds that money has not made her independent. In fact, because she has been allowed to progress halfway on the upward-mobility ladder she can see the rest of the distance that is denied her only because she is a woman. She can see the similarity between her oppression and that of other sections of the population. Thus, from their own experience, radical women in the movement are aware of more faults in the society than racism and imperialism. Because they have pushed the democratic myth to its limits, they know concretely how it limits them.

At the same time that radical women were learning about American society they were also becoming aware of the male chauvinism in the movement. In fact, that is usually the cause of their first conscious verbalization of the prejudice they feel; it is more disillusioning to know that the same contradiction exists between the movement's rhetoric of equality and its reality, for we expect more of our comrades.

This realization of the deep-seated prejudice against themselves in the movement produces two common reactions among its women: 1) a preoccupation with this immediate barrier (and perhaps a resultant hopelessness), and (2) a tendency to retreat inward, to buy the fool's gold of creating a personally liberated life style.

However, our concept of liberation represents a consciousness that conditions have forced on us while most of our sisters are chained by other conditions, biological and economic, that overwhelm their humanity and desires for self fulfillment. Our background accounts for our ignorance about the stark oppression of women's daily lives.

Few radical women really know the worst of women's condition. They do not understand the anxious struggle of an uneducated girl to find the best available man for financial security and escape from a crowded and repressive home. They have not suffered years of fear from ignorance and helplessness about pregnancies. Few have experienced constant violence and drunkenness of a brutalized husband or father. They do not know the day to day reality of being chained to a house and family, with little money and lots of bills, and no diversions but TV.

Not many radical women have experienced 9-11 hours a day of hard labor, carrying trays on aching legs for rude customers who may leave no tip, but leave a feeling of degradation from their sexual or racist remarks—and all of this for $80–$90 a week. Most movement women have not learned to blank out their thoughts for 7 hours in order to type faster or file endless numbers. They have not felt their own creativity deadened by this work, while watching men who were not trained to be typists move on to higher level jobs requiring "brain-work."

In summary: because male supremacy (assumption of female inferiority, regulation of women to service roles, and sexual objectification) crosses class lines, radical women are conscious of women's oppression, but because of their background, they lack consciousness of most women's class oppression.

III

The development of the movement has produced different trends within the broad women's liberation movement. Most existing women's groups fall into one of the four following categories:

(1) *Personal Liberation Groups*. This type of group has been the first manifestation of consciousness of their own oppression among movement women. By talking about their frustrations with their role in the movement, they have moved from feelings of personal inadequacy to the realization that male supremacy is one of the foundations of the society that must be destroyed. Because it is at the level of the direct oppression in our daily lives that most people become conscious, it is not surprising that this is true of women in the movement. Lenin once complained about this phenomenon to Clara Zetklin, leader of the German women's socialist movement: "I have been told that at the evening meetings arranged for reading and discussion with working women, sex and marriage problems come first."

But once women have discovered the full extent of the prejudice against them they cannot ignore it, whether Lenin approves or not, and they have found women's discussions helpful in dealing with their problems. These groups have continued to grow and split into smaller, more viable groups, showing just how widespread is women's dissatisfaction.

However, the level of politicization of these groups has been kept low by the very conditions that keep women underdeveloped in this society; and alienation from the male dominated movement has prolonged the politicization process. These groups still see the source of their oppression in "chauvinist attitudes," rather than in the social relations of capitalism that produce those attitudes. Therefore, they don't confront male chauvinism collectively or politically. They become involved solely in "personal liberation" attempts to create free life styles and define new criteria for personal relations in the hoped for system of the future. Bernadine Dohrn's criticism of these groups was a just one: "Their program is only a cycle that produces more women's groups, mostly devoted to a personal liberation/therapy function and promises of study which are an evasion of practice" (*N.L.N.*, V.4, No.9).

(2) *Anti-Left Groups.* Many women have separated from the movement out of bitterness and disillusionment with the left's ability to alter its built-in chauvinism. Some are now vociferously anti-left; others simply see the movement as irrelevant. In view of the fate of the ideal of women's equality in most socialist countries, their skepticism is not surprising. Nor is it surprising that individuals with leadership abilities who are constantly thwarted in the movement turn to new avenues.

These women advocate a radical feminist movement totally separate from any other political movement. Their program involves female counter-institutions, such as communes and political parties, and attacks upon those aspects of women's oppression that affect all classes (abortion laws, marriage, lack of child care facilities, job discrimination, images of women in the media).

The first premise of the theory with which these radical feminists justify their movement is that women have always been exploited. They admit that women's oppression has a social basis—*men as a group oppress women as a group*—therefore, women must organize to confront male supremacy collectively. But they say that since women were exploited before capitalism, as well as in capitalist and "socialist" societies, the overthrow of capitalism is irrelevant to the equality of women. Male supremacy is a phenomenon outside the left-right political spectrum and must be fought separately.

But if one admits that female oppression has a social basis, it is necessary to specify the social relations on which this condition is based, and then to change those relations. (We maintain that the oppression of women is based on class divisions; these in turn are derived from the division of labor which developed between the stronger and weaker, the owner and the owned; e.g., women, under conditions of scarcity in primitive society.) Defining those relations as "men as a group *vs*. women as a group," as the anti-left groups seem to do, is ultimately reducible only to some form of biological determinism (women are inherently oppress-able) and leads to no solution in practice other than the elimination of one group or the other.

(3) *Movement Activists*. Many radical women who have become full time activists accept the attitude of most men in the movement that women's liberation is bourgeois and "personalist." They look at most of the present women's liberation groups and conclude that a movement based on women's issues is bound to emphasize the relatively mild forms of oppression experienced by students and "middle class" women while obscuring the fundamental importance of class oppression. "Sure middle class women are oppressed," they say, "but how can we concentrate on making our own lives more comfortable when working class women and men are so much more oppressed." Others point out that "women cannot be free in an unfree society; their liberation will come with that of the rest of us." These people maintain that organizing around women's issues is reformist because it is an attempt to ameliorate conditions within bourgeois society. Most movement activists agree that we should talk about women's oppression, but say we should do so only in terms of the super-exploitation of working women, especially black and brown working women, and not in terms of personal, psychological, and sexual oppression, which they see as a very different (and bourgeois) thing. They also say we should organize around women's oppression, but only as an aspect of our struggles against racism and imperialism. In other words, there should not be a separate revolutionary women's organization.

Yet strangely enough, demands for the liberation of women seldom find their way into movement programs, and very little organizing of women, within or apart from other struggles, is actually going on:

—In student organizing, no agitation for birth control for high school and college girls; no recognition of the other special restrictions that keep them from controlling their own lives; no propaganda about how women are still barred from many courses, especially those that would enable them to demand equality in employment.

—In open admissions fights, no propaganda about the channeling of girls into low-paying, deadend service occupations.

—In struggles against racism, talk about the black man's loss of manhood, but none about the sexual objectification and astounding exploitation of black women.

—In anti-repression campaigns, no fights against abortion laws; no defense of those "guilty" of abortion.

—In analysis of unions, no realization that women make less than black men and that most women aren't even organized yet. The demands for equal wages were recently raised in the Women's Resolution (at the December SDS, NC), but there are as yet no demands for free child care and equal work by husbands that would make the demand for equal wages more than an empty gesture.

It is clear that radical women activists have not been able to educate the movement about its own chauvinism or bring the issue of male supremacy to an active presence in the movement's program any more than have the personal liberation groups.

The failure of the movement to deal with male supremacy is less the result of a conscious evaluation of the issue's impact than a product of the male chauvinism that remains deeply rooted in the movement itself. Most full-time women organizers work in an atmosphere dominated by aggressive "guerilla" street fighters and organizers (who usually have a silent female appendage), of charismatic theoreticians (whose ability to lay out an analysis is not hampered by the casual stroking of their girl's hair while everyone listens raptly), of decision-making meetings in which the strong voices of men in "ideological struggle" are only rarely punctuated by the voice of one of the girls more skilled in debate, and of movement offices in which the women are still the most reliable (after all, the men are busy speaking and organizing).

"Bad politics" and "sloppy thinking" baiting is particularly effective against women who have been socialized to fear aggressiveness, who tend to lack experience in articulating abstract concepts. And at the same time, a woman's acceptance in the movement still depends on her attractiveness, and men do not find women attractive when they are strong-minded and argue like men.

Many of the characteristics which one needs in order to become respected in the movement—like the ability to argue loud and fast and aggressively and to excell in the "I'm more revolutionary than you" style of debate—are traits which our society consistently cultivates in men and discourages in women from childhood. But these traits are neither inherently male nor universally human; rather they are particularly appropriate to a brutally competitive capitalist society.

That most movement women fail to realize this, that their ideal is still the arrogant and coercive leader-organizer, that they continue to work at all in an atmosphere where women are consistantly scorned, and where chauvinism and elitism are attacked in rhetoric only—all this suggests that most movement women are not really aware of their *own* oppression. They continue to assume that the reason they haven't "made it" in the movement is that they are not dedicated enough or that their politics are not developed enough. At the same time, most of these women are becoming acutely aware, along with the rest of the movement, of their own comfortable and privileged backgrounds compared with those of workers (and feel guilty about them). It is this situation that causes them to regard women's liberation as a sort of counter-revolutionary self-indulgence.

There is a further reason for this; in the movement we have all become aware of the central importance of working people in a revolutionary movement and of the gap between their lives and most of our own. But at this point our understanding is largely an abstract one; we remain distant from and grossly ignorant of the real conditions working people face day to day. Thus our concept of working class oppression tends to be a one-sided and mechanistic one, contrasting "real" economic oppression to our "bourgeois hang-ups" with cultural and psychological oppression. We don't understand that the oppression of working people is a total one, in which the "psychological" aspects—the humiliation of being poor, uneducated, and powerless, the alienation of work, and the brutalization of family life—are not only real forms of oppression in themselves, but reinforce material oppression by draining people of their energy and will to fight. Similarly, the "psychological" forms of oppression that affect all women—sexual objectification and the definition of women as docile and serving—work to keep working class women in a position where they are super-exploited as workers and as housewives.

But because of our one-sided view of class oppression, most movement women do not see the relationship of their own oppression to that of working class woman. This is why they conclude that a women's liberation movement cannot lead to class consciousness and does not have revolutionary potential.

(4) *Advocates of Women's Liberation Movement.* A growing number of radical women see the need for an organized women's movement because: (1) they see revolutionary potential in women organizing against their direct oppression, that is, against male supremacy as well as their exploitation as

workers; and (2) they believe that a significant movement for women's equality will develop within any socialist movement only through the conscious efforts of organized women, and they have seen that such consciousness does not develop in a male chauvinist movement born of a male supremacist society.

These women believe that radical women must agitate among young working class girls, rank and file women workers, and workers' wives, around a double front: against their direct oppression by male supremacist institutions, and against their exploitation as workers. They maintain that the cultural conditions of people's lives is as important as the economic basis of their oppression in determining consciousness. If the movement cannot incorporate such a program, these women say, then an organized women's liberation movement distinguished from the general movement must be formed, for only through such a movement will radical women gain the consciousness to develop and carry through this program.

The question of "separation" from the movement is a thorny one, particularly if it is discussed only in the abstract. Concretely, the problem at the present time is simply: should a women's liberation movement be a caucus within SDS, or should it be more than that? The radical women's liberationists say the latter; their movement should have its own structure and program, although it should work closely with SDS, and most of its members would probably be active in SDS (or other movement projects and organizations) as individuals. It would be "separate" *within* the movement in the same sense that say, NOC is separate, or in the way that the organized women who call themselves "half of China" are separate within the Chinese revolution.

The reason for this is not simply that women need a separate organization in order to develop themselves. The radical women's liberationists believe that the true extent of women's oppression can be revealed and fought only if the women's liberation movement is dominated by working class women. This puts the question of "separation" from SDS in a different light. Most of us in the movement would agree that a revolutionary working class movement cannot be built within the present structure of the student movement, so that if we are serious about our own rhetoric, SDS itself will have to be totally transformed, or we will have to move beyond it, within the coming years.

The radical women's liberationists further believe that the American liberation movement will fail before it has barely begun if it does not recognize and deal with the elitism, coerciveness, aggressive individualism, and class chauvinism it has inherited from capitalist society. Since it is women who always bear the brunt of these forms of oppression, it is they who are most aware of them. Elitism, for example, affects many people in the movement to the detriment of the movement as a whole, but women are always on the very bottom rung of participation in decision-making. The more they are shut out, the less they develop the necessary skills, and elitism in the movement mirrors the vicious circle of bourgeois society.

The same characteristics in the movement that produce male chauvinism also lead to class chauvinism. Because women are politically underdeveloped—their education and socialization have not given them analytic and organizational skills—they are assumed to be politically inferior. But as long as we continue to evaluate people according to this criterion, our movement will automatically consider itself superior to working class people, who suffer a similar kind of oppression.

We cannot develop a truly liberating form of socialism unless we are consciously fighting these tendencies in our movement. This consciousness can come from the organized efforts of those who are most aware of these faults because they are most oppressed by them, i.e. women. But in order to politicize their consciousness of their own oppression, and to make effective their criticisms of the movement, women need the solidarity and self-value they could gain from a revolutionary women's liberation movement involved in meaningful struggle.

What is the revolutionary potential of women's liberation?

The potential for revolutionary thought and action lies in the masses of super-oppressed and super-exploited working class women. We have seen the stagnation in New Left women's groups caused by the lack of the *need to fight* that class oppression produces. Unlike most radical women, working class women have no freedom of alternatives, no chance of achieving some slight degree of individual liberation. It is these women, through their struggle, who will develop a revolutionary women's liberation movement.

A women's liberation movement will be necessary if unity of the working class is ever to be achieved. Until working men see their female co-workers and their own wives as equal in their movement, and until those women see that it is in their own interests and that of their families to "dare to win," the position of women will continue to undermine every working class struggle.

The attitude of unions, and of the workers themselves, that women should not work, and that they do not do difficult or necessary work, helps to maintain a situation in which (1) many women who need income or independence cannot work, (2) women who do work are usually not organized, (3) union contracts reinforce the inferior position of women who are organized, and (4) women are further penalized with the costs of child care. As a result, most women workers do not see much value in organizing. They have little to gain from militant fights for better wages and conditions, and they have the most to risk in organizing in the first place.

The position of worker's wives outside their husbands' union often places them in antagonism to it. They know how little it does about safety and working conditions, grievances, and layoffs. The unions demand complete loyalty to strikes—which means weeks without income—and then sign contracts which bring little improvement in wages or conditions.

Thus on the simple trade union level, the oppression of women weakens the position of the workers as a whole. But any working class movement that does not deal with the vulnerable position of totally powerless women will have to deal with the false consciousness of those women.

The importance of a working class women's liberation movement goes beyond the need for unity. A liberation movement of the "slaves of the slave" tends to raise broader issues of peoples' oppression in all its forms, so that it is inherently wider than the economism of most trade union movements. For example, last year 187 women struck British Ford demanding equal wages (and shutting down 40,000 other jobs in the process). They won their specific demand, but Ford insisted that the women work all three rotating shifts, as the men do. The women objected that this would create great difficulty for them in their work as housekeepers and mothers, and that their husbands would not like it.

A militant women's liberation movement must go on from this point to demand (1) that mothers must also be free in the home, (2) that management must pay for child care facilities so that women can do equal work with men, and that (3) equal work *with* men must mean equal work *by* men. In this way, the winning of a simple demand for equality on the job raises much broader issues of the extent of inequality, the degree of exploitation, and the totality of the oppression of all the workers. It can show how women workers are forced to hold an extra full time job without pay or recognition that this is necessary work, how male chauvinism allows the capitalist class to exploit workers in this way, how people are treated like machines owned by the boss, and how the most basic conditions of workers' lives are controlled in the interests of capitalism.

The workplace is not the only area in which the fight against women's oppression can raise the consciousness of everybody about the real functions of bourgeois institutions. Propaganda against sexual objectification and the demeaning of women in the media can help make people understand how advertising manipulates our desires and frustrations, and how the media sets up models of human relationships and values which we all unconsciously accept. A fight against the tracking of girls in school into low-level, deadend service jobs helps show how the education system channels and divides us all, playing upon the false self-images we have been given in school and by the media (women are best as secretaries and nurses; blacks aren't cut out for responsible positions; workers' sons aren't smart enough for college).

Struggles to free women from domestic slavery which may begin around demands for a neighborhood or factory child care center can lead to consciousness of the crippling effects of relations of domination and exploitation in the home, and to an understanding of how the institutions of marriage and the family embody those relations and destroy human potential.

In short, because the material oppression of women is integrally related to their psychological and sexual oppression, the women's liberation movement must necessarily raise these issues. In doing so it can make us all aware of how capitalism oppresses us, not only by drafting us, taxing us, and exploiting us on the job, but by determining the way we think, feel, and relate to each other.

IV

In order to form a women's liberation movement based on the oppression of working class women we must begin to agitate on issues of "equal rights" and specific rights. Equal rights means all those "rights" that men are supposed to have: the right to work, to organize for equal pay, promotions, better conditions, equal (and *not* separate) education. Specific rights means those rights women must have if they are to be equal in the other areas: free, adequate child care, abortions, birth control for young women from puberty, self defense, desegregation of all institutions (schools, unions, jobs). It is not so much an academic question of what is correct theory as an inescapable empirical fact; women must fight their conditions just to participate in the movement.

The first reason why we need to fight on these issues is that we must serve the people. That slogan is not just rhetoric with the Black Panthers but reflects their determination to end the exploitation of their people. Similarly, the women's liberation movement will grow and be effective only to the extent that it abominates and fights the conditions of misery that so many women suffer every day. It will gain support only if it speaks to the immediate needs of women. For instance:

(1) We must begin to disseminate birth control information in high schools and fight the tracking of girls into inferior education. We must do this not only to raise the consciousness of these girls to their condition but because control of their bodies is the key to their participation in the future. Otherwise, their natural sexuality will be indirectly used to repress them from struggles for better jobs and organizing, because they will be encumbered with children and economically tied to the family structure for basic security.

(2) We must raise demands for maternity leave and child-care facilities provided (paid for, but not controlled) by management as a rightful side benefit of women workers. This is important not only for what those issues say about women's right to work but so that women who choose to have children have more freedom to participate in the movement.

(3) We must agitate for rank and file revolt against the male supremacist hierarchy of the unions and for demands for equal wages. Only through winning such struggles for equality can the rank and file *be* united and see their common enemies—management and union hierarchy. Wives of workers must fight the chauvinist attitudes of their husbands simply to be able to attend meetings.

(4) We must organize among store clerks, waitresses, office workers, and hospitals where vast numbers of women have no bargaining rights or security. In doing so we will have to confront the question of a radical strategy towards established unions and the viability of independent unions.

(5) We must add to the liberal demands for abortion reform by fighting against the hospital and doctors boards that such reforms consist of. They

will in no way make abortions more available for the majority of non-middle class women or young girls who will still be forced to home remedies and butchers. We must insist at all times on the right of every woman to control her own body.

(6) We must demand the right of women to protect themselves. Because the pigs protect property and not people, because the violence created by the brutalization of many men in our society is often directed at women, and because not all women are willing or able to sell themselves (or to limit their lives) for the protection of a male, women have a right to self-protection.

This is where the struggle must begin, although it cannot end here. In the course of the fight we will have to raise the issues of the human relationships in which the special oppression of women is rooted: sexual objectification, the division of labor in the home, and the institutions of marriage and the nuclear family. But organizing "against the family" cannot be the basis of a program. An uneducated working class wife with five kids is perfectly capable of understanding that marriage has destroyed most of her potential as a human being—probably she already understands this—but she is hardly in a position to repudiate her source of livelihood and free herself of those children. If we expect that of her, we will never build a movement.

As the women's liberation movement gains strength, the development of cooperative child care centers and living arrangements, and the provision of birth control may allow more working class women to free themselves from slavery as sex objects and housewives. But at the present time, the insistence by some women's liberation groups that we must "organize against sexual objectification," and that only women who repudiate the family can really be part of the movement, reflects the class chauvinism and lack of seriousness of women who were privileged enough to avoid economic dependence and sexual slavery in the first place.

In no socialist country have women yet achieved equality or full liberation, but in the most recent revolutions (Vietnam, Cuba, and China's cultural revolution) the women's struggle has intensified. It may be that in an advanced society such as our own, where women have had relatively more freedom, a revolutionary movement may not be able to avoid a militant women's movement developing within it. But the examples of previous attempts at socialist revolutions prove that the struggle must be instigated *by* militant women; liberation is not handed down from above.

Notes

1. *See Movement*, May 1969, p. 6—7.

2. We referred above to "middle class" forms of oppression, contrasting the opportunity for wasteful consumption among relatively affluent women, and superficial sexual freedom of college women to the conditions of poor and un-educated working women. Here "middle class" refers more to a life style, a bourgeois cultural ideal, than to a social category. Strictly speaking, a middle class person is one who does not employ other people but also does not have to sell his labor for wages to live, e.g., a doctor or owner of a small family business. Many people who think of themselves as "middle class," and who can afford more than they need to live on are, strictly speaking, working class people because they must sell labor, e.g., high school teachers and most white collar workers. There is, of course, a real difference in living conditions as well as consciousness between these people and most industrial workers. But because of the middle class myth, a tremendous gap in consciousness can exist even where conditions are essentially the same. There are literally millions of female clerical workers, telephone operators, etc., who work under the most proletarianized conditions, doing the most tedious female-type labor, and making the same wages, or even less, as sewing machine factory workers, who nevertheless think of themselves as in a very different "class" from those factory women.